NEW JERSEY'S
JEFFERSONIAN REPUBLICANS

The Institute of Early American History and Culture is sponsored jointly by the College of William and Mary and Colonial Williamsburg, Incorporated.

PUBLISHED FOR THE
Institute of Early American History and Culture
AT WILLIAMSBURG, VIRGINIA, BY
The University of North Carolina Press • *Chapel Hill*

NEW JERSEY'S JEFFERSONIAN REPUBLICANS

THE GENESIS OF AN EARLY PARTY MACHINE
1789-1817

by

CARL E. PRINCE

Copyright © 1964, 1967 by
The University of North Carolina Press
Library of Congress Catalog Card Number 67-15103
Printed by The Seeman Printery, Inc., Durham, North Carolina
Manufactured in the United States of America

For Sue
and my Mother and Father

ACKNOWLEDGMENTS

PARTS OF THIS WORK APPEARED IN *The William and Mary Quarterly* and the *Proceedings* of the New Jersey Historical Society. I am grateful for their permission to reprint parts of the above articles here.

It is a pleasure to pay my respects to the many individuals who spurred this effort. In the course of my research I have found the manuscript librarians in the various libraries I visited to be uniformly friendly and helpful. In this connection I am indebted in a special way to Mrs. Edith O. May, Librarian of the New Jersey Historical Society, and particularly to Donald A. Sinclair, Curator of Special Collections at the Rutgers University Library. Richard M. Brown of Rutgers University's History Department read the original manuscript as a dissertation and made several suggestions that I eventually incorporated into the revision. George L. A. Reilly, Chairman of the Department of History at Seton Hall University, went out of his way to obtain for me a reduced teaching schedule in order that I might revise the manuscript for publication. James M. Smith, formerly Editor of Publications at the Institute and now on the faculty of Cornell University, and Susan Lee Foard,

Associate Editor of Publications, both did yeoman work in getting this manuscript in shape for publication.

Bernard Sternsher, my friend and colleague at Seton Hall, read portions of the manuscript and offered penetrating and valuable suggestions, many of which I ultimately adopted. My sister, Mrs. Marcia P. Freedman of Brooklyn, New York, gave me the benefit of her professional editorial analysis. My greatest intellectual debt, accumulated over many years, is to Richard P. McCormick, my mentor at Rutgers. He first suggested the subject in a seminar, and directed the dissertation with acuteness and sensitivity. His knowledge of the subject and diligence as a dissertation director improved this work no end.

It is difficult to express feelings for one's loved ones in print, but I cannot finish without saying that my parents, Phillip and Anne Prince, always taught me that it is better to know than to have. My greatest debt, as is so often the case, is to my wife Sue. Over the years she has typed, proofread, corrected, and encouraged endlessly. She has at the same time maintained a stable household and held two children at bay, allowing me to work so much more effectively. I can't see how this book could have been completed without her.

CARL E. PRINCE

TABLE OF CONTENTS

LIST OF TABLES

———•—•———

INTRODUCTION

———•———

HISTORIANS NOW RECOGNIZE MORE CLEARLY THAN EVER BEFORE
that the development of American party machinery is most
accurately and profitably studied at the state level. Jeffersonian party organization in the states as well as the nation, as a
result, has been the focus of increasing attention in recent years
by Noble E. Cunningham, Jr., William N. Chambers, and
Joseph Charles, to name only three.[1] The present effort is pro-

1. Noble E. Cunningham, Jr., *The Jeffersonian Republicans: The Formation
of Party Organization, 1789-1801* (Chapel Hill, 1957) and *The Jeffersonian
Republicans in Power: Party Operations, 1801-1809* (Chapel Hill, 1963); William
N. Chambers, *Political Parties in a New Nation: The American Experience,
1776-1809* (New York, 1963); Joseph Charles, *The Origins of the American
Party System* (Williamsburg, 1956). The above books all intertwine, at least
to some extent, state and national Jeffersonian party developments. The follow-
ing are all relatively recent state studies: Harry M. Tinkcom, *The Republicans
and Federalists in Pennsylvania, 1790-1801: A Study in National Stimulus and
Local Response* (Harrisburg, 1950); Sanford W. Higginbotham, *The Keystone
in the Democratic Arch: Pennsylvania Politics, 1801-1816* (Harrisburg, 1952);
John A. Munroe, *Federalist Delaware, 1775-1815* (New Brunswick, 1954); Paul
Goodman, *The Democratic-Republicans of Massachusetts, Politics in a Young
Republic* (Cambridge, 1964); Alfred F. Young, "The Democratic Republican
Movement in New York State, 1788-1797" (unpubl. Ph.D. diss., Northwestern
University, 1958); Norman L. Stamps, "Political Parties in Connecticut, 1789-
1818" (unpubl. Ph.D. diss., Yale University, 1952); Harry Ammon, "The
Formation of the Republican Party in Virginia, 1789-1796," *Journal of Southern*

posed as one more link in a growing chain of state studies of our first political parties. New Jersey's Democratic-Republican party was one of several statewide Jeffersonian organizations that pioneered in the development of America's first permanent, institutionalized party system. An exposition and analysis of the apparatus of the New Jersey organization, it seems to me, is important to the effort to describe and explain early American political history.

Before the Revolution, ultimate responsibility for New Jersey's government rested with the English Crown. The achievement of independence, although it created new demands on the political machinery of the old colony, at first only slightly altered the factional political alignments and foundations. But, with the transition to stronger central government under the Federal Constitution, politics in New Jersey acquired a new dimension.

Events in New Jersey and in the nation during the years 1789-95 profoundly influenced the development of political organization in the state as it materialized in the latter part of the decade. Federalist domination of state (and national) politics triggered responsive anti-Federalist activity, democratic societies, and agitation over the Jay Treaty. The results of these efforts manifested themselves between 1796 and 1799, as the old system of factional politics gave way to emergent political parties at the local, county, and state levels; anti-Federalist factions matured into local Republican party organizations in some northern New Jersey counties, as the Alien and Sedition Laws precipitated the first important local Republican organizational efforts.

The structure of the local party apparatus eventually varied from region to region, ranging from the loosely formed township and county committee system prevalent in much of North

History, 19 (1953), 283-310, "The Richmond Junto, 1800-1824," *Virginia Magazine of History and Biography*, 61 (1953), 395-418, and "The Jeffersonian Republicans in Virginia: An Interpretation," *Va. Mag. of Hist. and Biog.*, 71 (1963), 153-67.

Jersey to the more tightly knit democratic associations which dominated local politics in the lower part of the state. At the point where party machinery dealt directly with the voters—in the towns and outlying countryside—the Republicans experienced their most difficult trials. These trials were in part offset by the encouragement local organizers received from developments elsewhere.

Responding to stimuli provided by national political developments—particularly the growing popular and organizational strength of the Jeffersonians in the federal government and in other states—the New Jersey Republican grass-roots factions coalesced into an institutionalized political party in 1800 and thereafter. A Republican congressional victory in New Jersey in 1800, climaxing an extensive and bitter series of campaigns, was followed in 1801 by the election of a majority of Republicans to the state legislature, signifying the demise of the last Federalist stronghold in the state. The Republican majority was checked only twice in the ensuing decade and a half: in 1802 when the Federalists temporarily managed to deadlock the legislature, and in 1812, when, for another brief year, they gained control of the state government for the last time.

In the interim, the Republican party extended the scope and depth of its organization, innovating extensively in a day when political parties were a dynamic and unique feature of American life. Beginning in 1800, the Republicans introduced and breathed life into the first continuous state nominating convention in the nation. This biennial adjunct of the party apparatus was widely emulated elsewhere and eventually became a major nominating device for most state and national organizations throughout the nineteenth and twentieth centuries. New Jersey Republicans, too, pioneered in the formation and utilization of the legislative caucus, a party device whose origins, significantly, coincided with the appearance of a Republican majority among the state's lawmakers.

Just as the state convention eventually controlled the nominating machinery for national elective offices in New Jersey, the caucus emerged, in the first years of the nineteenth century, as the party organ which exclusively controlled the distribution of patronage, focused the power of local party leaders, and, to an extent, secured Republican majorities for some key party measures. Both the convention and the caucus provided a cosmetic effect by carefully screening from the public many internecine party battles. The same effect, in a quite different sense, was also produced by the appearance of subsidized regional newspapers in pivotal areas of New Jersey—weeklies which, in the tradition of the American press of this period, served as propaganda organs for the parties of which they were parts. These newspapers were adjuncts of an increasingly widespread organized movement.

Parties, after all, were conceived as permanent, institutionalized, professional vehicles to political power, operating in the unique setting created by the need to win popular support for public office. The study of these original American parties at the state level can tell us much about the evolving American political system and the democracy and/or republicanism to which it owes its origins. Where our parties are going, it seems to me, can be understood more clearly if we can learn from whence they came.

NEW JERSEY'S
JEFFERSONIAN REPUBLICANS

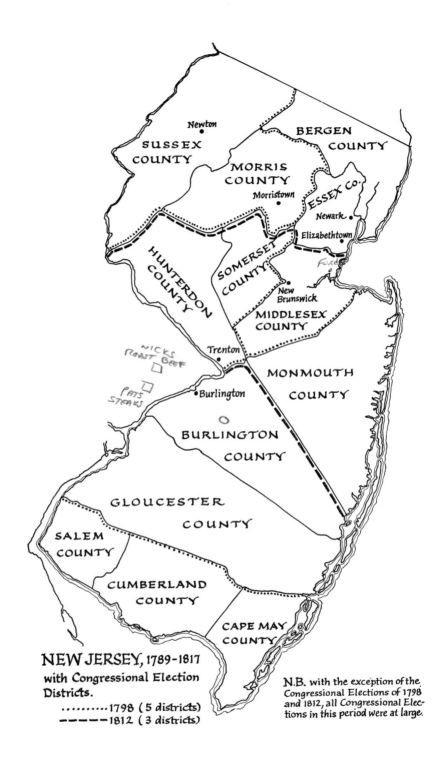

Newton

BERGEN
COUNTY

SUSSEX
COUNTY

MORRIS
COUNTY

Morristown

ESSEX CO.

Newark

Elizabethtown

HUNTERDON
COUNTY

SOMERSET
COUNTY

New
Brunswick

MIDDLESEX
COUNTY

NICKS
ROAST BEEF

Trenton

MONMOUTH
COUNTY

PATS
STEAKS

Burlington

BURLINGTON
COUNTY

GLOUCESTER
COUNTY

SALEM
COUNTY

CUMBERLAND
COUNTY

CAPE MAY
COUNTY

NEW JERSEY, 1789-1817
with Congressional Election
Districts.
.... 1798 (5 districts)
- - - - - 1812 (3 districts)

N.B. with the exception of the
Congressional Elections of 1798
and 1812, all Congressional Elections in this period were at large.

I

EIGHTEENTH-CENTURY
BEGINNINGS

———•———

ONE OF THE MOST DECEPTIVE OF FACTS ABOUT LATE EIGHTEENTH-
century New Jersey history was the unanimity with which the
Federal Constitution was greeted in 1789. This temporary
confluence of opinion masked a remarkably factious and com-
plex past. Revolutionary supporters came to power in the
colony in the 1770's but they by no means represented more
than a working majority of the state's residents; moreover,
their reforms, embodied in the State Constitution of 1776,
eliminated only a part of the structural weaknesses New Jersey's government inherited from its English past.

The Political Background

The Revolutionary movement thrust new responsibilities
and unprecedented authority upon the New Jersey electorate.
As the crisis with England mounted in 1774, county committees of correspondence made their appearance. These extralegal, revolutionary organizations exerted great political power
in New Jersey; they were to an extent legitimatized when
every county adopted more or less uniform articles of association, of the kind originally requested by the Continental Con-

[3]

gress meeting in Philadelphia. The new county "governments," reigning in fact with the consent of the majority, selected delegates in 1775 to attend the newly created colonywide Provincial Congress. On the national level, meanwhile, machinery to elect New Jersey representatives to the Continental Congress had been put in motion early in the summer of 1774 by mass meetings held in most counties pursuant to public notice. The delegates designated by these county meetings met immediately and appointed men to attend the Philadelphia meeting. The opening of the New Jersey Provincial Congress and the selection of representatives to attend at Philadelphia completed the first hesitant steps toward independence. These developments were not unlike the changes occurring in other colonies at the same time.

The ensuing months witnessed momentous changes as New Jersey completed the political transition from colony to state. For the most part, New Jersey's Constitution of 1776 reflected these changes and the aspirations that made independence possible. But the drafters of the State Constitution were practical, moderate men who adhered as much as possible to the colonial governmental framework. The Revolution in New Jersey as elsewhere aimed to end English interference rather than to turn topsy-turvy the existing order.[1]

The Constitution of 1776, nevertheless, clarified much that was uncertain when sovereign responsibility resided across the Atlantic. Elections for the legislature henceforth occurred annually instead of sporadically. The theoretically exclusive fifty pound or one hundred acre freehold requirement for voting—an uncertain and unevenly enforced provision dating back more than sixty years—was clarified and lowered to a simple

[1]. The background for the evolution of election machinery and politics generally is drawn from Richard P. McCormick, *The History of Voting in New Jersey: A Study of the Development of Election Machinery, 1664-1911* (New Brunswick, 1953), *passim*. The historical background for the Confederation period was garnered from the same author's *Experiment in Independence: New Jersey in the Critical Period, 1781-1789* (New Brunswick, 1950), *passim*. Also useful is Walter R. Fee, *The Transition From Aristocracy to Democracy in New Jersey, 1789-1829* (Somerville, N.J., 1933), 5-10.

requirement of fifty pounds of real *or* personal property to be eligible to vote. No longer did one have to be a freeholder to vote. Apart from the property qualification, anyone who was twenty-one years old and an inhabitant for one year of the county in which he voted could cast a ballot. Because the word "inhabitant" was undefined in the Constitution, and nothing more was said about who could (or could not) vote, it was possible for some women, slaves, and aliens to vote from time to time when sharper politics became the order of the day. All in all, the new electoral provisions in the Constitution, while not revolutionary, broadened the suffrage, extended the number of elective offices, and generally regularized the framework of government in the state.[2]

The new state's code emphatically vested supreme authority in a bicameral legislature. Property qualifications for the Council, the upper house, like those that had existed under the Crown, still required a candidate to possess a freehold worth one thousand pounds. A nominee for the Assembly under the new code, however, could now stand with property in his name worth five hundred pounds, not necessarily vested in a freehold, a liberal departure from colonial requirements. All state officials, including the governor, received their appointments from a joint meeting of the two houses. Each of the thirteen counties originally elected three assemblymen and one councilor, regardless of population differences. Subsequent changes in the Assembly representation, however, somewhat adjusted the original county equality in that body to population differences. The governor, who had no veto and few appointive powers, found his authority largely conditioned by his personal prestige.

The working consensus in New Jersey that had rendered possible the significant constitutional and political reforms

2. Despite the introduction of a judge of elections in place of the traditional sheriff to supervise the canvass, election procedures in 1776 were not entirely uniform. Independence, for example, did not affect the practice of keeping the polls open indefinitely, the continued prevalence of viva voce voting, nor occasional adjournment of the canvass from day to day until conditions were

accompanying the Revolution and independence was repeated only once—and then briefly—during the remainder of the century. Only the unanimous support in the state for the ratification of the United States Constitution provided a comparable situation. Indeed, the widespread espousal of the Constitution was an island of agreement surrounded by a sea of factional politics before 1788-89, and of party politics thereafter. Enduring disagreements, sometimes dating back to earliest colonial times, muddied post-Revolutionary politics, as they had before the Revolution. Only the Federal Constitution, with its promised reforms in such critical *national* areas as the disposal of state debts and western lands, federal control of commerce and revenues, and vitally needed executive powers and general governmental restructuring, could bring New Jersey factions together even temporarily. Except for this illusory oasis of togetherness, factional strife continued to hold New Jersey politics in its grip. This factionalism of long standing, well recounted in other studies of New Jersey, was part of the baggage accompanying New Jersey's emergence into the arena of party politics in the 1790's.[3]

The usual in-fighting prevalent among differing factions within the counties in the 1780's was compounded by a more basic and enduring source of disagreement: the long-standing hostility between East (North) Jersey and West (South) Jersey, which continued, as always, to find expression in the state legislature. A common source of contention was the location of the historic dividing line between the two formerly separate English colonies of East and West Jersey. The long-simmering

---

favorable to a given faction. Fraudulent election practices, moreover, were punishable only by relatively mild penalties which were rarely imposed, and "ticket voting" was not common. All of these debilities smacked of factional, not party, politics in the Revolutionary decade.

3. See sources in n. 1 above and Donald L. Kemmerer, *Path to Freedom: The Struggle for Self-Government in Colonial New Jersey, 1703-1776* (Princeton, 1940); Edgar J. Fisher, *New Jersey as a Royal Province, 1738-1776* (New York, 1911); John E. Pomfret, *The Province of West New Jersey, A History of the Origins of an American Colony, 1609-1702* (Princeton, 1956), and *The Province of East New Jersey, 1609-1702, The Rebellious Proprietary* (Princeton, 1962).

dividing line controversy was a manifestation of deep-rooted differences between the two sections; much of West Jersey was dominated by Quakers who were at odds religiously and culturally with their neighbors in East Jersey; moreover, in economic terms the state was situated between the great commercial cities of New York and Philadelphia, with each city exerting its pull on the essentially rural New Jersey population. These differences were compounded by a long-standing currency dispute between the two sections, exacerbated for obvious reasons by the problems of the Confederation. The majority of East Jerseymen, more inclined to mix mercantile and agrarian pursuits, generally favored "soft" money and easier credit policies, arousing time and again the more conservative and purely agrarian "hard" currency Quaker faction dominating West Jersey politics.

This cleavage, expressed often in bitter legislative politicking in the 1780's, came to a head in 1785. At that time, East Jersey agrarian-debtor interests led by Abraham Clark, a staunch champion of democratic causes, succeeded in capitalizing on the popular unrest caused by the all-too-familiar currency problems common to the Confederation. They won a tenuous control of the legislature annually for the greater part of the next four years. These East Jersey farmers' representatives emitted large quantities of paper money, alarming conservative-creditor interests in *all* parts of the state. The initial inability of the latter group to overcome historic sectional differences was an important factor in the continuing success of the East Jersey debtor group's efforts to stay in power. Although a temporary truce went into effect when all factions supported the Federal Constitution, factional politics once more became the order of the day in the first congressional elections held in 1789.

At this juncture, conservative East and West Jerseymen— for the most part creditors and their political followers—finally overcame their mutual hostility and faced together the more immediate threat posed by the East Jersey-dominated agrarian-debtor faction. The more well-to-do conservative group united behind the Junto Ticket, representing equally both sections of the state. The unprecedented factional alignment, it was hoped, could capitalize on the changes in government introduced by the Federal Constitution to end the suzerainty exercised by the East Jersey agrarian politicians, who were less prepared to adapt to the changes imposed by the recently ratified document. The East Jersey politicos were believed to be "radical," a term, like "conservative," with a wide variety of unclear meanings in this era.

The major change wrought in New Jersey politics under the new Constitution was the need to elect national representatives who now had to subject themselves to a popular vote, forcing elections above the county level for the first time in New Jersey's history. It was this development that made it possible for the more politically sophisticated Junto to surmount sectional differences in unifying its supporters. In the congressional election of 1789, then, the Junto—still a faction and not a party—better capitalized on recent improvements in the political machinery of the state. In addition to the need for a general congressional poll, other developments deserve mention: the number of polling places stood at fifty-three by 1788, for all practical purposes an expansion that broadened the electorate by making elections more accessible; by the same date eight of thirteen counties conducted elections secretly by ballot, permitting a freer expression of political choice for many more voters than heretofore.

The election of 1789, however, was characterized by unrestrained frauds. The Junto won an election that revealed the limitations of the existing electoral machinery. Fraudulent ballots were cast; in places where viva voce voting still prevailed open pressure was exerted; in other areas the poll was moved at will in order to favor one faction or another; some polling places remained open indefinitely in order to insure that all possible votes for a given faction were cast.

The turmoil accompanying the congressional election produced numerous demands for voting reforms. In 1790, a significant law provided for voting by township rather than by county for seven counties in the state, enhancing again the accessibility of the polls. Three more counties adopted the secret ballot, another change sanctified by the 1790 law. The act specified that polls should open on the second Tuesday in October and close on the evening of the following day, a provision eliminating both deferred elections in some areas and prolonged elections in others, and, in effect, forcing nearly uniform polling conditions on all parts of the state.

The work of codification was further advanced by the election law of 1797. Henceforth, voting everywhere in the state was by township and not by county; the written ballot or ticket was employed as the only means of voting; it was reaffirmed more explicitly that elections were to be held simultaneously in all counties; and the two-day limitation was restated more clearly. The 1797 statute did not clarify the meaning of the word "inhabitants" in defining suffrage eligibility, so that qualified women continued to vote in indeterminate numbers until 1807, when a new election law brought this practice to an end. The cumulative effect of these election laws was extremely important. They multiplied the number of polling places, making the poll more accessible than before, provided greater secrecy and therefore greater political independence for the average voter, eliminated the favored position of certain towns which could no longer boast of being the only polling place in a county, and insured more regular elections.

The Junto Ticket, the nucleus of the Federalist party, most ably took advantage of the shifting political tide characterized by the Revolutionary liberalization of the political structure. The faction was so successful in 1789 that it maintained its unity in the years following. It was this essentially conservative element which, after some political twists and turns, matured into the Federalist party. By the early 1790's the Federalists occupied the strategic middle ground in American politics by openly supporting the incumbent, unanimously elected administration. While vocally adulating George Wash-

[9]

ington, Federalist hearts, in New Jersey and throughout the nation, beat in tune with Secretary of the Treasury Alexander Hamilton's centralizing, commercially oriented political-economic programs. Hamilton's ultimate goals, embodied in his economic programs and in part realized before he left office in 1795, included strengthening federal power at the expense of the states and implementing American economic self-sufficiency through the encouragement of commerce and industry by an increasingly strong national government.

These goals sat especially well with the aspirations of the traditional ruling families from all parts of New Jersey that had supported the Junto. Moreover, even if many middling and agrarian Federalist supporters did not accept all of Hamilton's economic measures, he earned their support by encouraging stability, order, and national strength—appealing policies after the tumultuous experiences in most of the nation during the Confederation period. The emergent New Jersey Federalist party by the early 1790's reaffirmed the family leadership of the gentry and the continuing tradition of personal politics. Well-known families—including the Boudinots, Stocktons, Daytons, Ogdens, Elmers, Davenports, and Bloomfields—assumed command of the new statewide faction and, between 1790 and 1792, molded it into a party. For the second time, differences between East and West Jersey were at least buried if not forgotten; the landed, the wealthy, the conservative middling, and the easily led and relatively few poor all fell in line behind the strong economic-centralizing impulse provided by Alexander Hamilton.

Opposition throughout the nation, though a small minority at first, soon developed, particularly in key states like Virginia, New York, and Pennsylvania; this resistance was translated into opposition in Congress, led by James Madison, and equally cogently, in the cabinet, in the person of Thomas Jefferson. Political criticism of Hamiltonian "men and measures" soon appeared in most states, New Jersey included. Its origins in New Jersey were, not surprisingly, in East Jersey—particularly in Essex County—where, noted a Federalist writer in 1800, "from the very commencement of the Federal Government in March, 1789 . . . a party has existed, incessantly opposed to its operation, and indecent in their treatment of the constituted authorities."[4] This study attempts to trace the development of that opposition into the Democratic-Republican party.

Anti-Federalist Efforts, 1790-1795

The claim that an opposition party existed in 1789 was exaggerated. For one thing, support of the Constitution in the state was far too widespread; for another, hindsight colored in too sharply the outlines of a small faction opposing the Constitution that looked backward, not forward. Political opposition to the Hamiltonian interest did materialize, however, after the ratification of the Constitution. The antagonists, derisively called "anti-Federalists" by the budding Federalist party, were pitifully weak in 1792 when the first public cries of distress were sounded in New Jersey against Alexander Hamilton's financial policies. Resistance really mounted in 1794-95. A year later anti-Federalist endeavors culminated in the first "Republican" ticket competing for votes with the dominant New Jersey Federalist party. The last four years of this transitional decade witnessed the development of a party that permanently revolutionized the politics of New Jersey.

In 1792 the Federalists paid their respects to the first open anti-Federalist activity worthy of the name. Elias Boudinot, a staunch Hamiltonian, reported to the Secretary of the Treasury that the "Antis are making greater exertions than you perhaps are aware of, previous to the expected general [congressional] election." Boudinot cautioned Hamilton that "if the federalists sleep whilst their enemies are awake and vigilant, some mischief may be done." Boudinot's fear was well-founded. Circulating a broadside in West Jersey, the "Antis"

4. *Address to the Federal Republicans of the State of New Jersey* (Trenton, 1800), in New Jersey Pamphlets Collection, LXXIII, 9, New Jersey Historical Society, Newark, N. J.

pointed out the "dangerous consequences" following the implementation of Hamilton's economic program.[5] They warned against the dangers of electing such public creditors as Boudinot, Jonathan Dayton, and John Rutherford to Congress,[6] and leveled many other salvos at their adversaries' policies. Not infrequent references appeared through 1795 to Federalists who "have dipt [their] fingers deep into the cup of certificates," or supported ill-conceived "bank and funding schemes."[7]

In the first half of the decade, however, anti-Federalist agitation on economic issues was not translated into effective action at the polls. Elections through 1794, if newspaper coverage is an adequate guide, were rather tepid. There was almost no electioneering; ticket voting, a sure indication of strongly competitive politicking, seems to have been virtually unknown. In the congressional canvass of January 1795, for example, no factional alignments were publicized, and sixteen candidates for five seats all attracted significant electoral support. Resistance to Federalism prior to the latter part of 1795 continued to incubate well away from the polling places.[8]

Far more effective anti-Federalist organizational activity began in New Jersey with the formation of democratic societies in 1794 and 1795. These societies, organized in many states, served as vehicles for criticism of the national administration

5. Elias Boudinot to Alexander Hamilton, Sept. 13, 1792, in John C. Hamilton, ed., *The Works of Alexander Hamilton* (N.Y., 1850), V, 525-26; Noble E. Cunningham, Jr., *The Jeffersonian Republicans: The Formation of Party Organization, 1789-1801* (Chapel Hill, 1957), 29-30.

6. Walter R. Fee, "The Effects of Hamilton's Financial Policy upon Public Opinion in New Jersey," New Jersey Historical Society, *Proceedings*, 50 (1932), 32-44. This article, though useful, contains an exaggerated account of the importance of the debtor-creditor "struggle" in New Jersey.

7. See, for example, *Woods's Newark Gazette and New Jersey Advertiser*, Aug. 12, Sept. 16, Oct. 7, 1795, July 20, 1796. Hereafter cited as *Woods's Newark Gazette*, until issue of Nov. 8, 1797, when the editorial duties were assumed by Jacob Halsey, and the paper's name changed to the *Newark Gazette*.

8. New Brunswick *Guardian; or New Jersey Advertiser*, autumn, 1792-94, *passim*; hereafter cited as New Brunswick *Guardian*. *Woods's Newark Gazette*, July 21, 1791, Nov. 15, 1792, Oct. 16, 1793, Jan. 21, 1795. National party leaders were far more hopeful with regard to New Jersey than the facts warranted. See, for example, James Madison to Thomas Jefferson, Dec. 21, 1794, James Madison Papers, Library of Congress, Washington, D.C.

in the middle years of the decade. The three known New Jersey societies were all in populous and restive Essex County. They were not political parties in the true sense of the word, but they did foster a "general dissemination of political knowledge among the people" by trying to "acquire and diffuse political knowledge among [their] members."[9] Insofar as they stirred anti-Federalist sentiment in the state and laid the groundwork for party leadership and organization, they were close to the Republican movement.[10]

The Essex County Democratic Society—a merged unit of these three original organizations—grew out of the mounting opposition in the county to America's declaration of neutrality in 1793. An open meeting in Newark, just prior to the creation of the society, convened in August 1793 to discuss Washington's neutrality proclamation. "Why the people of the county are called upon to deliberate on a matter so foreign from their concerns is a subject of real astonishment," one critic observed. "The time for the people to meddle in affairs of government is the time of Election."[11] The gathering was an extremely tense one. When some opponents of neutrality (who favored partiality on the side of France) claimed the right to question the policies and judgment of the President and the Secretary of the Treasury, a large number of Federalists in attendance used a series of parliamentary maneuvers to still the "francophiles" and dominate the meeting. They eventually succeeded, but not before one dissenter, William S. Pennington, unsuccessfully introduced a series of resolutions which supported the French Revolution, called upon Americans to honor

9. *Woods's Newark Gazette*, Mar. 12, 1794. For a discussion of these societies nationally, with some attention to New Jersey, see Eugene P. Link, *Democratic-Republican Societies, 1790-1800* (N.Y., 1942), 61, 106, 114, 157-74, and *passim*. See also Fee, *Transition*, 40-49; Fee, "The Effects of Hamilton's Financial Policy upon Public Opinion in New Jersey," N.J. Hist. Soc., *Proceedings*, 50 (1932), 43-44.

10. Link, *Democratic-Republican Societies*, 61, 106, 114, 157-74, and *passim*; Fee, *Transition*, 40-49. The three Essex societies were the Republican Society of Newark, the Political Society of Mount Prospect, and the eventual successor to the first two, the Essex County Democratic Society.

11. *Woods's Newark Gazette, Supplement*, Aug. 14, 1793.

the French Treaty of 1778 by giving aid to France, and cast "reflections on the President."[12] The effort spurred Federalists to rush to the defense of neutrality by sponsoring public meetings in Newark, Princeton, Burlington, Morristown, and New Brunswick. But the damage had been done; not only had the resolutions of the Newark meeting made the issue a political one in Essex County, but the Newark dissidents also received aid and comfort later from two Morris County meetings in Rockaway and Hanover.[13]

Led by Pennington, many of the same opponents of neutrality invited "those persons desirous of forming themselves into a Republican Society" to assemble in Newark early in March 1794. The goad specifically referred to was "the conduct of a certain class of citizens" in the area, but undoubtedly the successful formation of democratic societies elsewhere in the Union provided most of the impetus.[14] Despite alleged Federalist efforts to prevent its organization, "upwards of thirty persons" banded together, electing Pennington and Matthias Ward officers and adopting a formal constitution. The document provided for monthly meetings, semi-annual elections, moderate annual dues, and, above all, the promotion of efforts to offer "political instruction" and to advance "political knowledge." The vital link to electoral efforts was articulated, although no evidence exists that it was ever applied; in keeping with "Republicanism," the constitution proclaimed, incumbent officeholders' "conduct would be examined . . . and of consequence [if they fail in their responsibility] they will be hurled from their easy situation."[15]

Just three months after its founding, the Essex County Democratic Society was embroiled in the public response evoked by the excise tax, the subsequent Whiskey Rebellion in western Pennsylvania, and the issue embracing the civil right to protest that grew out of the Rebellion. Even before

12. *Ibid.*
13. *Ibid.*, Sept. 4, 11, 25, 1793; Feb. 5, 19, 1794.
14. *Ibid.*, Feb. 26, Mar. 5, 12, 19, 1794.
15. *Ibid.*, Mar. 12, 19, 26, 1794.

armed resistance in the western country materialized, the Essex Society, in concert with similar societies around the nation, condemned the excise tax as incompatible with the spirit of a free people. When rioting flared in the mountains, the Essex organization condemned it "not for objecting, however, but for using violence." The Society went on to defend the right to oppose the government peacefully: "We are aware, that our governments are not infallible, but being under the controul of men . . . may DO WRONG." To prevent "enquiry into the conduct of the government," a Society statement summed up, "is as dangerous to civil liberty, as to raise in arms against its constitutional operations." The anti-Federalists were immediately condemned for condoning civil disorder, and in the political battle in the public prints in the autumn of 1794, they came out second best.[16] The most telling accusation against them was that the Essex organization, by justifying civil strife, "re-echoed the anathemas of the Demacratic Societies of the United States."[17]

Key spokesmen for the Society at this juncture were William S. and Aaron Pennington, the latter eventually becoming the permanent secretary of the organization. Both Penningtons— and particularly Aaron—were closely connected with the Newark *Centinel of Freedom* (Aaron was co-publisher and editor), the first really effective Republican newspaper in the state, and the editorial workhorse of the later Republican party organization. A third brother, Samuel, like William S., became a stalwart of the Essex Republican party for a good many years. William, indeed, rose to the top echelon of state leadership in the party. Aaron apparently died before the turn of the century. The fact that the Penningtons, closely connected to the *Centinel*, were also leaders in the Essex Democratic Society was not an unusual circumstance in this period. Many

16. *Ibid.*, Apr. 9, June 25, Sept. 3, 24, Oct. 8, 15, Nov. 12, Dec. 10, 17, 24, 31, 1794.
17. *Ibid.*, Jan. 21, 1795.

Jeffersonian journalists got their start in similar societies in other states.[18]

The continuing leadership of the Penningtons was markedly in evidence when, in the ensuing spring of 1795, the Society —and anti-Federalists generally—turned to belaboring Jay's Treaty. The treaty was a much more fruitful issue than the Whiskey Rebellion, and one that went a long way toward revolutionizing public opinion in the state. Opponents of the treaty tapped a deep wellspring of anti-British sentiment, natural among farmers and artisans nurtured on Revolutionary propaganda. The treaty "has become the common topic of conversation in every company," "Candor" disclosed in May 1795.[19] By summer, petitions were circulating "signed by thousands" in West Jersey, asking the President to refuse to submit the treaty to the Senate on the grounds that while it reiterated British promises to evacuate the northwest forts and established Anglo-American trade on a firmer footing, it offered no guarantees of American neutral rights on the high seas.[20] Residents of Morris County and Amwell and Hopewell townships in Hunterdon County took up the call and circulated petitions of their own.[21]

Public concern increased as a result of two spirited meetings convened to voice opposition to Jay's Treaty in August 1795. In Flemington a copy of the treaty was ceremoniously burned and the throng "erected the [liberty] pole, hoisted

18. See Donald H. Stewart, *Jeffersonian Journalism: Newspaper Propaganda and the Development of the Democratic-Republican Party, 1789-1801* (unpubl. Ph.D. diss., Columbia University, 1950), 9-12. For a treatment of the Penningtons in New Jersey politics, see Lucius Q. C. Elmer, *The Constitution and Government of the Province and State of New Jersey . . .* (Newark, 1872). For accounts of the Penningtons vis-à-vis the Republican party, see chapters three and seven.

19. *Woods's Newark Gazette*, May 13, 1795.

20. Mount Pleasant, Monmouth County, *Jersey Chronicle*, July 25, 1795; hereafter cited as Mount Pleasant *Jersey Chronicle*. This newspaper was edited by Philip Freneau, the former editor of the *National Gazette*, Philadelphia organ for Jefferson and Madison's budding party in 1792. For an account of Freneau's editorial activities in this period see Lewis Leary, *That Rascal Freneau: A Study in Literary Failure* (New Brunswick, 1941).

21. Mount Pleasant *Jersey Chronicle*, Sept. 5, 1795.

the petition, and set fire to the tar-barrel."[22] In Trenton a much larger but more sedate crowd of dissidents satisfied themselves by merely denouncing and vilifying the treaty, and by forwarding a petition to the President requesting that he not submit it to the Senate. The chairman of the latter meeting was Moore Furman, a Hunterdon County merchant; the chairman of the resolutions committee was James Mott, treasurer of the state. Significantly, both men were destined to become leading organizers of the Democratic-Republican party in 1800.[23]

In Essex County the Democratic Society marshaled the opponents of the treaty. The Society sponsored one successful convocation in Orange early in August and scheduled a larger, countywide meeting for later in the month that was called off when word arrived that the treaty had already been accepted. Nevertheless, Federalists reported that "Society patriots" were stirring "the minds of the people to anarchy, disorder, and confusion." These "irregular Jacobin societies," the New Brunswick *Guardian* protested, were guilty of "horrid ingratitude" for the blessings they were determined to undermine.[24]

With the treaty ratified and operative by the fall elections of 1795, immediate public concern died out; because of the lack of the proper party machinery to channel popular enthusiasm toward the polling places, the issue had little effect on the local elections. Many people in the state, however, questioned for the first time the wisdom of existing governmental policies; to the Federalists looking back after many years of political change, the Jay Treaty loomed large as the turning point in their political fortunes. The agitation surrounding it, the Federalists alleged, was the signal for the inception of party strife in New Jersey.[25] Although New Jersey

22. *Ibid.*, Aug. 18, 1795; New Brunswick *Guardian*, Aug. 11, 1795.
23. *Ibid.*
24. *Woods's Newark Gazette*, Aug. 5, 19, 1795; New Brunswick *Guardian*, Aug. 11, 1795, Oct. 4, 1796.
25. Trenton *True American*, July 19, 1813. The belief that Jay's Treaty

lagged behind several states in organizing resistance to the Federalists, preparations for the national and local elections of 1796 aided the creation of Republican party machinery.

Beginnings of Republican Party Organization, 1796-1798

The first concerted challenge to entrenched Federalism in New Jersey materialized in the presidential election of 1796. Rising party tensions in Congress and opposition to the Jay Treaty stimulated Republican resistance which rallied round Thomas Jefferson. New Jersey was no exception, even though the Republican movement lacked leadership and party machinery at the beginning of 1796. The most notable indication of Jeffersonian support was a pamphlet printed in Newark by the publishers of the Newark *Centinel of Freedom*, endorsing Jefferson's candidacy and attacking that of Adams. The pamphlet was widely, though surreptitiously, circulated.[26] A moderate Federalist noted that the pamphlet displayed "judgment and much ingenuity," but assured his political brethren that it would not meet with favorable public approval because it sent "from it evidences of [party] prejudice."[27] The critic was quite correct. There still prevailed, according to Aaron Ogden, a leading Federalist, a "tried attachment to . . . the federal party [that] seemed to preclude all doubt upon the subject of the Election, and to insure the vote of every elector."[28] The local Adams supporters were confident of success since presidential electors were not elected by popular vote but by the legis-

---

triggered a massive party organizational movement is an interpretation widely held and generally applied to the nation as a whole by historians today. Such agitation was not limited to New Jersey alone but was current throughout the Union. See Joseph Charles, *The Origins of the American Party System* (Williamsburg, 1956); William Nisbet Chambers, *Political Parties in a New Nation: The American Experience, 1776-1809* (N.Y., 1963); John C. Miller, *The Federalist Era, 1789-1801* (N.Y., 1960); Cunningham, *The Jeffersonian Republicans, 1789-1801.*

26. *President II* (Newark, 1796), Imprint Collection, New York Public Library, N.Y.C.

27. New Brunswick *Guardian*, Dec. 6, 1796.

28. Aaron Ogden to Jonathan Dayton, Dec. 10, 1796, Park Collection, Morristown National Historical Park, Morristown, N. J.; *Woods's Newark Gazette*, Dec. 1796, Jan. 1797.

lature. John Adams easily carried the vote of the joint meeting of the legislature in 1796 for New Jersey's presidential electors.[29]

During the campaign of 1796, Republican leadership and organization took hold in Essex and Morris counties. John Condit, a candidate running as a Republican, won a place in the Legislative Council from Essex County, the first candidate to run successfully in New Jersey under that banner. As the "Newark candidate," Condit defeated his Federalist opponent from Elizabethtown by a narrow margin.[30] The canvass, as it had in the past, had locked the rival cities in a struggle for ascendancy in Essex. Newark and environs were led by prominent families of recent vintage—the Penningtons and the Condits appeared significantly in New Jersey politics only after the Revolution. Elizabethtown, on the other hand, was the seat of many staid, well-to-do colonial families such as the Ogdens, the Daytons, the Williamsons, and the Boudinots. A distinctly fresh dimension was added to the old rivalry when Newark, generally endorsing Condit, indicated its growing sympathy with the emergent Republican interest, for Condit was by 1796 becoming well known as a local leader of that interest. Thus the combatants were designated Republicans and Federalists as well as Newark men and Elizabethtown men.[31]

Republican gains at the polls were, in large part, attributable to the efforts of a maturing cadre of leaders, the foremost being Aaron Kitchell. Elected to Congress in 1794 as a Federalist, this former blacksmith was converted to Republicanism and became the only representative from New Jersey actively opposed to the Jay Treaty. In fact, he acted in concert with

29. *Minutes and Proceedings of the Joint Meeting of the Legislature of the State of New Jersey*, 1796 (Trenton, 1797), 87; Newark *Centinel of Freedom*, Oct.-Nov., 1796. No roll-call legislative vote was recorded.

30. Newark *Centinel*, Oct. 1796; *Woods's Newark Gazette*, Oct. 1796; Elizabethtown, *New Jersey Journal*, Oct. 1796.

31. Edward R. Turner, "Women's Suffrage in New Jersey, 1790-1807," *Smith College Studies in History*, 1 (1916), 170; Newark *Centinel*, Oct.-Dec., 1796; *Woods's Newark Gazette*, Oct.-Dec., 1796; Elizabethtown *N.J. Journal*, Oct.-Dec., 1796.

Republicans in the House from other states, and probably attended at least one Republican congressional caucus in the early months of 1796 to lay organizational plans to strengthen the opposition party throughout the Union. John Beckley, among the foremost Republican organizers in Philadelphia, found Kitchell useful as a party contact for New Jersey;[32] Kitchell, after all, could be instrumental in hastening the development of a full-blown Republican interest in New Jersey.

Kitchell did not have to be told how to take advantage of the ripening political situation at home. A consummate politician, he was in touch with local New Jersey leaders at least as early as March 1796, suggesting retaliation against "leading gentlemen in the Legislature" who had been "seeking opportunities to embarrass New Jersey by their [proposed] Resolutions" supporting the Jay Treaty. Another way to affect public sentiment, Kitchell said, was to accuse Federalist colleagues in the House of extravagance, evinced by their votes favoring government expenditures. These, Kitchell concluded, would make good campaign issues in the pending congressional elections of 1797. In order to aid that campaign the resourceful Congressman forwarded literature from Philadelphia to his anti-Federalist friends in the state. This material was earmarked for use to discredit the New Jersey Federalists.[33]

32. John Beckley to James Monroe, Apr. 2, 1796, James Monroe Papers, N. Y. Pub. Lib.

33. Aaron Kitchell to Ebenezer Elmer, Mar. 7, May 3, May 24, 1796, Gratz Collection, Historical Society of Pennsylvania, Philadelphia, Pa.; Joseph F. Folsom, *et al.*, comps., *Cyclopedia of New Jersey Biography*, 6 vols. (N.Y., 1923), I, 141; James J. Wilson to William Darlington, Nov. 6, 1804, William Darlington Papers, Lib. Cong. Aaron Kitchell, the lone New Jersey congressman who discreetly directed the Republican movement in the formative year of 1796, was descended from New Jersey yeomanry who had settled in Hanover Township, Morris County. Kitchell started out as an apprentice blacksmith. After his master's death the run-down forge went to Kitchell by default, for no one else wanted it. He invested his hard-earned profits in land, which eventually provided him with a comfortable living. He then turned to politics. He was described as "a man of the people, dealing in the plainest speech." Kitchell's plain speech soon gained for him a reputation as the New Jersey Republicans' best orator. He was active in legislative politics during the Confederation, and was elected to Congress in 1794, before party lines had hardened in New Jersey. Because of his involvement in Republican politics in the House, he lost his seat in the Jan. 1794 election, but was returned in 1798, this time as

Although Kitchell in 1795 and early 1796 increasingly identified with the Republican interest in Congress, he still hoped to maintain his standing with the Federalists who had elected him their representative from Sussex and Morris counties. The Federalists, however, noting his Republican sympathies with regard to the Jay Treaty and his quiet aid to Republicans in local campaigns, sought and found evidence of his alleged duplicity and exposed him publicly as a "trimming, time-serving politician."[34] Middlesex Federalist Anthony White charged openly that Congressman Kitchell "had written, while in Congress, on the same day, different political sentiments to different persons in this state." The Federalist papers picked up the allegation and attributed it to Kitchell's "trimming conduct," concluding that he "was a very unfit man to represent them in Congress." Despite his repeated denials that he had written the two letters, Kitchell was through as a Federalist.[35] His future was thus necessarily charted for him: Kitchell would run as a Republican. "I myself have been indicted by the grand jury of Middlesex," Kitchell remonstrated facetiously in a public statement, "and the lawyers of that, and the adjacent counties have found me guilty of voting against the omnipotence of the President and Senate, vis-a-vis the Jay Treaty and have passed sentence upon me, which is to

---

an out-and-out Republican. After 1800, he served in the state legislature. The ex-blacksmith was sent to the United States Senate in 1804 by a grateful Republican legislative majority; he served in the Senate until poor health forced him to retire in 1809. See H. D. Kitchel, *Robert Kitchel, and His Descendants, from 1604 to 1879* (N.Y., 1879), 76-78; Folsom, *et al.*, comps., *Cyclopedia of New Jersey Biography*, I, 141; Fee, *Transition*, 97-98; and scattered correspondence from Kitchell to various New Jersey Republicans in the Gratz Collection, Hist. Soc. of Pa.

34. Newark *Centinel*, June 14, July 19, 26, Aug.-Sept., 1797; Newark *Centinel Supplement*, July 12, 1797; Trenton *State Gazette and New Jersey Advertiser*, Jan. 3, 1797; Aaron Kitchell to Ebenezer Elmer, Mar. 7, May 3, 24, 1796, Gratz Collection, Hist. Soc. of Pa. The story was detailed retrospectively in the *Centinel*.

35. Newark *Centinel Supplement*, July 12, 1797; Newark *Centinel*, July 19, 1797; *Woods's Newark Gazette*, Jan. 11, 1797; Trenton *State Gazette*, Jan. 3, 1797.

be executed the first time I am a candidate for any appointment in the future."[36]

With Kitchell in the van, embryonic Republicanism made strenuous efforts in the unsuccessful congressional campaign of January 1797. Aided by the Newark *Centinel of Freedom,* founded by the Pennington brothers in 1796, the Republicans boldly attacked the "Federalist Ticket, alias the Aristocratical, alias the Lawyer ticket."[37] In December 1796 a "Morris County Farmer" (Kitchell?) boldly suggested the first truly Republican ticket: "may we not with greater safety place our confidence in an [Ebenezer] Elmer, a [Joseph] Cooper, a Kitchell, a [William] Helms, a Dr. Condit?[38] Significantly, it was at this time that the term "Republican" came into common use in referring to anti-Federalists in New Jersey, although it long since had been introduced elsewhere in the nation.

Shortly before Christmas, a meeting of Newark electors took the cue and resolved that the five men (except for the substitution of James Linn for William Helms) receive the meeting's "suffrages at the ensuing election for members of Congress, and [did] . . . earnestly recommend them to the electors in every part of the state."[39] The Federalist *Newark Gazette,* though still claiming impartiality, deprecated the effort: "The number of persons at the above meeting did not exceed fifty, and those (except six persons) from the town of Newark—the votes to support the above Ticket were about twenty five."[40] The convocation did not give itself a party label, but merely called its members a group of "electors" or "freeholders."

36. Newark *Centinel Supplement,* July 12, 1797.

37. Newark *Centinel,* Nov. 30, 1796. Congressional elections were still scheduled arbitrarily by the legislature prior to the expiration of the terms of office of incumbent congressmen. The election law of 1790 clearly stated that county elections were to begin on the second Tuesday of October, but the law was silent about the date for the election of congressmen. This silence was responsible for the leeway given the legislature in scheduling national elections throughout the Republican era.

38. Newark *Centinel,* Dec. 14, 1796; William DeHart to Ebenezer Elmer, Dec. 14, 1796, Gratz Collection, Hist. Soc. of Pa.

39. Newark *Centinel,* Dec. 21, 1796.

40. *Woods's Newark Gazette,* Dec. 28, 1796.

Another meeting, this one composed of residents of Bloom-field and Cranetown (Montclair), gathered a week before the election; they departed from the Newark choices to a degree (substituting Joseph Bloomfield and William Crane for Elmer and Cooper), just as the Newark ticket differed from that of a "Morris County Farmer," indicating a fundamental lack of organization and Republican communication. The Bloomfield men, in their plea to unite behind their ticket, noted that in their slate "the agricultural, mechanical and common interests of our country are blended." The *Centinel* expressed "full confidence in the military, civil and political virtues" of the nominees—its endorsements, significantly, conforming exactly to the choices of the Newark meeting.[41]

Outside Essex County only Morris County Republicans hinted at even nominal organized support of the ticket.[42] Nevertheless, individual Republicans in many parts of the state tried to rally support for the ticket. The effort of William DeHart of Morris County typified the unsatisfactory nature of individual politicking. Despite his assurances to Ebenezer Elmer, a nominee and Cumberland County's leading Republican, that "this *ticket* will be run strong in [Morris] county," and his promise "that I and all my friends here will make every exertion for you," he called no public meetings. DeHart closed his letter with the well-chosen admonition, "I hope you are a tough Democrat and a good Whigg."[43] Elmer and all Republican nominees would have to be, to run so hopelessly in 1796 in a statewide contest.

Even though widespread organization was lacking, issues continued to enliven the public prints. A Republican sum-

41. *Ibid.*, Dec. 28, 1796; Newark *Centinel*, Jan. 4, 1797; J. N. Cumming to Jonathan Dayton, Jan. 1, 1796 [1797], Lloyd W. Smith Collection, Morristown National Hist. Park.

42. Newark *Centinel*, Dec. 14, 1796; William DeHart to Ebenezer Elmer, Dec. 14, 1796, Gratz Collection, Hist. Soc. of Pa.

43. William DeHart to Ebenezer Elmer, Dec. 26, 1796, Emmet Collection, N.Y. Pub. Lib. One newspaper, striving to retain subscribers of all shades of opinion, reported only *after* the election that a "Farmer's Ticket" had been run. Trenton *State Gazette*, Jan. 10, 1797.

marized many of the gravest questions of the day in answering in the *Centinel* a plea by the *Newark Gazette* to support "good government." Taking exception to editor John Woods' definition of good government, the writer averred: "But what must be [the voter's] surprise and indignation when he shall be told that . . . good government only means the Hamiltonian administration; by good order, submission to his administration; by federal ticket, a ticket favorable to this administration, and by peace, peace with England and war with France."[44]

Ticket voting was still not the order of the day. The appearance of "mixed" tickets—containing the names of both Federalists and Republicans—indicate that factions and not parties were competing in New Jersey in 1796.[45] Perhaps Aaron Kitchell understood this best: "My situation with respect to the Election is not very pleasant . . .," he said. "At present I am alone in politicks from Jersey." Among other things, he expected to lose running with Republican outsiders.[46] But Federalist leaders, unruffled by scattered opposition, were sanguinely confident of success. They slighted the "Farmer's [Republican] Ticket" and belittled Jeffersonian electioneering, noting that in Essex "Pennington is shouting loudly of the necessity of changing men in order to change Measures." One Essex Federalist predicted the "whole Ticket will go to the Wall," adding "Doctr. Condet—Kitchell—Linn—Cooper and Elmer are the Ticket, and the Lord have mercy on us if New Jersey is not better represented than by them."[47]

Federalist hopes were borne out as the entire Republican ticket went down. The top five Federalists tallied from 4,090 to 7,100 votes, while Kitchell led the losers with 3,860 votes;

44. Newark *Centinel*, Jan. 11, 1797.

45. For example, see Newark *Centinel*, Oct.-Dec. 14, 1796, and New Brunswick *Guardian*, Jan. 10, 1797.

46. Aaron Kitchell to Ebenezer Elmer, Dec. 14, 1796, Gratz Collection, Hist. Soc. of Pa.

47. Richard Howell to Jonathan Dayton, Dec. 22, 1796, Gratz Collection, Hist. Soc. of Pa.; J. N. Cumming to Jonathan Dayton, Jan. 1, 1796 [1797], Lloyd W. Smith Collection, Morristown National Hist. Park

the remainder of the Republican ticket trailed far behind, finishing with a high of 2,485 to a low of 2,076.[48] Despite their victory, however, the Federalists knew they had been in a fight.

In the interim between the campaigns of 1796-97 and 1798, the XYZ Affair pressed a new issue on potential voters. The Federalists naturally capitalized on the increasing threat of hostilities with France by attacking the Republicans for their well-known sympathy for the French. Moderate Federalist meetings in Newark, New Brunswick, and Trenton in May 1798 passed resolutions supporting the policy of negotiation advocated by John Adams. These were naturally publicized in the Federalist press: "Unhappy partiality for the French nation," the *Newark Gazette* concluded happily, "is waning more rapidly than it grew." More militant party men, following the lead of Alexander Hamilton, demanded war and not negotiation. Federalists in Burlington collected money to build "A Ship of War" for the government. Equally ardent Federalists denounced "the wretches who cry peace—peace—when there is no peace." Despite these evidences of a strong Federalist offensive, Republicans in Essex, at least, held ther own—an indication of the young movement's ability to adjust to changing conditions and retain organizational solidarity at a time of great stress. This became clear when, at a second Newark meeting, Republicans were able to vote down a resolution supporting the President's policies in the crisis. The XYZ issue, in New Jersey at least, had not ruptured exisiting Republican unity prior to the fall elections of 1798.[49]

The Federalists, having written off the opposition of the Jeffersonians completely in 1797, were troubled by the considerable energy Essex Republicans continued to display. To forestall a more widespread Republican effort in the 1798

48. Trenton *State Gazette*, Jan. 31, 1797; Elizabethtown *N.J. Journal*, Jan. 25, 1797; Newark *Centinel*, Jan. 18, 25, Feb. 1, 1797.

49. *Newark Gazette*, May 1, 15, June 12, July 17, 24, 31, 1798. For treatments of the XYZ Affair nationally, see Manning J. Dauer, *The Adams Federalists* (Baltimore, 1953); Stephen G. Kurtz, *The Presidency of John Adams: The Collapse of Federalism, 1795-1800* (Philadelphia, 1957).

congressional elections, the Federalist legislature districted the state (see map, p. 2) and decreed that the national and state polls should be held at the same time in an effort to spur a greater Federalist vote in the increasingly Republican areas of Essex and Morris counties. Populous and Republican Essex was bracketed with strongly Federalist Bergen and Middlesex counties; Morris and Sussex were paired off to elect a representative, as were Hunterdon and Somerset counties. To the south, Monmouth, Burlington, and Gloucester counties joined to choose a congressman; and the remaining counties, Cumberland, Salem, and Cape May, made up the final district of the state.[50] Republican efforts were more widespread and organized than in 1796; the emergent party designated congressional candidates in all of the five districts.

Both Federalist and Republican candidates were supported "by formidable and well disciplined phalanxes" in the district embracing Essex, Bergen, and Middlesex.[51] Beginning early, the Republicans focused their efforts to elect a congressman in the tri-county area. Machinery was created to conform to the congressional district, but only Essex County added a slate to compete in the concurrent legislative elections. At the end of August "a large meeting of inhabitants from different parts of the county of Essex, and committees from the counties of Middlesex and Bergen convened" at Springfield, Essex County, to designate John Condit their congressional candidate.[52]

Condit, a doctor who entered politics at the age of forty, like Kitchell was descended from an old New Jersey family. Like the Morris politician also, he was attacked bitterly and personally by his opponents. Typical was the advice of "Veritas," who cautioned the doctor "to heal the bodily diseases of [your] patients, not to endeavor to diffuse [your] political poison into their minds." Another detractor described him as "in a state of mental derangement." Condit, like Kitchell, survived

50. Newark *Centinel*, Sept. 4, 11, 18, 25, 1798; Trenton *State Gazette*, Sept. 18, Oct. 2, 1798.

51. Newark *Centinel*, Oct. 9, 1798.

52. *Ibid.*, Sept. 4, 25, 1798.

the bitter political trials of the 1790's to serve in the House and then the Senate continuously from 1799 to 1820. A poor speaker, he made his way in Republican circles by means of his taciturn nature and party regularity. As one Federalist observed discerningly of Condit, "it may truly be said no man knows his sentiments."[53]

By September 1 the campaign to elect Condit was well under way. Republican efforts naturally focused on Essex County, for if Condit prevailed by a big margin there he would win the district. On September 21 a county meeting convened at Orange comprising "delegates from the townships of Essex and other inhabitants of the county," indicating that even in Essex a standard form for county meetings did not yet exist. Condit's nomination was endorsed and a slate designated for legislative and county offices.[54] The Federalists in the district responded by renominating and campaigning for the incumbent, James Schureman. His membership in the Continental Congress in the 1780's, his attractive Revolutionary military record, Dutch ancestry, and "substantial mercantile interests" made this "staunch Federalist" an imposing opponent.[55]

In addition to state and national party machinery, the foundations for township party apparatus, spurred by the changes in the election law of 1797, were also erected at this juncture. The first township Republican meeting was held in Newark at the end of September, and the meeting ratified the slate adopted at the county level. Such extraordinary efforts to certify the ticket arose, apparently, from a general uncertainty regarding its acceptance by Republican voters. The Newarkers read aloud an address issued by the tri-county district meeting, attesting in this way to the source of their organiza-

53. New Brunswick *Guardian*, Sept. 18, 1798; *Newark Gazette*, July 3, 31, Oct. 9, Nov. 6, 1798. For brief biographies of Condit, see J. Henry Clark, *The Medical Men of New Jersey, in the Essex District, from 1666 to 1866* (Newark, 1867), 65-67; *The Biographical Encyclopaedia of New Jersey of the Nineteenth Century* (Phila., 1877), 280.

54. Newark *Centinel*, Sept. 25, 1798.

55. New Brunswick *Guardian*, Sept. 25, 1798; *Newark Gazette*, Sept. 11, 25, Oct. 2, 9, 1798; McCormick, *Experiment in Independence*, 199.

NEW JERSEY'S JEFFERSONIAN REPUBLICANS

tional efforts. After approving the address without dissent, they ordered one thousand copies struck off and circulated within the district.[56] The Tri-County Address eulogized Condit and lashed out at entrenched Federalism. Other local meetings at Caldwell, Aquackanonk, and Springfield convened at the same time, shamelessly emulating the Newark meeting in most details, including a reading and endorsement of the address; each assembly expressed its support of the county slate of candidates and its concurrence in Condit's nomination.[57]

It is evident that each gathering proceeded according to a prearranged format, probably laid down by the leading Essex politicos. The effects of these efforts may be judged by the Federalist reaction: "In Essex county indeed no stone has been left unturned, no exertion has remained untried to vitiate and corrupt the public mind. Falsehood and calumny against our government have been circulated among the inhabitants of Essex with the most malignant and industrious profusion."[58] Newspaper propaganda, campaign songs, and word of mouth all supplemented organization meetings. In Essex, at least, a Republican machine was effectively sinking roots. The same could not be said for Bergen and Middlesex, the Federalist counties in the district, for which there is practically no evidence of Republican activity.[59]

Organizational efforts in the Morris-Sussex district were marred by the inflexibility of many Sussex Republicans; they wanted their choice to run for Congress in place of Morris County's perennial candidate, Aaron Kitchell. Silas Dickerson, a leading Sussex politico, was instrumental in finally making Kitchell's candidacy acceptable to other Sussex Republicans;

56. Newark *Centinel*, Sept. 4, 11, 18, 25, Oct. 2, 1798.
57. *Ibid.*, Oct. 2, 1798.
58. New Brunswick *Guardian*, Oct. 23, 1798; Newark *Centinel*, Sept.-Oct., 1798, *passim*.
59. A party meeting was held in Bergen County, and a slate of local candidates was designated, but the small meeting broke up without authorizing steps to support the ticket. Republicans charged that the Federalists intimidated many who attended the meeting, and the entire effort collapsed. Newark *Centinel*, Sept. 11, 1798.

early in August he endorsed Kitchell, saying that "I shall confer my little influence on the Morris County Candidate," and adding that he would, like other Republicans in the district, "uniformly oppose all who prefer a war with France or any other Nation."[60]

Dickerson's efforts to cement party harmony proved decisive only after a good deal of turmoil. A "large number" of Sussex and Morris citizens with difficulty agreed to meet at Flanders in Sussex County on September 8. There are indications that there was not a little friction at the open meeting: Kitchell was nominated only after "full deliberation"; he was "approved of by a large majority present" from the outset but unanimity came only at the end of the lengthy meeting, when it was agreed, "he [should] be supported as the candidate for the district." Only then was his nomination made "unanimous."[61]

Despite the scramble backstage, however, Republican differences never openly reached the public and the region aligned itself behind Kitchell. This was impressive evidence of growing party discipline. Other proofs of growing party consciousness also manifested themselves. At Mendham, energetic Republicans erected a liberty pole and an effigy of Anthony W. White, Kitchell's former nemesis, which they proceeded to abuse. The zealous party men went so far that a spokesman present announced that the "[Mendham Republican] committee disapproved of such proceedings." This sort of activity led a Federalist to conclude that Morris County "servilely copies after Essex in all its infamy and disgrace."[62]

In the normally Federalist Hunterdon-Somerset congressional district, some informal machinery existed among Republicans, who designated James Linn their candidate by some unexplained means. Linn was an often controversial, but very

60. Silas Dickerson to Mahlon Dickerson, July 25, Aug. 5, 1798, Dickerson Letter Book, N.J. Hist. Soc.
61. Trenton *State Gazette*, Sept. 18, 1798; Silas Dickerson to Mahlon Dickerson, July 25, Aug. 5, 1798, Dickerson Letter Book, N.J. Hist. Soc.
62. New Brunswick *Guardian*, Sept. 4, Oct. 23, 1798.

adept Jeffersonian party organizer. Originally a resident of Federalist Somerset County, he moved in 1801 to neighboring Hunterdon County, where there existed a stronger and more promising Republican interest, and where he soon took the initiative in strengthening Republican efforts. He retired from Congress in 1801 to undertake this task, aided by one of the most prized appointments in President Jefferson's power to confer: the job of supervisor of internal revenue for the state, a position which kept Linn in the county. In 1798, he was aided by a split which produced two Federalist candidates for Congress. But only fragmentary open support for Linn developed; Republican newspapers remained silent. It is possible that the newspaper silence was deliberate, for the Republicans may have hoped to perpetuate Federalist differences by lulling them into complacency. Republicans in Bridgewater, in fact, sparked the only known organized effort for the candidate when they took the initiative at a local gathering to suggest a meeting for the whole of Somerset County—a meeting the results of which were not made known, however. Some of these deficiencies, Federalists alleged, were remedied by Linn, who took the unpardonable step of compaigning for himself. A candidate is a "detestable and dangerous wretch," noted one opponent, "when his popularity has been 'sought after,' by *day light* and by *candle light*."[63]

In the district embracing Monmouth, Burlington, and Gloucester counties, another Federalist area, Thomas Henderson of Monmouth was the Republican candidate. The only way to measure the stir he made is to evaluate the Federalist assaults on his candidacy; no other evidence of Republican activity in this district has come to light. But these attacks and the apparently unanimous Republican backing of his candidacy indicate at least minimal party machinery. Even so,

63. *Ibid.*, Sept. 11, 18, 25, 1798; Trenton *State Gazette*, Nov. 20, 1798; Walter Lowrie and Walter S. Franklin, eds., *American State Papers*, Class X, *Miscellaneous*, I (Washington, 1834), 282. See also descriptions of Linn's local role, chapter three, and patronage efforts, chapter eight.

Henderson fared very badly, for he was accused of a cardinal sin of the 1790's—an expressed lack of faith in George Washington and his policies. Mute testimony to the weakness of the campaign mounted for Henderson was the absence of election returns for the district in either Republican or Federalist newspapers.[64]

In the national and state elections in New Jersey held simultaneously in the middle of October 1798, the Republicans scored their first major triumph by electing three of the five-member New Jersey delegation to Congress. It was not surprising that John Condit won his election in the Essex-Bergen-Middlesex district, nor was it startling that Aaron Kitchell was victorious in increasingly Republican Morris and Sussex counties. The real upset occurred in the Hunterdon-Somerset district where James Linn emerged with a slim majority over two Federalist candidates. Many Federalist voters, perhaps disgusted with the schism in their party, stayed away from the polls.[65] The Federalists, viewing the wreckage, admitted a serious blunder: the Republicans won, a commentator reported, because of "an advantage which they derived from the new method of election of representatives in Congress by Districts, which never could have been obtained in a general election."[66] In short, earlier Federalist fears of the impact of the vote from populous and Republican Essex County in an at-large election had resulted in the districting which was now blamed for the defeat. Whatever the reason, New Jersey Republicans were encouraged by the capture of a majority of the state's seats in Congress even while elsewhere in the nation

64. Trenton *State Gazette*, Oct. 2, 1798; New Brunswick *Guardian*, Oct. 2, 1798. There were no indications of any Republican efforts in the lower district embracing Cumberland, Salem, and Cape May counties.

65. Trenton *State Gazette*, Nov. 20, 1798. Linn gathered 1,613 votes to his opponents' totals of 979 and 554 respectively. Earlier and later elections indicate an appreciably stronger Federalist showing in this area, lending credence to the assumption that the Federalists were apathetic as well as divided. Republicans were also successful in the state elections in Morris and Essex counties. See Newark *Centinel*, Oct. 16, 23, 30, 1798.

66. *Newark Gazette*, Nov. 6, 1798.

many better organized Republican parties went down to defeat.[67]

Politics in the Legislature

The consolidation of Republican party apparatus in the legislature occurred in the late 1790's, along with that in the counties; yet it lagged behind the party growth in some counties discussed above. There was no Republican attempt to undermine Federalist authority in the legislature in 1796 and 1797. The results of the congressional and state elections of 1798, however, inspired Republican confidence. In small ways in 1798 and 1799 opposition legislators indicated their willingness to stand up and be counted.

The political infirmities among Democratic-Republican legislators in 1796 and 1797 and their growing strength in 1798 can be summed up by the terse sentences inserted in the minutes of the joint meetings of the legislature in 1796, 1797, and 1798 regarding the election of Richard Howell as governor. In 1796 and 1797, the sentence read: "Richard Howell was unanimously re-elected as Governor of the state of New Jersey."[68] In 1798, however, the word "unanimously" was omitted—a telltale omen in view of other developments. The Republicans for the first time had mustered resistance to Richard Howell, nominating several candidates. The effort was more noteworthy than the result: "Notwithstanding the intrigues, artifices and manoeuvers of our democrats to turn out the virtuous Howell, he was reelected Governor by a very large majority."[69]

The same joint meeting of 1798 faced the task of designating two United States senators, and although Jonathan Dayton was elected to a full term, once again the word "unan-

67. Miller, *The Federalist Era*, 255. While New Jersey returned Republicans as such to Congress for the first time, Virginia, South and North Carolina, and Georgia all increased their Federalist congressional delegations.

68. *Minutes and Proceedings of the Joint Meeting*, 1796, 87ff; *ibid.*, 1797 (n.p., n.d.), 77ff.

69. *Newark Gazette*, Oct. 30, 1798; New Brunswick *Guardian*, Oct. 30, Nov. 6, 1798; *Minutes and Proceedings*, 1798, 37ff.

imously" was conspicuously missing from the minutes.[70] The second senatorial election in 1798, to fill the seat vacated by John Rutherford's resignation, stirred impressive Republican activity. There were eleven Republicans among the fifty members of the joint meeting. When the Federalists, caught unawares, split their votes among three candidates, the Republicans cast their ballots for Ebenezer Elmer, in the first recorded roll-call vote in at least three years.[71] The Federalists quickly rallied against this unexpected opposition and elected James Schureman to the Senate, but they were badly shaken. For the first time in a decade factional politics had appeared in the legislature, the Federalists charged. One added prophetically that "the present Legislature are very much managed by Kitchell and Condit."[72]

Republican unity again appeared in the early months of 1799, when the Democratic-Republican faction in the Assembly used the legislature as a forum to debate the Virginia and Kentucky Resolves. The Resolves had been drafted by Thomas Jefferson and James Madison as a ringing defense of civil liberties and states' rights in answer to the Adams administration's employment of federal power to enforce the highly controversial Alien and Sedition Acts. The Resolves of both states were circulated to the legislatures of the remaining states in the Union for discussion and possible endorsement. The Alien and Sedition Laws appeared first in New Jersey as a party issue briefly in 1798 when they were passed by Congress, but they did not stir widespread public interest, apparently, until the beginning of 1799 when the effects of their enforcement were first felt.[73] In January of the latter year the issue broke with a vengeance upon New Jersey politics.

As might be expected, Essex Republicans took the lead by

70. *Minutes and Proceedings,* 1798, 37ff.
71. *Ibid.*
72. Richard Stockton to John Rutherford, Jan. 30, Feb. 20, 1798, N.J. Hist. Soc., *Proceedings,* 2d Ser., 3 (1872), 181, 184; *Minutes and Proceedings,* 1798, 37ff.
73. For early indicators of public interest, see *Newark Gazette,* Mar. 27, July 31, 1798.

calling a public meeting "for the purpose of taking into consideration the propriety of Remonstrating to Congress on the subjects of the Alien and Sedition Acts." A rousing—even startling—reception greeted the call, indicative of the volatile political overtones of the Acts, and typical of the reaction to them throughout the country. A hostile Federalist newspaper reported that three to four hundred Essexites turned out to protest the laws, which were "held up *in terrorum*" to the meeting. The potential evils flowing from the acts described to the throng ranged from "an imaginary horde of malicious informers" to "the prejudices and caprices of an arbitrary President—with all the evils of Pandora's box." Those who chose to defend the laws were hissed and laughed at. The meeting voted to censure the hated legislation and to reiterate support of a free press.[74] Popular disaffection with administration policy manifested itself even in strongly Federalist Bergen County, where a gathering denounced the Acts and raised a "Sedition Pole" (Liberty Pole) in protest. The scene was for the most part repeated in Morris County, and in all probability elsewhere in the state as well.[75]

Capitalizing on the concurrent wave of popular disapproval, Republican legislators brought the issue before the Assembly for discussion early in 1799, in an obvious appeal for public favor. It was a subject which Republicans could indeed squeeze for propaganda purposes, for by early 1799 controversy boiled up throughout the country over the repressive measures.[76]

Republican strategists in the Assembly, led by William S. Pennington and Henry Southard, did not endorse the Virginia and Kentucky Resolves. Indeed, they, like the Federalists,

74. *Ibid.*, Jan. 22, 1799.
75. *Ibid.*, Mar. 5, 1799; New Brunswick *Guardian*, Aug. 21, 1799.
76. Two monographs dealing with the Alien and Sedition Acts generally (both touch also on New Jersey specifically) are: James M. Smith, *Freedom's Fetters: The Alien and Sedition Laws and American Civil Liberties* (Ithaca, 1956), and John C. Miller, *Crisis in Freedom: The Alien and Sedition Acts* (Boston, 1951). For a more detailed account of the temper of the times in New Jersey, particularly among New Jersey legislators, see the otherwise outdated F. M. Anderson, "Contemporary Opinion of the Virginia and Kentucky Resolutions," *American Historical Review*, 5 (1900), 52-55.

ostensibly opposed approving them. To create an issue, however, Republican legislators also resisted "affronting a sister state" by merely dismissing the Resolves as the Federalists intended to do, without some explanation for the Assembly's actions. Clearly, no adherence to principle was at issue in this instance; the Republican minority simply was playing the political game to the hilt.

The Federalists moved to dismiss the Resolves forthwith. Pennington eloquently opposed the motion on the grounds that the House "ought to treat a sister state, and especially one of so much importance as that of Virginia, with common decency and respect." "Even if indecent," Pennington continued, "let us not retort upon them [the Resolves] indecency." A Federalist member was "almost" led "to suspect the sincerity of their [Republican] declarations," for if the minority was opposed to the Resolves then why consider them? "It is at least a strange inconsistency." Applying the balm of sweet reason and moderation as thickly as he dared, Pennington summed up the Republican position by pointing out that "the duty of New Jersey [is] to endeavor to appease, not to irritate, and a well-reasoned reply will be the most likely means of preserving harmony between the states."[77]

The Federalist majority, as expected, gained dismissal of the Resolves without explanation by a vote of twenty to fifteen. The tactical victory went to the Republicans, however. Their stand was moderate and popular; they were joined by some moderate Federalists on the vote, a fact which helped to legitimatize their position. A final tactical advantage accrued when the imaginative William Pennington introduced a resolution calling for a national constitutional convention to amend and delimit the respective powers of the state and federal governments. The Federalists dismissed the motion, but not before it was broadcast by party newspapers throughout the state.[78]

77. *Newark Gazette*, Jan. 29, 1799; Anderson, "Contemporary Opinion of the Virginia and Kentucky Resolutions," *Amer. Hist. Rev.*, 5 (1900), 52-55.
78. *Ibid.* See also Newark *Centinel*, and Elizabethtown *N.J. Journal*, Jan.-May, 1799, *passim.*

It was during this same legislative session of 1799 also that Republican members first took quarters together, evincing a consciousness of their party affiliation. Once again they were "determined to give [Governor] Howell a sweat."[79] The Republicans supported the moderate Federalist Andrew Kirkpatrick for governor, knowing that they could not elect one of their own but hoping to deepen the Federalist split. Howell was re-elected despite their efforts although fifteen votes were mustered for Kirkpatrick. Notwithstanding a deluge of petitions favoring Republican appointments engineered by Republican legislators, the Federalists remained "determined against every thing that is Republican."[80]

Republican legislative rapport was carefully cultivated by Joseph Bloomfield, one of the few Federalist leaders in the state to make the transition to Republican ranks. This former Congressman was, like Kitchell, a magnet to whom Republicans were drawn. He made himself indispensable by meeting with dissident legislators and planning with them a design for legislative action. His fine hand was evident in the parrying over the Sedition Laws and the challenges to legislative appointments of a governor and a senator. Described later as "old and rich," Bloomfield certainly had the stature and means to carry out his ambitious project. "The General," as he liked to be called, frequently invited Republican legislative leaders to his Burlington home with its "fine library and . . . many curiosities," where he wined and dined them. Such Jeffersonians as the Dickerson and Pennington brothers, Ebenezer Elmer, Aaron Kitchell, Henry Southard, and others visited him at one time or another in this formative period. By 1799 these episodes had become a regular occurrence among Republican legislators and strategists, and were in fact early Republican caucuses of a sort.[81] It was these men who laid

79. Silas Dickerson to Mahlon Dickerson, Oct. 22, 1799, Dickerson Letter Book, N.J. Hist. Soc.

80. *Minutes and Proceedings*, 1799, 37ff; Mahlon Dickerson to Silas Dickerson, Oct. 28, 1799, Silas Dickerson to Mahlon Dickerson, Nov. 1, 1799, Dickerson Letter Book, N.J. Hist. Soc.

81. Ephraim Bateman to John W. Taylor, Oct. 15, 1816, John W. Taylor

the groundwork for improved Republican organization.

Bloomfield's transition to Republicanism after 1796 lent the party a degree of respectability. Having served the government prominently the General was in the public eye, and during this period of transition he tried to straddle the political fence while he made up his mind. As late as December 1796, he publicly denied any anti-Federalist leanings, protesting "I am a friend of the President and Government, [as] I have already evinced, by voting as an elector for the President in 1792, and marching under his orders in 1794."[82] Soon after making this public declaration, however, he openly severed his Federalist ties anyway. Perhaps he disliked the Federalist position on the Jay Treaty. Whatever his motives, he helped to cultivate anti-Federalist sentiment in the state. Because of his active political past and his initial coyness regarding his Republicanism, Bloomfield was viewed with suspicion by many Jeffersonians until as late as 1804.[83]

Papers, New-York Historical Society, N.Y.C.; Silas Dickerson to Mahlon Dickerson, Nov. 1, 1799, and *passim*, Dickerson Letter Book, N.J. Hist. Soc. For information about the evolution of the legislative caucus, see relevant sections of chapters four, five, seven, and eight. Joseph Bloomfield, like Kitchell and Condit, had roots deep in New Jersey. He had served actively with the state militia in the Revolution; after Washington became President, Bloomfield joined the Federalist cause, leading New Jersey troops against the Whiskey Rebellion in 1794. He was an officer in the New Jersey (and national) Society for the Abolition of Slavery. After the Republican triumph in 1801, he served as governor of the state for ten years and spent four years more in Congress. For three years he was a major general in the American army during the War of 1812, serving without distinction in a number of posts. For aspects of Bloomfield's life, see Joseph Bloomfield, *To the Public*, Dec. 1, 1796, New Jersey Broadsides Collection, N.J. Hist. Soc.; *Biographical Encyclopaedia of New Jersey*, 273; Elmer, *The Constitution and Government of New Jersey*, 124; Isaac W. Crane to Joseph Bloomfield, Nov. 7, 1796, Lloyd W. Smith Collection, Morristown National Hist. Park.

82. Joseph Bloomfield, *To the Public*, N.J. Broadsides Collection, N.J. Hist. Soc.; New Brunswick *Guardian*, Jan. 3, 10, 1797.

83. Silas Dickerson to Mahlon Dickerson, Nov. 10, 1801, Mahlon Dickerson to Silas Dickerson, Nov. 28, 1801, Dickerson Letter Book, N.J. Hist. Soc.; Ebenezer Elmer to George Burgin, n.d. [1801], Emmet Collection, N.Y. Pub. Lib.; Joseph Bloomfield to Ebenezer Elmer, July 6, 1802, Ely Collection, N.J. Hist. Soc.; John Condit to Ebenezer Elmer, Sept. 29, 1802, Gratz Collection, Hist. Soc. of Pa.; Joseph Bloomfield to Silas Dickerson, Mar. 19, 1804, Ely Collection, N.J. Hist. Soc.

Parties and People

The emergence of effective Republican opposition inside and outside the legislature between 1795 and 1800 brought an immediate Federalist reaction. The proponents of John Adams used with particular delight the term "anti-Federalist" to describe their foes, an epithet which galled Republicans more as they grew in strength. One party man protested that "to call a man an anti-federalist because he may think some act of the general government is unjust or impolitic is . . . absurd." Another Republican reacted in much the same way. "May true Republicans only be known by that appellation," he asserted, "and the names of Federalist and Anti-Federalist be obliterated."[84]

Federalist abuse was not limited to words of scorn. A running feud of the kind typical in this initial party era broke out between the editors of the Republican *Centinel* and the Federalist *Newark Gazette.* Aaron Pennington, one of the editors of the *Centinel,* resentful of personal allusions to his crippled leg, capped the mounting antagonism by challenging the editor of the rival weekly to a duel in the summer of 1797. The latter declined, but promised to horsewhip Pennington the "first time I met with him." Although this particular threat was never carried out, the following summer Pennington was attacked and beaten by an unknown assailant, part of a group the *Centinel* editor bitterly referred to as "the order of the knife." The assault, he said, occurred as a result of his unrelenting public criticism of Governor Howell. This same criticism made Daniel Dodge and Pennington early but by no means singular victims of the Sedition Acts. Both were arrested and, like so many other Republican newspapermen, charged with seditious libel for refusing to divulge the name of the author of an article attacking the Governor.[85]

The co-editors were by no means the best known New

---

84. Newark *Centinel,* Nov. 2, 1796; *Woods's Newark Gazette,* July 16, 1794.
85. *Woods's Newark Gazette,* Aug. 9, 1797, and *passim;* Newark *Centinel,* Aug. 7, 14, 21, 28, 1798; New Brunswick *Guardian,* Aug. 28, 1798.

Jersey victims of the Sedition Laws. That distinction belonged to Luther Baldwin of Newark. While drunk one day in the fall of 1798, this otherwise inconspicuous individual (in his more sober moments he was "captain" of a garbage scow plying the Passaic River) publicly expressed a wish to see President Adams, then passing through town, "shot through the arse" by a cannon salute. He was promptly clapped in jail (and later convicted) for sedition. In a few short months Baldwin became one of the most celebrated victims of the Federalist Sedition Laws in the United States. Republicans everywhere for years thereafter reminded their antagonists of this miscarriage of justice; they claimed the last word on the subject when they queried, "Can the most enthusiastic Federalists or Tories suppose that those who are opposed to them would feel any gratification in firing at such a disgusting target as the [arse] of John Adams?"[86]

Party feelings were expressed most violently at Fourth of July celebrations. Coming at a time when campaign preparations were just getting underway, the celebration of American independence "drew the line of division between the parties, and fanned the flame of party spirit." It was, in the words of another participant, a day of "political wrangle."[87] Republicans could take the offensive as well as their opponents when the occasion arose. In the Fourth of July festivities at Morristown in the summer of 1798, the Republicans were provoked by some Federalists, whereupon "some loaded Whigs, some [with] cudgels some [with] fists . . . was engaged in the fray sometimes all up sometimes all down."[88]

Even in this period of ferment not everyone chose sides. A "moderate," writing in the *Centinel* in September 1799, made a plea for the end of "derision, confusion and noise" resulting from the divergent politics of the day. Pre-dating

86. Miller, *Crisis in Freedom*, 112-14; Smith, *Freedom's Fetters*, 270-74; *Newark Gazette*, Jan. 29, 1799; New Brunswick *Guardian*, Nov. 13, 1798.
87. Newark *Centinel*, Aug. 28, 1798, July 2, 1799.
88. Silas Dickerson to Mahlon Dickerson, July 12, 1798, Dickerson Letter Book, N.J. Hist. Soc.

Jefferson by more than a year he asked plaintively, "are we not all federalists and republicans?"[89] It was too late, however. The Republicans of New Jersey smelled victory. Silas Dickerson, one of the first Republicans of the state, wrote in November 1799, "the high tone of federalism begins to flag in this State and I think will finally become as unpopular as toryism in seventy six."[90]

Much of the impetus for the crystallization of party formations in New Jersey was national in origin. Included among the causes was the agitation of such key issues as Hamiltonian economic policies, the Jay Treaty, the Alien and Sedition Acts, and incipient Republican direction from the House of Representatives. Still, the strength of the party was bound up with the momentous changes taking place at the local level. The activities of the Democratic Society and of men like Kitchell, Bloomfield, Condit, and Pennington were highly important in giving direction to the aroused political passions of a changing New Jersey; this was especially true in Essex County. Many of these men of like outlook came together in the legislature where some effective organizational activities were promoted. It was here that leadership centered, where depth soundings were made, and a coherent and unified program of organization was undertaken. When the personal ambition and self-interest of men like Kitchell, Bloomfield, Condit, and Pennington merged with key issues, party formations appeared in the precincts. A useful republican Revolutionary tradition and bitterly anti-English prejudices proved excellent vehicles for these men in creating the mood necessary for the formation of a highly developed statewide political force that was to come to fruition in 1800.

89. Newark *Centinel*, Sept. 17, 1799.
90. Silas Dickerson to Mahlon Dickerson, Nov. 11, 1799, Dickerson Letter Book, N.J. Hist. Soc.

II

ORGANIZING FOR VICTORY
IN 1800

FOR THE THIRD DAY IN A ROW, A WEARY JOSEPH BLOOMFIELD
guided his plodding horse along the dirt paths that passed for
roads in Monmouth County. His errand was vital—to coax
and cajole a reluctant and insecure county organization and its
leaders to unify and step up their efforts to elect Republicans
in what Bloomfield knew was a pivotal set of elections in
New Jersey.[1] The elections of 1800 were, because of the efforts of men like Bloomfield, contested with a thoroughness
and vigor new to the local scene. Emergent party managers
recognized that the party faithful liked to share in the excite-
ment of political campaigns, and local captains endeavored
to provide a role for all to play, promoting *esprit de corps* at
the grass roots and encouraging the growth of functioning
party machinery in many counties by boosting the use of newspapers, broadsides, pamphlets, and other electioneering aids.

In 1800 the annual local contests for the state legislature
and the biennial congressional elections coincided with the
presidential campaign. New Jersey's Republicans strove to elect

1. Joseph Bloomfield to Ebenezer Elmer, Aug. 25, 1801, Ely Collection, N.J.
Hist. Soc.

presidential electors pledged to Thomas Jefferson, but the task was particularly difficult, for the legislature had the option of providing for the popular election of electors or choosing them itself. A Federalist legislature, it was virtually certain, would follow the latter course. Therefore, the Republicans prepared to contest each seat, hoping to secure a legislative majority as a prerequisite to carrying New Jersey for Jefferson.

In most counties, however, there were no Republican organizations prior to 1800. Those organizations that did exist, notably in Morris and Essex counties, lacked established means of communication with Republicans of like feeling outside their respective areas. Therefore, Republican managers were unprepared at the beginning of 1800 to contest the election of presidential electors by the legislature. Faced with the difficult trial and little time, party leaders worked rapidly to form a network of local party machines in as many counties as possible. By the end of the year, a number of counties had succeeded in establishing party apparatus, thus introducing a vital Republican interest stretching from Sussex County in the north to Salem and Cumberland counties in South Jersey.

The attempt to build a statewide Republican organization got underway in April 1800, spearheaded by a comparatively small but closely knit activist group who had been laying the groundwork for party development for five years, men like Aaron Kitchell of Morris County, William S. Pennington of Essex, Silas Dickerson of Sussex, and Ebenezer Elmer and Joseph Bloomfield farther south in the state. By midsummer, the coordination established by the leaders was paying dividends. Mahlon Dickerson confided to his brother, "I hear from . . . a number of other gentlemen who are well informed on the subject, that the Republicans in Gloucester County and even in Burlington County [and Salem, Cumberland, and Cape May as well] are raising their heads."[2] Elmer and Bloomfield, in conjunction with lesser southern county leaders, were doing their

2. Mahlon Dickerson to Silas Dickerson, July 28, Aug. 14, 1800, Dickerson Letter Book, N.J. Hist. Soc.; Joseph Bloomfield to Silas Dickerson, Nov. 17, 1800, Mahlon Dickerson Papers, *ibid.*

[42]

job well. "You may be assured," Kitchell promised Elmer, "that the Eastern Counties will Support the Republican Ticket —and I hope that they will not want in Exertions."[3] Silas Dickerson, a prominent Sussex Republican, also vowed that "every exertion will be used in support" of the Republican candidates.[4]

These men, and others from nearly every county, met together many times in the course of the year. What was not discussed personally was taken up through the mails. In these tangible ways, New Jersey's Republican managers succeeded in coordinating their efforts to form a thoroughgoing statewide machine.[5]

The initial public call to arms appeared on April 1, 1800, when the "Sussex and Morris subscribers" to the Newark *Centinel of Freedom* proclaimed that,

Whereas the republican citizens of New Jersey, have in many instances, been disappointed in their hopes and expectations of having men elected to office who should represent their sentiments and interests in our State and National Councils, owing entirely to the want of unanimity in their plans of election; therefore in order to unite their exertions, and enable them to act in concert throughout the state, and by that means secure an entire representation in the next Congress and Legislature.

Resolved that a Committee of three persons be appointed in this township [Morristown] to act in concert with such other committees as may be appointed in other townships for the like purpose of recommending to the people suitable persons to be supported as Candidates, for members of our next Legislature.

3. Aaron Kitchell to Ebenezer Elmer, Dec. 11, 1800, Gratz Collection, Hist. Soc. of Pa.

4. Silas Dickerson to Mahlon Dickerson, Dec. 11, 1800, Dickerson Letter Book, N.J. Hist. Soc.

5. Joseph Bloomfield to Ebenezer Elmer and George Burgin, Sept. 29, 1800, Moore Collection, Princeton University Library, Princeton, N.J.; Elizabethtown *N.J. Journal*, Oct. 14, 1800; Joseph Bloomfield, *To the People of New Jersey*, Sept. 30, 1800, New Jersey Political Broadsides Collection, 1746-1805, Rutgers University Library, New Brunswick, N.J.; Newark *Centinel*, Oct. 1800, *passim*, Dec. 9, 1800; Silas Dickerson to and from Mahlon Dickerson, 1800, *passim*, Dickerson Letter Book, N.J. Hist. Soc.; Aaron Kitchell to ?, Apr. 23, 1800, Dreer Collection, Hist. Soc. of Pa.; Aaron Kitchell to Ebenezer Elmer, May 12, 1800, Ebenezer Elmer to David Moore, May 12, 1800, Gratz Collection, Hist. Soc. of Pa.; Joseph Bloomfield to Ebenezer Elmer, Apr. 20,

The announcement summoned a meeting of the proposed Morris County committees for July 4. The delegates, the call to arms continued, then could appoint a three-man county committee, "to consult and correspond with similar committees, which may be appointed in the different Counties of this State, for the purpose of recommending suitable persons to the people, to be supported as Candidates at the next election for Representatives in Congress."[6] The employment of such committees of correspondence was reminiscent of the organizations which had appeared in New Jersey prior to the Revolution.[7]

The *Centinel*, editorializing on the appeal of the Sussex and Morris subscribers, expected that the plan would "contribute greatly to the success of the republican ticket at the ensuing election, by uniting the strength of the republicans *in every part of the state*."[8] The Morris formation, then, was designed to serve as an example to other counties.

Its apparatus was almost certainly the brainchild of Aaron Kitchell, who, as we have seen, was directing party efforts in Morris County in the spring of 1800, and was striving to establish local machinery everywhere in New Jersey. On April 23, Kitchell wrote to a South Jerseyman,

1800, Ebenezer Elmer Papers, Rutgers Univ. Lib. These are selected examples of statewide coordinated activity. The evidence supporting this point is ample. See also the discussions of county and local organizations, chapters three, five, and seven.

6. Newark *Centinel*, Apr. 1, 15, 1800.

7. In the summer of 1775, the extralegal Provincial Congress seized control and "gradually usurped the powers" of the colonial government. At the same time "the local government passed into the hands of revolutionary 'Committees of Correspondence or of Observation.'" These local revolutionary committees associated on a statewide level in the form of the Provincial Congress. The Democratic-Republican local committees meeting in the spring and summer of 1800 followed the same path. The Provincial Congress served as the focus for the local committees of correspondence from May 1775 until the adoption of the New Jersey Constitution in 1776. The Democratic-Republican state conventions of 1800 and thereafter helped to maintain unity of purpose among the local party machines in generally the same way. The latter-day local and state committees differed in that they were not merely temporary expedients, however. See Leonard Lundin, *Cockpit of the Revolution: The War for Independence in New Jersey* (Princeton, 1940), 71, 110.

8. Newark *Centinel*, Apr. 1, 15, 1800.

I am informed that Morris and Essex have chosen Committees and it is Expected that Sussex, Bergin and Somerset have also. My informant is anxious to know whether any measures will be taken in any of the western counties. It is not Expected that Committees will be chosen at any publick meetings. All they request is that some persons of information and influence will Correspond with them and propose to them Such measures as appears to them most proper to preserve an Union of the Republican interest.[9]

Other confidential indications of coordinated effort followed. Less than three weeks later, Kitchell requested Ebenezer Elmer to contact Doctor Lewis Condict of Morristown when seeking advice on the best means of promoting party activity. He added, "I hope to hear from some of our Republican friends in Cumberland [and] . . . I hope that measures will be taken to Bring Jersey forward both for President and Members of the next Congress."[10] Elmer took the hint and launched an extensive but judicious letter-writing campaign to Republicans in Cumberland and Salem counties, reminding them that "the most important national concerns" were at stake. He suggested an organizational plan and then sought tactical suggestions, indicating his own position as final arbiter for the area: "If any other arrangement shall promise better success I shall wish to adopt it."[11]

Activists like Elmer and Kitchell were busy indeed, if a Federalist appraisal has any validity: "The one [party organizer] who lives near me is very industrious and secret; he is sending off letters almost every day to the different Townships, and receiving expresses from New-York, Essex County and Morris County; but he keeps them all secret from everybody but his Republicans."[12] Republicans were "ever assiduous to diffuse

9. Aaron Kitchell to ?, Apr. 23, 1800, Dreer Collection, Hist. Soc. of Pa. The recipient of this key letter almost certainly was Ebenezer Elmer. The first public appeal for party organization in 1800 appeared in the Newark *Centinel*, Apr. 1, 1800.

10. Aaron Kitchell to Ebenezer Elmer, May 12, 1800, Gratz Collection, Hist. Soc. of Pa.

11. Ebenezer Elmer to David Moore, May 12, 1800, *ibid.* There are indications in this letter that similar missives went to others in South Jersey.

12. *Newark Gazette*, Sept. 30, 1800.

their mischievous doctrines," complained another alarmed opponent, who added that they "are lavish in expense to hire the most flagitious men, who are stationed in divers parts."[13]

Events in Morris County moved rapidly after April 1. A reporter disclosed that before the month was out "the Republicans [were] gaining ground in Morris."[14] The local delegates of five Morris towns (Morristown, Hanover, Washington, Mendham, and Pequanock) met on Independence Day. Their most important act was to create from their number a county committee to constitute a committee of correspondence to integrate the activities of county Republicans and supervise preparations for the coming canvasses.[15]

Ultimately a sophisticated and enthusiastic Republican party was developed in Morris County. But it proved something of a mixed blessing. Six weeks after it originated the organization was engaged in a dispute over the nomination of candidates, evidencing a fact of political life that always plagued even the best Republican party managers. As long as the Republicans had remained amateurs at party politics, there was never much question of their ability to unite behind a ticket. However, once a powerful political in-group appeared, the struggle for leadership led to violent internal feuds which often resulted in split tickets on election day. This was true in county after county; a direct correlation developed between the authority wielded by the party in its bailiwick and the violence and depth of the struggle for control of the machinery. A situation arose that was long to trouble New Jersey Republi-

13. *Ibid.*, May 13, 1800.
14. Mahlon Dickerson to Silas Dickerson, Apr. 24, 1800, Dickerson Letter Book, N.J. Hist. Soc. The reporter was "B[ernard] Smith," later a Republican congressman.
15. Newark *Centinel*, Oct. 7, Dec. 16, 1800. Kitchell's organizational efforts in Morris County did not go unchallenged. A bizarre counter-proposal appeared in the public prints on Apr. 10, unique for its grand phrasing. Each town, instead of electing delegates to represent them, would choose "Tribunes." These Tribunes from each township would then hold annual "grand Associate meetings" on July 4 to choose "legislative eligibles" (candidates). The simpler scheme forwarded by the "subscribers" was adopted anyway. See the Morristown *Genius of Liberty*, Apr. 10, 1800.

cans: in the most solid Republican counties, there existed the deepest cleavages in party unity.[16]

Coincident with political developments in Morris County, Essex Republicans perfected their organization. Because they had a head start, Essex Republicans temporarily achieved the best local organization in the state. At a town meeting in Newark on April 14, a committee was chosen to form an organization capable of nominating and electing a slate of Republican candidates. The meeting acknowledged in its summons that the initiative came from Morris and Sussex. Aquackanonk Township also organized a local committee at the same time, Caldwell followed suit a week later, and shortly thereafter Springfield fell into line; other towns joined as the year wore on.[17] Each township party was led by a chairman and two, three, or even four additional committee members chosen by a vote of the town's Republicans. At the county committee meeting, it was ordained that each town would have an equal voice.[18]

On August 4, the first meeting of the Committee of the County of Essex convened in Newark. Only Elizabethtown and Bloomfield were unrepresented. The committeemen, in emulation of the Morris gathering, designated three of their number as a county committee of correspondence. Before adjourning, the representatives issued a long address touching on a number of sensitive issues. It attacked Adams' foreign policy which, the remonstrance proclaimed, favored England, and condemned the waste of public money (especially insofar as public funds were used to sustain a standing army), denounced sedition laws, and glorified sedition martyrs. State issues were not ignored; the Essex delegates found it "inexpedient at this time" to revise the state constitution, but chastised the legislature for ignoring Republican petitions

16. Mahlon Dickerson to Silas Dickerson, May 18, 1800, Dickerson Letter Book, N.J. Hist. Soc. The pattern described was present in all areas of the state with but few exceptions. See discussions of local party organization for confirmation, chapters three, five, and seven.

17. Newark *Centinel*, Apr. 1, 15, 22, June 10, Aug. 19, 1800.

18. *Ibid.* See also *ibid.*, Oct. 6, 13, 1801.

requesting a popular vote in New Jersey for the presidency. Agreeing to meet again in September to nominate candidates, the new organization ended its labors with a demand for action and unity in every township.[19]

The county nominating convention gathered in Newark on September 15. Nominations were read aloud "and due deliberation had thereon" before each township cast its two votes for each nominee of its choice. All Republican candidates not endorsed by the organization at that point succumbed to party needs and declined to run for office. The whole effort was well managed; county Federalists fumed in vain at this "self created society of bastard republicans." The state elections in October vindicated the Essex machine by sweeping into office all of its nominees. Federalist resistance never materialized. However, the unexpectedly easy victory cut deeply into the sense of sacrifice exhibited by Essex party men, and they would never again prove so tractable.[20]

Republican organization efforts in Sussex County were underway in April,[21] although they developed at a much slower pace. "Combustible matter," however, was "gathering which by and by will catch the flame," said Silas Dickerson.[22] Perhaps the material was too combustible, for at the Republican nominating meeting in August, "Major Ogden and a number of others dealing freely with the jolly God and singing a number of patriotic songs . . . and giving loose to their political sentiments a quarrel ensued between the Major and one Stephen Little . . . . They came to blows and 'fought' terribly for 15 minutes and 'bled' most copiously in freedom's cause." Such was the stuff of Republicanism that "the next morning they [the combatants] breakfasted together in the utmost harmony and friendship."[23] This meeting did not give itself

19. *Ibid.*, Apr. 1, 15, 22, June 10, Aug. 19, 1800.
20. *Ibid.*, Sept. 23, 30, Oct. 7, 14, 21, 28, 1800.
21. Aaron Kitchell to ?, Apr. 23, 1800, Dreer Collection, Hist. Soc. of Pa.
22. Silas Dickerson to Mahlon Dickerson, Apr. 30, 1800, Dickerson Letter Book, N.J. Hist. Soc.
23. *Ibid.*, Aug. 22, 1800.

over entirely to bloodshed. The participants arranged for the fall elections and designated a complete legislative ticket. The difficulties attendant to maintaining party discipline in a county which had never known such regularity became evident almost at once. "It is not very unlikely," Silas Dickerson disclosed, that the Republican opposition to the nominations "will form an entire new ticket and carry their point."[24] At the least, however, Republicans were assured one way or another of gaining legislative adherents to their cause from the refractory but Republican county.

In Bergen County, Republican party development followed an even more tortuous course, although it was not apparent at the outset. Newspaper appeals, primarily in the *Centinel*, continually urged the Republican interest to mobilize. At the same time, Silas Dickerson, prompted by his brother Mahlon, spent many days in the county lending the weight of his experience to novice Bergen Republicans. Other Republicans did the same throughout the spring of 1800, according to a Federalist report: "As to the people of Essex County and Morris County, who are continually riding about our County [Bergen], and meeting with our Republicans, I don't thank them at all for saying that we are a parcel of Dutch Fools."[25] These auspicious efforts heartened state leaders. Mahlon Dickerson was optimistic that "the Republicans will carry their election in Bergen County."[26]

Encouraged by outside support and following the lead of Essex and Morris counties, many Bergen townships organized committees. Hackensack took the initiative in May, followed by Harrington and Pompton in June. By the end of July, Franklin Township, Saddle River, and New Barbadoes had also formed committees. The delegates convened at the end

24. *Ibid.*
25. *Newark Gazette*, Sept. 30, 1800; Mahlon Dickerson to Silas Dickerson, July 28, Aug. 14, 1800, Dickerson Letter Book, N.J. Hist. Soc.; Newark *Centinel*, May 6, June 3, July 22, Aug. 26, 1800.
26. Mahlon Dickerson to Silas Dickerson, Sept. 17, 1800, Dickerson Letter Book, N.J. Hist. Soc. Federalist efforts had continued apace, however, throughout the spring and summer. See the *Newark Gazette*, May-Oct., 1800, *passim.*

of August to nominate a legislative and local ticket and to designate a county committee from their number. Emulating Essex, all the Republican candidates not endorsed by the county meeting declined to run.[27]

Despite these auspicious beginnings, the whole structure collapsed before the month was out. With the election only three weeks away, the township committees were suddenly called into emergency session by the county group. They were told that two candidates for the legislature named by the earlier convention now declined to run. Shamefaced, the delegates had to confront a more serious defection. A third member of the ticket, James Jay, informed the county committee (of which he was also a member) that he could not run for the Assembly on the Republican ticket inasmuch as he had agreed to run for the same office on the Federalist slate.[28] The organization, broken by this rapid sequence of events, would not recover its composure or its initial promise of success for some time to come. Needless to say, the Republicans lost Bergen County in 1800.[29]

The effort to redraw the political lines of North Jersey was repeated in the southern part of the state as well. Aaron Kitchell, writing to Ebenezer Elmer on April 23, was "anxious to know whether any measures will be taken in any western [southern] counties." Hoping to aid the cause, he disclosed that "some persons of information and influence will correspond with them [South Jersey Republican leaders] and propose to them such Measures as appears to them most proper to preserve an Union of the Republican Interest." He added parenthetically, "I do not wish you [a would-be candidate for Congress] to take an active part [but] only to communicate

27. Newark *Centinel*, May 6, June 3, 17, 25, July 1, 8, Aug. 5, Sept. 2, 9, 1800.
28. *Ibid.*, Sept. 30, Oct. 7, 1800. The *Centinel* explained weakly that James Jay "for some motive, best known to himself, is determined to ruin his own interest in opposition to the Ticket formed by the General Committee of which he is a member." Although no more direct evidence exists, it is clear that the Federalists succeeded in infiltrating the party at its inception, and when the proper time came, simply shattered the organization in Bergen from within.
29. *Ibid.*, Oct. 14, 21, 1800.

those Ideas to Such in whom you can Confide—and to write to me if it is provable that any Union can be formed."[30] The fact that impetus was supplied by a small cadre of North Jerseymen did not deter South Jerseymen from responding to the formation of a Republican machine in much the same way as their compatriots had done in the northern counties.

The political fever sweeping the state can be charted in the diary of a young man from Fairfield, Cumberland County. Ephraim Bateman, eventually to rise through Republican ranks to the legislature, the House of Representatives, and the Senate, in 1800 was a struggling twenty-year-old schoolteacher who responded strongly to the rising tide of Jeffersonian enthusiasm. In 1799, Bateman and a group of young adults from Cumberland had formed a Juvenile Society to discuss major (and minor) issues of the day. Their debates reflect the problems that were foremost in their minds and constitute a good barometer for Republican feeling among the otherwise historically inarticulate men of the area. Interspersed among such timeless questions as, "Is it right to marry a girl because she is rich?" or "Which are the most deceitful the men or the women?" were questions of much more (or less) serious import. The Society debated such problems as "Ought any man in this U. S. to be debarred from the privilege of voting for public officers because he is not worth a certain Sum?" or "Ought a man in a public station to act agreeable to his own opinions or those of his constituents?" and ominously for the lawyer-ridden Federalist cause, "Are Lawyers any advantage to the Community?"[31] The debaters came to feel that perhaps the answers to these questions could be best expressed through political action.

By the middle of May 1800, the drive to organize the southern counties was well underway. The absence of a Republican newspaper hampered the effort, but the Republicans moved

30. Aaron Kitchell to ? [Ebenezer Elmer], Apr. 23, 1800, Dreer Collection, Hist. Soc. of Pa.

31. "Journal of Ephraim Bateman of Fairfield Township, Cumberland County," *Vineland Historical Magazine*, 13 (1928), 82-89.

quickly to propagandize the area by circulating information in other ways. The "Proceedings of Congress," a broadside drafted by Kitchell, was an example. The author hoped that "the citizens of the western [southern] Counties would examine [the proceedings] . . . and votes of their Representatives and turn out such as does not appear to have acted for the Best Interest of the State."[32]

In Cumberland and Salem counties, Ebenezer Elmer emerged as the prime mover. He maneuvered behind the scenes to organize the most appealing tickets in these areas. Elmer considered himself influential enough to revert to the first person in reporting to Aaron Kitchell that "if there is any probability of carrying [George] Burgin for Council, I shall be running him there [in Salem County]."[33] Although few details can be gleaned from the sources, it appears that the Salem party structure rested entirely on township committees patterned after the plan of the Morris and Sussex subscribers. This, at least, was the permanent form on which the county organization finally settled.[34] By midsummer "a very favorable change [had] taken place in Salem, Cumberland, Cape May and even in Gloucester."[35]

In Gloucester County, a Republican Committee met on July 28, vowing "to unite with our Republican brethren in this state and the United States." The meeting was chaired by that anomaly among Republicans, James Sloan, a Quaker Jeffersonian politician. Later to serve in Congress, he was one of four men who constituted a committee of correspondence

32. Aaron Kitchell to Ebenezer Elmer, May 12, 1800, Gratz Collection, Hist. Soc. of Pa.

33. Ebenezer Elmer to [David] Moore, May 12, 1800, *ibid.*; Joseph Bloomfield to Ebenezer Elmer, Apr. 20, 1800, Ebenezer Elmer Papers, Rutgers Univ. Lib. The letter to Moore contained extracts from a letter to Kitchell.

34. Newark *Centinel*, Aug. 26, 1800; Ebenezer Elmer to [David] Moore, May 12, 1800, Gratz Collection, Hist. Soc. of Pa.; Mahlon Dickerson to Silas Dickerson, July 28, 1800, Dickerson Letter Book, N.J. Hist. Soc. Although Salem went Federalist, the new Republican party made a good showing (929-798) at the polls, indicating the existence of a fairly sturdy party machine.

35. Mahlon Dickerson to Silas Dickerson, July 28, 1800, Dickerson Letter Book, N.J. Hist. Soc.; "Journal of Ephraim Bateman," *Vineland Hist. Mag.*, 13 (1928), 89.

in Gloucester. He was bitterly attacked in the Federalist press for slandering Washington and preaching revolution. Republican prints reported, however, that "the spirit of genuine republicanism has arisen" in the county.[36]

Burlington party men also responded to the efforts of the Jeffersonian leadership cadre, forming a county corresponding committee at a Republican meeting during the summer presided over by Joseph Bloomfield. Although an elaborate organization developed initially employing, according to one report, fifty-three workers, the organization appeared much better on paper than it was in fact. Despite Bloomfield's sanguine report that "we have good hope of sending a Republican representation" to the legislature, Burlington's Federalist majority soon swamped Bloomfield's organization in a deluge of party activity.[37] The county long remained a Federalist stronghold. The future governor was on far safer ground when boasting of South Jersey's political progress generally: "We have adhered to our promise with our Eastern [northern] Friends, and not only kept our numbers but have gained ground of the Feds.—Notwithstanding their scores of tales, Committeemen in every township, and of deception imposed on the ignorant."[38] The Republicans in North and South Jersey had made great strides in preparation for the presidential election.

36. *Gloucester County, State of New Jersey*, July 28, 1800, New Jersey Imprints Collection, N.J. Hist. Soc.; Newark *Centinel*, Aug. 26, 1800; *Newark Gazette*, Oct. 21, 1800; Frank H. Stewart, ed., "Dairy of Samuel Mickle," Apr. 5, 1800, in *Notes on Old Gloucester County*, 3 vols. (Camden, 1917), I, 166; Mahlon Dickerson to Silas Dickerson, Aug. 14, 1800, Dickerson Letter Book, N.J. Hist. Soc.

37. Joseph Bloomfield to Ebenezer Elmer and George Bergen [Burgin], Sept. 29, 1800, Moore Collection, Princeton Univ. Lib.; Joseph Bloomfield to Ebenezer Elmer, Aug. 25, 1801, Ely Collection, N.J. Hist. Soc.; Mahlon Dickerson to Silas Dickerson, Aug. 14, 1800, Dickerson Letter Book, *ibid.*; *To the People of the County of Burlington* (Mount Holly, 1800), Imprint Collection, N.Y. Pub. Lib. The Federalists made a special effort to save Burlington. See *Address to the Federal Republicans of Burlington County* (Trenton, 1800), *ibid.*; *Newark Gazette*, Sept. 16, and Sept.-Oct., 1800, *passim*. The vote in the Burlington state elections (2806-520) indicated the existence in fact of a very weak Republican organization.

38. Joseph Bloomfield to Ebenezer Elmer, Dec. 28, 1800, Joseph Bloomfield Papers, N.J. Hist. Soc. "The General" was abused terribly in the Federalist

The Presidential Election of 1800

The presidential canvass in New Jersey scheduled for October 1800 hinged on control of the legislature. If the Republicans could gain a majority of the seats, they could either appoint Jeffersonian electors or provide for a general canvass for President, as they claimed they wanted to do. It was generally acknowledged, on the other hand, that if the Federalists could hold their seats, the legislative majority would choose Adams electors. The key to the presidential vote being bound up with a legislative victory in October, the Republicans agreed that the county elections should be decided, where possible, on the presidential question rather than on local issues.

After the Republican victory in the New York elections of May 1800, it appeared that New Jersey might be pivotal in deciding the fate of Thomas Jefferson. Ebenezer Elmer predicted that "if New Jersey will give her vote for Jefferson it [the election] is done—or if New Jersey will divide or not vote at all [by deadlocking the legislature, as in Pennsylvania] it will answer."[39] A Philadelphia coterie of Jeffersonian Republicans, supervising the presidential campaign on something of a national scale, exhorted Jerseymen to win the state for Jefferson. Their New Jersey liaison, Mahlon Dickerson, wrote to his brother Silas: "If the republicans are only vigilant there can be no doubt of their success. No exertions should be spared in New Jersey." He repeated his message to other key Republicans in the state.[40]

Philadelphia Republicans exerted a great influence on New Jersey party men. Mahlon Dickerson, a native Jerseyman who practiced law in Philadelphia, coordinated his efforts with John Beckley. Beckley, working diligently with many Republicans in Philadelphia for Jefferson's election, provided

press as an apostate and rank party man. See, for example, the New Brunswick *Guardian*, Oct. 8, 15, 1800.

39. Ebenezer Elmer to Col. [David Moore], May 12, 1800, Gratz Collection, Hist. Soc. of Pa. Elmer quotes a letter he received from Aaron Kitchell.

40. Mahlon Dickerson to Silas Dickerson, May 6, 1800, Dickerson Letter Book, N.J. Hist. Soc.

Dickerson with quantities of campaign literature which the latter forwarded to New Jersey either directly or through his brother, Silas; Mahlon also advised local Republican cadremen on the national outlook, suggesting campaign strategy or remedies as the need arose; he visited the state periodically to confer with leading Democratic Republicans.[41]

Dickerson's long career in national and state politics spanned the first half of the nineteenth century. A bachelor all his long life, he was a man of many parts. Aside from his career as a lawyer, Dickerson operated an iron mine at a profit, and he was also an amateur botanist and naturalist. Above all, he was a polished and durable politician.[42] In Philadelphia he had first become involved in politics by aiding the Jeffersonian cause prior to 1800. His Republican ties led him into the camp of Governor Thomas McKean of Pennsylvania, who bestowed numerous offices on his protégé. When Mahlon returned to New Jersey in 1808, he rose rapidly—even spectacularly— through the Republican ranks, being elected to the legislature in 1811 from his native Morris County. In 1815 he became governor, and in 1817 he was sent to the Senate where he served two full terms. He was among the many Jeffersonian Republicans who made the transition to the Jackson banner between 1824 and 1828, and was rewarded with a cabinet post, serving as secretary of the Navy until Jackson's retirement from office.

With the aid of men like Mahlon Dickerson, New Jersey Republicans were stirring by early summer. The Philadelphia *Aurora*, a Republican paper widely circulated in South Jersey, printed a telling series of assaults on New Jersey's Senator

41. Mahlon Dickerson to and from Silas Dickerson, 1800-1801, *passim, ibid.* See especially letters of May 6, July 28, and Aug. 14, 1800. Other evidence confirming the existence of a Philadelphia group running Jefferson's campaign may be found in Charles O. Lerche, Jr., "Jefferson and the Election of 1800: A Case Study in the Political Smear," *William and Mary Quarterly*, 3rd Ser., 5 (1948), 467-91; John Beckley to James Monroe, Aug. 26, 1800, Monroe Papers, N.Y. Pub. Lib.; Cunningham, *The Jeffersonian Republicans, 1789-1801*; Chambers, *Political Parties in a New Nation*.

42. See Charles R. Erdman, Jr., in *DAB* s.v. "Dickerson, Mahlon."

Jonathan Dayton. These were later reprinted in the *Centinel* and in pamphlet form for distribution throughout the state.[43] Abraham Bishop's strikingly effective and celebrated denunciation of Federalism was broadcast widely in New Jersey, for it was reprinted by Pennington and Gould and Company, the publishers of the *Centinel*. It is not known how many copies were struck off in Newark, but often as many as one thousand at a time were published elsewhere.[44] The publication was late, catching only the tail end of the presidential campaign, but it proved of great value in the congressional election that followed. This tract, put to effective use, was only one of several.

From the Philadelphia headquarters of John Beckley, additional party literature was distributed far and wide throughout the United States. New Jersey received its share, as we have seen, via Mahlon Dickerson, who forwarded to his brother and others in quantity for distribution not only Beckley's own *Epitome . . . of the Life of Mr. Jefferson* but such potent political reprints as Albert Gallatin's *View of the Public Debt* and copies of John Adams' damaging *Letter to Tench Coxe*.[45] The copies of Beckley's pamphlet that Silas received, his brother instructed, were to be distributed in the area of Sussex County. Mahlon also forwarded fifty copies to John Condit for circulation in Essex and Bergen counties. Both recipients obeyed Mahlon Dickerson's instructions; Silas reported: "after keeping one [of Beckley's pamphlets] for myself [I] distributed the remainder through the County [Sussex] by sending them to a Republican meeting." The younger Dickerson was "much pleased with . . . the Pamphlets."[46] Mahlon Dickerson was in contact with leading Republicans in South Jersey also, and

43. Mahlon Dickerson to Silas Dickerson, July 28, 1800, Dickerson Letter Book, N.J. Hist. Soc.

44. Lerche, "Jefferson and the Election of 1800," *Wm. and Mary Qtly.*, 3rd Ser., 5 (1948), 467-91.

45. John Beckley to James Monroe, Aug. 26, 1800, Monroe Papers, N.Y. Pub. Lib.; Mahlon Dickerson to Silas Dickerson, July 28, Aug. 14, 1800, Dickerson Letter Book, N.J. Hist. Soc.

46. Silas Dickerson to Mahlon Dickerson, Aug. 22, 1800, Dickerson Letter Book, N. J. Hist. Soc.

it may be assumed that the same circulation pattern was employed in that area.[47]

To combat the unprecedented activity by the Republicans, the Federalists undertook a campaign of unparalleled activity to save the state for John Adams. A prominent Federalist, Lucius Horatio Stockton, "rode throughout the state with Parson Linn's poisonous pamphlets, preaching that Religion was in danger, etc. if Jefferson was elected." The Republicans themselves later admitted that Stockton "did more injury [to the Republican cause] with his pen and tongue, than any man in N. Jersey."[48] William Griffith of Burlington County also actively traversed the state in Adams' behalf.[49]

During the summer and fall of 1800 nationally prominent Federalists invaded New Jersey to watch a telling campaign. The state became a haven for residents of Philadelphia trying to escape the yellow fever, and many highly placed Federalist officials, including President Adams himself, found Trenton or Princeton a desirable refuge from the scourge. At least one Republican thought their presence spurred local Federalists to greater efforts in the hope of drawing attention to themselves and their obvious claims on the party's gratitude.[50] The quantity of anti-Jefferson material available for distribution in the state must have been enormous; at least one hundred different campaign pamphlets, totaling thousands of issues, were in print nationally in 1800, the majority of them supporting the Federalist cause.[51]

47. *Ibid.*, June-Oct., 1800, *passim*. See especially letters dated July 28, Aug. 14, 22, 1800.

48. Joseph Bloomfield to "Dear Doctor" [Ebenezer Elmer], Jan. 25, 1802, Gratz Collection, Hist. Soc. of Pa.

49. *Ibid.*

50. Silas Dickerson to Mahlon Dickerson, Oct. 22, 1799, Dickerson Letter Book, N.J. Hist. Soc.

51. Lerche, "Jefferson and the Election of 1800," *Wm. and Mary Qtly.*, 3rd Ser., 5 (1948), 467-91; Cunningham, *The Jeffersonian Republicans, 1789-1801*, 158, 253-54, and *passim*. At least one Federalist pamphlet was published in New Jersey: *Serious Considerations on the Election of a President* (Trenton, 1800), which proved especially useful in the state. See the New Brunswick *Guardian*, Sept. 17, 1800. No copy of the Trenton edition could be found by the author in existing collections, although other editions are extant.

The Republicans, emulating the Federalists, sent spokesmen to the doubtful counties. Stephen Sayre was one campaigner who "was active [for] several months before the general election . . . [for] the choice of a President."[52] Silas Dickerson, who labored in Bergen County on Jefferson's behalf,
in a questionable burst of enthusiasm anonymously posted
Jefferson's likeness in his church in Sussex County. This pleased
the Democrats of the flock but had a dubious effect indeed
on Federalist parishioners.[53] Judging by the Federalists' warnings to their supporters, the Republicans employed any number
of electioneering ruses. "Be watchful that false or imperfect
tickets are not imposed on you," the incumbents cautioned,
"lest you get swindled."[54]

Despite the intense campaign waged for Jefferson, it became painfully obvious toward the end of the summer that
the Republicans were underdogs. The counties were approximately equal in legislative representation, so the heavy vote
turned out for Jefferson in Morris and Essex counties would
be canceled by Federalist victories in smaller counties when
the Federalist lawmakers chose Adams' electors. The Republicans made one final effort to attract new voters by calling a
state convention, the first ever held in New Jersey and one
of the earliest in the nation. The few leaders who promoted
the meeting assumed it would draw influential Republicans

52. Joseph Bloomfield to Thomas Jefferson, Nov. 10, 1801, Thomas Jefferson Papers, CXVII, 20262, Lib. Cong.

53. Silas Dickerson to Mahlon Dickerson, July 28, Aug. 14, 1800, July 31,
1801, Dickerson Letter Book, N.J. Hist. Soc. Electioneering campaigns such
as these were usually made with as little fanfare as possible throughout the
period of Republican rule. Although it was fairly common practice, it was
still not respectable, and, usually, the campaigner disguised his motives by
transacting other business along the way. James Linn would thus appear in
Sussex County in 1806, or Joseph Bloomfield would turn up in Monmouth
County in 1801 and 1803. See the New Brunswick *Guardian*, Sept. 15, 1803.
A clear example of this sort of activity occurred in 1820 when Warren Scott
of New Brunswick appeared in Morris County. David Thompson, Jr., Assemblyman from Morris, reported: "I did not see him [Scott] but suppose from the
inquries he made that he was on an electioneering campaign—whom does
he want for senator?" David Thompson, Jr., to Samuel L. Southard, Sept.
4, 1820, Samuel L. Southard Papers, Princeton Univ. Lib.

54. *Newark Gazette*, Sept. 30, Oct. 21, 1800.

from most or all of the state's thirteen counties. The practicality of such a device seems to have occurred early to Republican managers, but the idea hung fire until the last minute; only some early hints indicate that a meeting was in the offing. At the beginning of August, some Republicans in Essex County, aware that a state convention was a possibility, appointed a committee of correspondence specifically to act in unison with party men from other counties upon the forthcoming congressional and presidential elections. Bergen Republicans designated a similar committee to "correspond with the Committees of other such Counties as they may deem necessary and expedient, and in *conjunction* with them, to nominate a suitable person or persons as the case may require, to represent us in Congress." Gloucester also did the same.[55]

Regardless of these activities there never was a formal public call for all counties to elect delegates, nor were there any particular qualifications outlined for those who attended this initial state gathering. Apparently delegates filled only two requirements: they were Republicans and representatives of their respective counties. The original meeting mustered late in September at Kingston but proved a failure because there was no quorum (seven counties were not represented). The small group adjourned and the convention was rescheduled for a few days later at Princeton.[56] Republicans from all counties except Cape May finally met at Princeton on September 30, just two weeks before the poll for members of the state legislature. Despite its patchwork quality it represented a major innovation in American political techniques.

Joseph Bloomfield presided at the convention and signed its address to the voters, which protested against the incumbent national administration's waste of public money, the creation and extension of a huge national debt, and the levying of

55. Morristown *Genius of Liberty*, Aug. 28, 1800; Newark *Centinel*, Sept. 2, 1800; *Gloucester County, State of New Jersey*, July 28, 1800, N.J. Imprints Collection, N.J. Hist. Soc.

56. Joseph Bloomfield to Ebenezer Elmer and George Burgin, Sept. 29, 1800, Moore Collection, Princeton Univ. Lib.

heavy taxes (the Carriage Tax was cited as an example). The Republicans asserted that so long as the incumbents remained in power the nation would not be free of foreign (British) dictation. The Federalists' method of choosing presidential electors through the New Jersey legislature was introduced as an example of that party's "aristocracy" in action.[57] Naturally, Republicans, like Federalists, proclaimed that they alone could preserve the "sacred and glorious" Revolution and Constitution. The leadership of the lawyers was denounced once again. Finally, the Jeffersonians dismissed the Federalist assertion that the major question of the campaign was "GOD—AND A RELIGIOUS PRESIDENT; or . . . JEFFERSON—AND NO GOD!!!"[58]

The Princeton meeting closed with an invitation to a state nominating convention to be held prior to the congressional election later that fall. A final appeal was made to New Jersey voters to elect Republican legislators who would either vote for a Jeffersonian slate of presidential electors or call for a general popular vote for president. Although the convention worked for a Republican victory, the delegates were "aware that the time allotted us is disproportionate to the list of objects which demand our attention."[59]

The Republican attempt to rally the voters came too late. The legislature remained Federalist. Huge Republican majorities in Sussex, Essex, and Morris counties, and Republican representation in the legislature from these counties, could not offset the other counties which again returned Federalists. The Federalist majority stood at thirty-eight, to twelve for the Jeffersonians. In the vote for electors in the joint meeting, the Adams slate triumphed by the same margin, and all five

57. Joseph Bloomfield, *To the People of New Jersey*, Sept. 30, 1800, N.J. Political Broadsides Collection, Rutgers Univ. Lib.; Newark *Centinel*, Oct. 7, 1800; Elizabethtown *N.J. Journal*, Oct. 14, 1800; Fee, *Transition*, 100-116.

58. *Newark Gazette*, Sept. 22, 1800. Fee, *Transition*, 100-116, contains a full discussion of the issues posed by the two parties in 1800.

59. Elizabethtown *N.J. Journal*, Oct. 14, 1800; Joseph Bloomfield, *To the People of New Jersey*, Sept. 30, 1800, N.J. Political Broadsides Collection, Rutgers Univ. Lib.

electoral votes from New Jersey went to Adams and Pinckney.[60]

If New Jersey Republicans could not swing the state to Jefferson and Burr, they took courage from the fact that their candidates had won the election without them. Thus they entered the pending congressional election in the state with redoubled energies and a great deal of confidence that, at last, with a strong local boost, a majority of the state's citizens would get the Republican message from other sections of the country. The Republican position in New Jersey was immeasurably strengthened by Jefferson's victory.

The Congressional Election

After winning control of the legislature, the Federalists took hold of the proverbial tiger by the tail. They not only denied the voters a canvass for the presidential election but also risked further embarrassment in designating a battleground for the congressional poll. A district canvass, even with the districts carved to their liking, would concede two, and possibly three, of five congressional seats to the Republicans. The elections of 1798 offered proof of this distinct likelihood. A general canvass meant gambling for an all-or-nothing stake. Populous Morris, Essex, and Sussex counties might prove decisive in electing all five Republican candidates. The Federalist legislative majority nevertheless chose the latter risk in drafting an election law; Federalists were willing to gamble all the seats rather than concede the certainty of at least two Republican congressmen retaining their offices. The Republicans responded with relief. "It is a measure," the *Centinel* announced, "which has been brought forward by the federal party under full confidence that their strength is sufficient to turn out the old republican members, and to elect in their room five [Federalists]."[61]

Even before the Federalist legislature drafted its at-large election law for the congressional contest, the Republicans

60. Newark *Centinel*, Oct. 21, 28, Nov. 4, 11, 1800.
61. *Ibid.*, Nov. 11, 1800.

had anticipated the move and made preparations for it. At the Republican state convention on September 30, the party managers had put in motion a second meeting should an at-large congressional election materialize. The September group agreed to meet with the Republican minority in the state legislature to fix "on the most popular characters to be run for Congress."[62] This was the usual method employed to select a political ticket among the nation's Jeffersonians.[63] Other leading Republicans in the state apparently decided, however, that a day-long convention more broadly based than one composed merely of Republican legislators and a few others would have more popular appeal. Also, a legislative caucus would be dominated by the northern counties and surely northern men could not speak authoritatively for all of New Jersey's Republicans. In any event, sometime between the first convention on September 30 and the announcement of a second meeting, a new format was definitely and permanently adopted. Each county organization was urged to designate its own delegates for the December 2 meeting. The delegations were not limited in size, but representatives to the convention voted by county, each county possessing two votes cast by the majority of the delegation. With ten counties attending the Trenton convention, it was counted a success. Only Cape May, Bergen, and Sussex counties did not respond to the roll call when the chairman called the convention to order.[64]

The second state convention of 1800 differed markedly from the original in two important respects: first, it was called specifically and publicly to nominate a slate of congressional candidates; New Jersey's Republican party was the first to implement a permanent state nominating convention, establishing a precedent for the convocation of similar state con-

62. Joseph Bloomfield to Silas Dickerson, Nov. 17, 1800, Dickerson Letter Book, N.J. Hist. Soc. Among those making the decision were Bloomfield, John Morgan, Stephen Sayre, and James Sloan.

63. Cunningham, *The Jeffersonian Republicans, 1789-1801,* 160-65, 205-6, and *passim.*

64. Newark *Centinel,* Dec. 9, 1800; New Brunswick *Guardian,* Dec. 17, 1800.

ventions to be held in succeeding years; secondly, party captains made it clear that each county was empowered to designate its delegates by means of its own choosing. Delegates were not necessarily legislators since it was not a legislative caucus. Many counties resorted to a popular choice of representatives at open county meetings.[65]

The Republican managers did not leave the choice of a congressional slate in the hands of a group of unpredictable delegates, however. A few men handpicked a ticket long before the convention actually met. It is patently obvious that this first convention was only a shrewd attempt to secure a sanction for the ticket from a general and authoritative party agency. More than two weeks *before* the convention met to adopt a ticket, General Bloomfield speculated with Silas Dickerson on the qualifications of the future Republican ticket—clearly already designated—compared to that of the Federalists: "Our friend General [William] Helm[s], has equal pretensions with A[aron] Ogden as a Soldier—Messrs. Kitchell and Condit, gather more votes than their colleagues [in the House of Representatives] Imlay and Davenport—and, I think, the two other Republicans proposed [Henry Southard and Ebenezer Elmer], have better claims, than a man lately come into the State a Bankrupt—and whose family were No-Tory-ously disaffected [in the Revolution]."[66] This estimate of the Republican ticket two weeks in advance of its nomination was too accurate to be guesswork. The "balanced" pre-convention slate and the earlier organizational pattern leaves a strong impression that the Republican party in New Jersey started out as a hierarchy-dominated organization in the hands of a few powerful captains. The cosmetic touch provided by the convention indi-

65. Elizabethtown *N.J. Journal*, Oct. 14, 1800; Joseph Bloomfield, *To the People of New Jersey*, Sept. 30, 1800, N.J. Political Broadsides Collection, Rutgers Univ. Lib.; Newark *Centinel*, Oct. 1800. For the development of the state convention into a permanent party institution, see chapters four, five, and seven.

66. Joseph Bloomfield to Silas Dickerson, Nov. 17, 1800, Dickerson Letter Book, N.J. Hist. Soc.

cated that this leadership was not only powerful but also highly sensitive to the ways of the new politics and voter response.

The convention sanctioned the ticket placed before it with the only changes in it occasioned by the declination of Aaron Kitchell. His refusal to seek another term left the way open for Helms of Sussex County to run alone from the northern portion of the state.[67] The five who were nominated were Condit of Essex, Helms, Henry Southard of Somerset, Ebenezer Elmer of Cumberland, and James Mott of Monmouth; the latter was added both to bring the number of candidates up to five, in effect replacing Kitchell after his decision had left an unfilled opening, and to provide representation on the ticket from a part of the state heretofore overlooked. The officers of the convention which sanctioned the ticket were again Joseph Bloomfield, chairman, and John Morgan, secretary. The short address to the public warned the voters that each ballot counted, even in the Federalist counties, for it was an at-large election.[68]

The Republicans set to work to augment expected solid pluralities in the three northern counties, totaling "near five thousand," with at least nominal majorities in some of the southern counties. Congressman Kitchell felt that there was "little doubt of success" if the expected pluralities materialized. In order to shore up morale in South Jersey, he enclosed for general circulation in a letter from Philadelphia a remarkably accurate forecast of the vote in Congress that would finally elect Thomas Jefferson President. Kitchell's estimate was coupled with Abraham Bishop's campaign pamphlet and given wide circulation in southern New Jersey; the congressional campaign was off to a good start. Joseph Bloomfield of Burlington was optimistic that his county and Gloucester would not turn out "so great a majority against the Republicans, as at the last [legislative] election." The Quakers, he felt, were un-

67. Jonathan Dayton to Aaron Ogden, Nov. 28, 1800, Aaron Ogden Papers, Rutgers Univ. Lib.
68. Newark Centinel, Dec. 9, 1800.

happy with the Federalist attack on Jefferson's lack of religion, for any assault on religious toleration, according to the General, was abhorrent to the sect.[69]

The Federalists, meanwhile, called attention to the alleged hypocrisy of the address from the Republican nominating convention in referring to the Republican ticket as a slate of farmers. "This old, worn out pretext of 'farmer' candidates, wont do," commented the *Guardian*. "John Condict [Condit] and Ebenezer Elmer, are by all accounts . . . Doctors. . . . As to Jemmy Mott, it will be hard to prove he has seen a plough for many a day. . . . This Mr. Helms [is] . . . a General; and as to Henry Southard, he has long since abandoned the peacable profession of a farmer for the trade of Jacobinism."[70]

The First Statewide Victory

The Republicans emerged barely victorious in their first organized statewide contest. All five Republican candidates were elected to Congress with a total vote ranging from 14,547 to 14,726, against a Federalist vote of 14,037 to 14,177. Approximately 71 per cent of the eligible male voters in the state were polled in this hard-fought canvass, indicating the effectiveness of both parties' campaigns for Congress.[71] Close as it was, the victory nevertheless was highly significant in terms of the Republicans' future. After defeat of the Federalists in congressional districts of that party's design in 1798, this new triumph eradicated any remaining doubt about the numerical equality of the parties, whether or not the state was carved into districts. The flow of federal patronage into the state, to be dispensed in the future by a sympathetic Republican national administration, would be enhanced by the pres-

69. Aaron Kitchell to Ebenezer Elmer, Dec. 11, 1800, Gratz Collection, Hist. Soc. of Pa.; Joseph Bloomfield to Silas Dickerson, Nov. 17, 1800, Silas Dickerson to Mahlon Dickerson, Dec. 11, 1800, Dickerson Letter Book, N.J. Hist. Soc.
70. New Brunswick *Guardian*, Dec. 17, 1800.
71. Newark *Centinel*, Jan. 6, 1801; Fee, *Transition*, 120. The figure indicating the percentage of eligible male voters in this election was taken from manuscript material in the possession of Richard P. McCormick, Rutgers University, New Brunswick, New Jersey.

ence of Republican representatives from New Jersey seated in Washington; this was especially true in 1800 when the rules governing federal patronage were yet to be laid down, and when both United States senators from the state remained Federalist. Also, the successful effort justified the extension and innovation of Republican party machinery. Finally, the real boost given the most embattled counties by an emergent state Jeffersonian organization with some claim to success, and the symbolic prod provided by the party's first victory in any general election, went a long way in transforming the image of the party from a struggling and often hopeless minority to a party not only with a pleasing present but a very promising future; few Republicans, if the exuberance of the small number who remain recorded is any indication, doubted that this was the turning point.

Their expectations were borne out by the statistical evidence. There were only a few scattering votes cast (that is, votes not delivered for an entire ticket or votes for a candidate other than a party nominee)—a significant development indicating the growing strength of party appeals. The incidence of straight ticket voting was in some measure attributable to the printed tickets that were employed in this election, as they were in contemporary elections elsewhere in the country. Printed prior to the canvass, the tickets were distributed by party workers either before the election began or at the polls.[72] The three northern counties of Essex, Morris, and Sussex cast a disproportionately large share of the Republican vote. These were the same counties that the Republicans in former years carried in the legislative elections. At this point, the parties in Hunterdon, Monmouth, Salem, and Cumberland were closely matched, though the Federalists still maintained a slight edge. The other counties remained clearly Federalist.[73]

The poll for congressional representatives climaxed a year-

72. Morristown *Genius of Liberty*, Dec. 18, 1800; Newark *Centinel*, Dec. 16, 23, 1800; *Newark Gazette*, Sept. 30, Oct. 21, Dec. 23, 1800; McCormick, *History of Voting*, 104; Fee, *Transition*, 120.
73. See Table I, pp. 76-78.

long Republican campaign to reach the voter. Semiprofessional state managers, guiding amateur local leaders, did their work well in awakening political interest. The introduction of the nominating convention was a distinct contribution by Jerseymen to the art of building a party machine. It marked the state's Republican leaders in 1800 as pioneers in party development.[74] These men were no party hacks, following old and outmoded forms. They possessed the imagination necessary to adapt new forms of political action to the needs and conditions imposed by a new political era. This original convention justified itself as a potent political device, and it ultimately spread to other states. Often, it replaced as a nominating mechanism the more restrictive legislative caucus. The representative nature of this machinery on the county level ostensibly offered wide-ranging participation to the lowliest Republican activists, and for this reason it remained popular with Republican voters. With the passing years, it proved one of the most enduring political contributions made by the state's Republicans to the evolution of the American party system, coming as it did when operative political machinery was first gaining a foothold in the United States.[75] New Jersey's Republican organization would have been far less potent and its ultimate triumph in the state much more doubtful had such exertions not been made by Jeffersonian party men.

The effective use of party machinery and propaganda to increase voter participation was amply demonstrated in New Jersey in 1800. Every effort was made to bring the voter actively to the fore in the struggle for "Jefferson and Liberty." But there remained unfulfilled two major goals to establish Re-

74. State conventions were held in Pennsylvania in 1788, and in Delaware in 1802 but neither resulted in an institutionalization of the apparatus. See Robert L. Brunhouse, *The Counter-Revolution in Pennsylvania, 1776-1790* (Harrisburg, 1942); Harry M. Tinkcom, *The Republicans and Federalists in Pennsylvania, 1790-1801: A Study in National Stimulus and Local Response* (Harrisburg, 1950); John Munroe, *Federalist Delaware, 1775-1815* (New Brunswick, N.J., 1954); George Luetscher, *Early Political Machinery in the United States* (Phila., 1903).

75. Another original effort by New Jersey Republicans resulted in the evolution of the legislative caucus.

publicanism triumphant in New Jersey. The first was to gain control of the legislature in order to dominate the political and patronage machinery of the state. The second was to expand the Republican apparatus to cover all of New Jersey's counties as the best means of insuring and perpetuating a party following. Both goals were achieved in the years following 1800.

III

THE EXPANSION
OF GRASS-ROOTS MACHINERY
1801-1806

———•———

THE REPUBLICAN PARTY'S FORTUNES HAD BEEN DECIDEDLY BOOSTED
by the progress made in the elections of 1800. Even though
the party had lost the state legislative elections and consequently failed to secure New Jersey's electoral vote for Jefferson,
Republican confidence and initiative had been redeemed by
the election of five congressmen. It was with redoubled energies, therefore, that the Republicans continued to expand
and strengthen their grass-roots organization. Although local
party organization stretched from North to South Jersey,
serious weaknesses would be eliminated in the years following
1800; often this would be accomplished by restructuring the
county organization to conform with local needs rather than
statewide uniformity. Much of the improved organizational
machinery was introduced in response to the growing need
for intraparty discipline and unity. Electoral success brought
power to the Republican party, but with power, in-fighting
for control of the party materialized as well. This was acutely
evident at the county level. The extent to which activists in
the counties surmounted this difficulty was a measure of the

depth of the local interest that Republican professionals were able to plumb.

The Nature of Local Party Formations

The county organization in New Jersey was the keystone of the state Republican party.[1] Most units were well designed to meet the peculiar problems they faced. Although there were many common features that all county organizations shared, each county machine was ultimately unique; all claimed a common genesis, but none developed in quite the same way. Their ability to mesh in a legislative caucus or a state convention behind a common issue or set of candidates enabled New Jersey Republicans to retain political power long and effectively.

Despite the many variations from county to county, it is possible to generalize about some dominant elements common to all local organizations in New Jersey. This was natural in a state where party machinery originally developed in response to planned, statewide, coordinated efforts.

First, the earliest state leaders were also county leaders, regardless of region. William S. Pennington, Silas Dickerson, Aaron Kitchell, James J. Wilson, Ebenezer Elmer, and Joseph Bloomfield were not only active in state and national politics, but they were also initially and throughout the Republican period foremost party leaders in their respective counties. County politics usually revolved around a small coterie of party managers, a single manager, or competing leadership factions. In each county in New Jersey political organization was unquestionably hierarchical.

Second, the uniform township committee system, provided by New Jersey party captains in April 1800, was initially

1. For the sake of brevity without sacrificing depth, I will describe local politics by discussing five of the state's thirteen counties as generally representative of the remainder. The five are Essex, Sussex, Hunterdon, Middlesex, and Burlington counties. For a discussion of all the state's counties, see Carl E. Prince, New Jersey's Democratic-Republicans, 1790-1817: A Study of Early Party Machinery (unpubl. Ph.D. diss., Rutgers University, 1963).

common to nearly all counties as the first blueprint for party organization. The five counties described below—Essex, Sussex, Hunterdon, Middlesex, and Burlington—all adopted the proposed structural pattern in 1800 or thereafter as an organizational starting point for the construction of Republican county machinery. Changes governed by local and regional needs followed only thereafter. Only *after* initial organization, then, were variations introduced from county to county and region to region, to conform to local needs and circumstances. Even after the changes, a basic committee structure of local and county organization remained intact, at least nominally, in most counties. In those areas where the township committee system disappeared or never really gained a foothold—Essex is a good example—party effectiveness declined appreciably. In Sussex, Middlesex, Hunterdon, and Burlington, strong parties operated, for local committees took hold for long periods. In the counties of South Jersey, exemplified by Burlington, the committee system was in fact strengthened and formalized even more than party leaders first planned for, by the introduction of democratic associations. The same generalization is true, to a lesser degree, of centrally located counties like Hunterdon and Middlesex. In each case, regardless of the degree of formality or adherence, local organizations were supposed to integrate into a formal county machine.

Third, the forces of disintegration working on county Republican organizations likewise were no respecters of region. Essex, Sussex, and Burlington Republican parties all buckled as the "Era of Good Feelings" dawned nationally in 1817. Middlesex's Republican element gave way for good in 1820-21. Only Hunterdon's strong party survived until 1824, and this despite a concerted if unsuccessful attempt to undermine James J. Wilson's organization in 1817. In New Jersey, the era was clearly one of deep factional feelings. This was not always clear when viewed from a national perspective, but it was certainly apparent at the local and state levels.

Fourth, local and regional variations notwithstanding, only

two basic nominating procedures were employed—the open county meeting and the delegate convention. From 1800 to 1817, each county unit of the Republican party adopted one or the other procedure, cutting across regional lines in doing so. In the great majority of elections, Essex, Sussex, and Hunterdon adopted the open county meeting. Middlesex County utilized only the delegate convention. In a sense, Burlington Republicans combined both types effectively, although formally they employed the open meeting. Whatever the nominating device, evidence supports the conclusion that both types fell victim early to political domination by party bigwigs. Neither device guaranteed a democratic system of nominations.[2] One might well conclude that in most—if not all—counties, democratic practices were more apparent than real, rather elaborate facades notwithstanding.

Fifth, Republican newspapers did much to arouse and maintain local party sentiment. It is noteworthy that in counties where Republican weeklies were published the party benefited greatly. The Newark *Centinel of Freedom* in Essex County and the Trenton *True American* in Hunterdon County both successfully stimulated their respective local causes. In Middlesex, Republicans succeeded initially in 1811, the first year the New Brunswick *Fredonian* was published. Despite later losses, Republican activity and sentiment in Middlesex increased thereafter. Burlington County, like most South Jersey locales, suffered from want of an effective organ of propaganda and information. Republican leaders often alluded to the lack of a newspaper as one cause of their difficulties.

Sixth, local party practices indicate the early development in every section of the state of sophisticated electioneering practices to get out the vote. Each county produced favored

2. Dealing with a few local representatives behind closed doors opened clear possibilities for control, as developments in Middlesex suggest. The democratic association in Burlington openly controlled the county meeting. James J. Wilson's authority at Flemington was more subtle but just as real. In Essex County, both the Pennington and Kollock factions exerted significant pressure. The group that convened at Newton in Sussex County during August Court was accused by dissident factions of manipulating nominations.

techniques, and all county parties employed committees and poll watchers to advantage. A well-understood need to get out the vote helped to inspire a rather elaborate party superstructure for that purpose. Jackson men generally and New Jersey Whigs in their campaign of 1840 would not have to innovate much, and in fact they had to go to great pains to improve upon local electioneering techniques already practiced in New Jersey.[3] Propaganda devices likewise were well developed; the rapport existing between Republican editors and party leaders (indeed the two functions were often synonymous) indicated a close political connection between the two.[4]

Seventh, Federalist resistance knew no sectional boundaries, although it tended to endure longer in the south. In counties where Federalists continued to give battle, local Republican party lines were drawn much tighter. The formal democratic associations of South Jersey were in large part a response to Federalist strength. Sussex, Middlesex, and Hunterdon counties all exhibited strong party formations to combat comparable Federalist alignments. Conversely, in Essex County, where opposition disappeared early, the Republican party found its emergent organization weakened by the absence of Federalist resistance.

In order to convey a sense of the diversity of local units within the state organization, it is necessary to describe party formations in key counties and townships. Moreover, it is vital to view developments at the grass roots in order to place in proper perspective the important developments taking place at the same time at the state level.

Essex County

Essex County from 1796 to 1800, as we have seen, was the incubator of incipient Republicanism in New Jersey. Jeffer-

3. The 1840 campaign has been viewed as something of a millennium for party electioneering tactics, surpassing even those of the Jackson period. See William J. Chute, "The New Jersey Whig Campaign of 1840," N.J. Hist. Soc., *Proceedings*, 77 (1959), 223.

4. See chapter eight for patronage rewards coming the way of New Jersey

sonians in this first North Jersey Republican enclave built the earliest local party machine in the state and elected some of New Jersey's first proclaimed Republicans to the legislature and Congress. These political successes were accomplished by a congeries of township organizations that achieved at least partial integration at a county nominating meeting. The brightening Republican horizon in Essex in 1800 did not obscure the fact that much organizational work remained to be done in this populous Republican county. After 1800, however, the rules changed somewhat; by 1802, Federalism as a vital force had clearly disappeared.

The finely tuned Republican organization of 1800 proved in the long run to be of a delicate nature.[5] Lacking significant Federalist opposition, it ran into difficulties in 1801 and 1802—difficulties from which the county party would never quite escape. The county convention in 1801 attracted delegates from Aquackanonk (Passaic), Caldwell, Newark, Springfield, and Westfield, who gathered in Newark on September 21. In theory, each town cast two votes for each candidate in forming a ticket, regardless of the number of delegates present. In fact, places on the ticket were allocated regionally within the county; nominees were selected according to a prearranged agreement among the townships in a region. This arrangement triggered the first split in the Essex Republican party.[6]

The major source of disaffection emanated from the Springfield Township committee, whose members were also delegates to the Essex convention. They issued a handbill a few days after adjournment charging Newark Republicans with greed and the convention generally with "want of liberality in forming the general ticket." Springfield desired two places on the county ticket to satisfy two local factions in town, despite the

newspaper editors. The careers of Shepard Kollock, James J. Wilson, and James Fitz Randolph reinforce the conclusion that a close institutional relationship between newspapers and party machinery existed during the Republican era.

5. See chapter two for a description of Essex party organization in 1800. Chapter one contains a description of Republican machinery prior to 1800.

6. Newark *Centinel*, Sept. 1, 8, 15, 29, Oct. 6, 13, 1801; *Newark Gazette*, Oct. 6, 13, 1801.

fact that Newark, with which Springfield was paired in dividing county representation, had cast three times as many Republican votes in the election of 1800. With three places allocated to the two towns, Newark offered to limit herself to two places on the ticket. The Springfield men countered that unless they received two spots, schism in the township (and, it was implied, in the county) was inevitable.[7] A second disagreement enhanced the importance of the first. Delegates from Caldwell and Aquackanonk could not decide among themselves which town should provide the "northern man" on the ticket. The convention, caught in a crossfire, left it to the two towns to decide on a man after adjournment and to inform the Essex committee of their decision.[8]

The lack of unanimity among the delegates, augmented by the continued absence of local committees from key towns such as Bloomfield and Elizabethtown, underlay events developing in 1801. Internal Republican weaknesses came home to roost when a second nominating meeting was held, a gathering essentially in competition with the first. The second meeting, in contrast to the first, was an open meeting of residents of Elizabethtown, Westfield, and Springfield. They were joined by disgruntled Caldwell adherents who renounced their allegiance (as did one Springfield faction) to the earlier county delegate convention. Elizabethtown Republicans, conspicuously absent from organizational politics up until then, assumed the leadership of these dissident Essex Jeffersonians. A second Republican ticket resulted. Although the original Newark-led Essex committee ticket won the election, the damage to party unity was irreparable.[9]

The rift widened in 1802, despite the abandonment of the county delegate convention. Apparently it had proved too restrictive for the tastes of the Elizabethtown-led minority, and its passing was in the nature of an olive branch offered by the

7. Newark *Centinel*, Oct. 6, 1801; *Newark Gazette*, Oct. 6, 13, 1801.
8. Newark *Centinel*, Oct. 6, 1801.
9. *Ibid.*, Oct. 6, 20, 1801. The vote was 1770 for the Essex committee ticket to 719 for the Elizabethtown-led faction.

majority Republican contingent dominated by Newark. Instead, an open nominating meeting convened in Newark. It

TABLE I

County Voting Statistics—Votes for Legislative Council, 1800-1815

Year	Adult White Males	Votes Cast	Per cent Voter Partic.	Fed. Vote	Rep. Vote
		ESSEX			
1800	4333	1678	39%	12	1666*
1801	4428	2489	56%		2489*
1802	4523	1600	35%		1600*
1803	4618	2260	49%	263	1997*
1804	4713	1708	36%		1708*
1805	4808	1869	38%		1869*
1806	4903	3941	80%		3941*
1807	4998	4970	99%		4970*
1808	5093	3122	61%	378	2744*
1809	5188	1876	36%	126	1750*
1810	5283	2048	39%		2048*
1811	5390	2040	38%		2040*
1812	5497	2282	42%		2282*
1813	5604	2207	39%	97	2110*
1814	5711	3181	56%		3181*
1815	5818	2225	38%		2225*
		SUSSEX			
1800	4405				
1801	4472	2537	57%	1230	1307*
1802	4539				
1803	4606	3484	76%	1087	2397*
1804	4673				
1805	4740				
1806	4807				
1807	4869	3212	65%	1443	1769*
1808	4941	3832	76%	1747	2085*
1809	4954	2977	60%	835	2142*
1810	5070	1514	30%		1514*
1811	5212	2474	47%	810†	1668*
1812	5354	3886	73%	1426	2460*
1813	5496	3377	61%	1188	2189*
1814	5638	3371	58%	1294	2077*
1815	5780	3304	57%	1253†	2051*

County Voting Statistics—Votes for Legislative Council, 1800-1815

Year	Adult White Males	Votes Cast	Per cent Voter Partic.	Fed. Vote	Rep. Vote
		HUNTERDON			
1800	4087	2498	61%	1217	1281*
1801	4168	3387	81%	1552	1835*
1802	4248	3689	87%	1834	1855*
1803	4330	5271	122%	2406	2865*
1804	4411				
1805	4492				
1806	4573	4477	98%	2171	2306*
1807	4657	5470	117%	2520	2950*
1808	4735	4166	88%	2043	2123*
1809	4816	3897	81%	1780	2117*
1810	4900				
1811	4985				
1812	5070	4465	88%	2208	2257*
1813	5155				
1814	5250	4401	84%	2130	2262*
1815	5325	4142	76%	1932	2210*
		MIDDLESEX			
1800	3362	2401	71%	1589*	812
1801	3425	1998	58%	1129*	869
1802	3488	1640	47%	955*	685
1803	3551	3037	86%	1662*	1375
1804	3614	1569	43%	852*	717
1805	3777	1741	47%	916*	825
1806	3740	1470	39%	897*	573
1807	3862	2147	56%	1098*	1049
1808	3886	2879	74%	1590*	1280
1809	3929	2202	56%	1172*	1030
1810	3991	2152	54%	1149*	1003
1811	4027	2457	61%	1206	1251*
1812	4063	3199	79%	1776*	1423
1813	4099	2811	69%	1560*	1251
1814	4135	2905	70%	1723*	1182
1815	4171	2462	59%	1340*	1122

County Voting Statistics—Votes for Legislative Council, 1800-1815

Year	Adult White Males	Votes Cast	Per cent Voter Partic.	Fed. Vote	Rep. Vote
		BURLINGTON			
1800	4389	3326	76%	2806*	520
1801	4447	2624	59%	1783*	841
1802	4505	2734	61%	1627*	1107
1803	4563	3869	85%	2431*	1438
1804	4621	2253	49%	1295*	958
1805	4679	1560	33%	814*	746
1806	4737				
1807	4793				
1808	4843	3172	65%	2191*	981
1809	4911	2091	43%	1394*	697
1810	4967				
1811	5046				
1812	5125				
1813	5204				
1814	5283				
1815	5264				

*denotes winning ticket †combined Rep.-Fed. ticket
SOURCES: Votes cast were extracted from the following newspapers: Newark *Centinel of Freedom*; Trenton *True American*; *Newark Gazette*; *Trenton Federalist and New Jersey Gazette*; Morristown *Genius of Liberty*; *Guardian, or New Brunswick Advertiser*; New Brunswick *Fredonian*. Eligible voters were determined by taking the total of free white males over the age of twenty-one from the census returns. The following sources were employed: *Return of the Whole Number of Persons Within the Several Districts of the United States*, [1800 Census] (Washington City, 1802), 48. *Aggregate Amount of Persons Within the United States in the Year 1810* (Washington, 1811), 32. *Census for 1820* (Washington, 1821). Reprint of Return in the American Antiquarian Society, Worcester, Mass. found in Princeton University Library.

was open to the public and a large number attended, but it still retained a vestige of its earlier form, for the participants chose a committee of conference from among their number to represent each town. The committee reported a ticket, but, before it was approved, Springfield Republicans once again touched off a violent controversy when they objected to the ticket and accused the committee of conference of being "a complete aristocracy."[10] Essex Republicans, despite efforts to

10. John Condit to Ebenezer Elmer, Sept. 29, 1802, Gratz Collection, Hist. Soc. of Pa.; Newark, *Centinel*, Sept. 28, Oct. 5, 1802.

compromise differences between regional factions in the county, could not avoid controversy within the organization. No other Republican ticket appeared, however, and the lid, for the time being, remained firmly clamped in place.[11]

Further rents in the county organization in the next few years signified a continuing deterioration from within, despite successful efforts to keep the feud from the public. In 1803, William S. Pennington resigned from the legislature to accept an appointment as attorney for the New Jersey federal district. At the interim election to fill his seat in January 1804, the Republicans in the county openly divided once more. Voters in the vicinity of Newark pitted their candidate against a candidate representing the old coalition headed by Elizabethtown party men. The Newark candidate once again defeated his opponent.[12] By October 1804, however, the Republican county machinery existed only nominally. The fall elections of that year and the year following witnessed a continuation of the same difficulty. The Newark faction struggled successfully to maintain its edge over the opposition of Elizabethtown "and her satellites."[13]

It was less a particular issue that kept Essex Republicans embroiled than it was the clash of two personalities representing different areas of the county. William S. Pennington of Newark—former editor of the *Centinel of Freedom*, Essex County's earliest Republican organizer, and later its leading office-holder—remained the guiding hand of the dominant Newark group. Aided by his brothers Samuel and Aaron, before the latter's death around the turn of the century, William ruled his organization with an iron hand.[14] Pennington was a Revolutionary hero and a hatter by trade. When the Republicans came to power in 1800, Pennington, though middle aged, studied law and became a member of the bar. Thereafter, in

11. Newark *Centinel*, Oct. 19, 26, 1802.
12. *Ibid.*, Jan. 10-24, 1804.
13. *Ibid.*, Sept. 18-Oct. 9, 1804, Sept. 10-24, Oct. 8, 1805.
14. Pennington's power in the county has been well documented. See Stewart, Jeffersonian Journalism, 7; Elmer, *The Constitution and Government of New Jersey*, 162; *Newark Gazette*, July 27, 1802, and 1797-1804, *passim*.

[79]

the decade prior to the War of 1812, he served in various legal and judicial capacities in the state, reaching the high point in his political career when he became governor in 1813. Only in 1815 did he give up the reins of authority in the county and, to an extent, in the state, when he retired from the governorship to accept the lucrative federal judgeship for the state-wide district.[15]

William S. Pennington was often vexed by Shepard Kollock, the venerable editor of the Elizabethtown *New Jersey Journal.* Kollock drew support for both his paper and his politics from outlying towns in Essex County. Although he served in the legislature occasionally and his paper was the oldest Republican sheet in the state, Kollock remained a stranger to the inner circle that controlled New Jersey's Republican party.[16] Pennington remained a part of that inner circle so long as he could muster the dominant Republican majority in a county nearly devoid of Federalists.

Sussex County

Sussex County, on the other hand, was most emphatically not without Federalists. In fact, a rock-ribbed, two-party system prevailed for most of the Democratic-Republican period. Nevertheless the Republicans dominated the county in the early years of party organization between 1800 and 1806 despite continuing Federalist exertions. The latter party broke into the victory column only once and then partially, in 1806, when they elected a councilor. Vigorous contests each year fortified an already energetic Republican party apparatus. Indeed, both depth and flexibility were mandatory elements if the Repub-

15. For accounts of William S. Pennington's political career, see *ibid.,* and John Whitehead, *The Judicial and Civil History of New Jersey* (Boston, 1897), 411-14; *Biographical Encyclopaedia of New Jersey,* 28; Folsom *et al.,* comps., *Cyclopedia of New Jersey Biography,* I, 31; Newark *Centinel,* July 13, 1813.
16. For Shepard Kollock's long-time role in Essex politics, see his newspaper, the Elizabethtown *N.J. Journal,* for the entire period of his tenure from well before 1790 through 1818. See also David Thompson, Jr., to Samuel L. Southard, Mar. 8, 1816, Southard Papers, Princeton Univ. Lib.; Newark *Centinel,* Sept. 17, 1816, Sept. 23, 1817; Trenton *True American,* Sept. 14, 1818.

licans hoped to maintain their edge. Although schism in the Republican organization did produce a disquieting attack of quidism, or "third partyism" in the words of contemporaries, which in the long run contributed to the weakening of the Republican interest, in its heyday the Sussex Republican party was the strongest and best structured political machine in northern New Jersey.

Republican party machinery in Sussex appeared early in 1800 in response to the urgings of the "Morris and Sussex Subscribers" to the *Centinel*. Little is known about the party in the first two years of its existence, but it is definite that by 1802 it had adopted the open nominating meeting characteristic of North Jersey. This procedure prevailed for most of the period through 1815. The meetings were usually held at Newton in August of each year so that they would coincide with the annual County Court; this scheduling insured that the most prominent political figures of the county would be in attendance. The well-attended meetings proved to be a good barometer for party enthusiasm.[17]

Enthusiasm, however, did not preclude local squabbling among party factions. The first of many internal stresses on the organization appeared in 1801, and it, like so many future difficulties, revolved around the figure of Silas Dickerson, an influential Sussex Republican in the formative years of party development. The youthful Speaker of the Assembly, who possessed a stubborn streak and often acted first and thought later,[18] made many enemies. Some Sussex Republicans, Silas claimed in 1801, took "pains [unsuccessfully] to keep me out [of the legislature]."[19] Silas managed to fend off this and subsequent

17. Trenton *True American*, Sept. 27, 1802, July 7, 1806, Aug. 31, 1807, Sept. 13, 1809, July 30, 1810, Aug. 12, 1811; Newark *Centinel*, Sept. 21, 1802, Sept. 20, 1803, Aug. 30, 1808, July 31, 1810, July 28, 1812, Sept. 26, 1815; Silas Dickerson to Mahlon Dickerson, June 22, 1804, Dickerson Letter Book, N.J. Hist. Soc.

18. See the Dickerson Letter Book, N.J. Hist. Soc., *passim*; Ebenezer Elmer to David Moore, Mar. 24, 1803[2], Gratz Collection, Hist. Soc. of Pa.; Newark *Centinel*, Sept. 1, 1801.

19. Silas Dickerson to Mahlon Dickerson, Oct. 4, 1801, Dickerson Letter Book, N.J. Hist. Soc.

threats to his position, but eventually his ambition betrayed him.

In 1804, Dickerson, an assemblyman, decided to elevate his status and run for Council even though he might "interfere with [William] McCullough," the Republican incumbent.[20] Although he was dissuaded at the last minute, the incident provided a foundation for the charge leveled the following year that Silas Dickerson, along with many of his followers, was a quid. Silas' previous lapses were recalled in 1805, when it was learned in the county that his brother Mahlon, residing in Philadelphia, was supporting Governor Thomas McKean against the "regular" Republican candidate Simon Snyder. This situation removed any doubts from the minds of many voters, and Silas lost his bid for re-election to the legislature. He wrote his brother, "The County in general is so in favor of Snyder and from their knoledge of your Opposition to him I have been set down as a tertium quid." Although only Republicans were elected, the damage to the party organization was not easily repaired.[21]

In 1806, Sussex Republicans looked for quids behind every bush. Early in July, Republicans were warned to form only a genuine Republican ticket. "Your old enemies will be on the alert (perhaps not openly) to create a division," a Sussex Republican warned. He added, "You have that heterogenious monster 'quidism' or third partyism to oppose; and you have a host of office hunters [including Dickerson] to defeat among those who appear friendly to republicans." Even the prudent *True American* cautioned editorially that "through the malevolent designs of your enemies, your strength may be divided."[22] Silas Dickerson, now out of office but still a leading figure in the disruptive element of the county organization, shed a few

20. Mahlon Dickerson to Silas Dickerson, Aug. 5, 1804, *ibid.*

21. Silas Dickerson to Mahlon Dickerson, Oct. 15, 1805, *ibid.* See also Cunningham, *The Jeffersonian Republicans in Power: Party Operations, 1801-1809* (Chapel Hill, 1963), 162-64.

22. Trenton *True American*, July 7, Oct. 6, 1806; Newark *Centinel*, Sept. 30, 1806.

crocodile tears in reporting to his brother that "the Democrats of Sussex have behaved verry rascally in consequence of which I think Jacob S. Thompson [a Federalist] will represent us in Council this year."[23] Indeed the Sussex Republican organization was so busy looking for quids that it neglected to watch out for the Federalists, and the first and only Federalist was elected to the legislature in this heyday of Jeffersonian sentiment.

Hunterdon County

Republicans in Hunterdon County in central New Jersey challenged a Federalist interest initially even stronger than that opposing their Sussex brethren to the north. The early years of party conflict in Hunterdon County were marked by bitter contests and efforts to establish a proper organization. In 1801 Republicans briefly flirted with a delegate nominating convention; each town's Republicans elected men to represent them at a closed countywide nominating convention, thus paralleling maiden developments in Essex County. The delegates also served on their respective township correspondence committees which organized the election campaign. This nominating machinery did not meet the Republicans' needs, however, for it did little to foster any widespread feeling of participation in the nominating process among the voters. The need to develop a sense of inclusion among Republicans was made clear to party managers in 1801 and 1802, when the Federalists were able to elect most of their ticket to office.[24]

In 1802, the Hunterdon Republicans had fallen short of electing a legislator by one vote. As a result, the state legislature was tied, and the state government was deadlocked for the year. This election had been distinguished by widespread

23. Silas Dickerson to Mahlon Dickerson, Oct. 12, 1806, Dickerson Letter Book, N.J. Hist. Soc.; Trenton *True American*, Oct. 13, 20, 1806; Newark *Centinel*, Oct. 14, 21, 1806.

24. Trenton *True American*, Sept. 1, 1801, Aug. 23, Sept. 6, Oct. 11, 18, 25, 1802, Jan. 3, 17, 1803; Newark *Centinel*, Oct. 12, 1801, Oct. 26, 1802.

frauds; it served notice on Republican leaders that a broader but tighter county organization was in order.[25]

The highly competitive political situation in Central Jersey and the inability of the Hunterdon Republicans to break into the Federalists' strength spurred efforts toward revision of the party apparatus, and in January 1803 a new type of machinery resulted. The changes made in 1803 and the modifications that followed in 1804 provided a foundation for a Republican party that served the county well for almost twenty years. Emanating from a proposal made by Trenton Republicans at the end of 1802, the new organization originally took the form of an "Association for the Preservation of Our Electoral Rights." This association drafted a constitution governing nearly every area of political activity. The men behind the effort were James Linn and James J. Wilson.[26]

An organizational meeting that convened early in January 1803 was open to all eligible voters in the county who were sympathetic to the Republican cause. James J. Wilson presented to the assembled crowd an outline for the new organization. Each town was to form a committee, but one in name only, for all Republicans in town were eligible for membership. The member was to "assist all in his power to disseminate correct information on public affairs among his fellow citizens."[27]

25. The Republicans, striving to have the election set aside, declared before a legislative investigating committee that "women voted, citizens of Philadelphia, negroes and slaves, and those possessing less than fifty pound freeholds." Votes, one witness added, "were accepted in the open from carriages on the streets." The Federalists asserted that the Republicans received as many illegal votes as they did. The legislature dismissed all charges because both sides appeared to be equally guilty of wholesale violation of the election laws. Petitions and Reports of the Legislative Committee of Elections Investigating Irregularities in Hunterdon County, Nov. 16, 1802, Assembly Minutes Papers, No. 1979, New Jersey State Library, Trenton, N.J. Republican petitioners even charged the committee with conducting the investigation unfairly.

26. Trenton *True American*, Jan. 3, 17, Feb.-Apr. 1803, *passim*; James J. Wilson to William Darlington, 1802, *passim*, Darlington Papers, Lib. Cong.; Anon., *To the Republicans of the County of Hunterdon* (Phila., 1812), New Jersey Pamphlets Collection, Rutgers Univ. Lib.; James Linn to Ebenezer Elmer, Jan. 3, 1803, and *passim*, Gratz Collection, Hist. Soc. of Pa.

27. Trenton *True American*, Jan. 3, 17, 1803; James Linn to Ebenezer Elmer, Jan. 3, 1803, Gratz Collection, Hist. Soc. of Pa.

Trenton and Maidenhead (now, understandably, Lawrence-ville), the first two towns to form committees—or, more correctly, organizations—did so by April 1803. It appears that all other towns in Hunterdon County established local organizations by July, for at the end of that month committees from the several townships convened.[28]

The blueprint for the association was an extremely detailed one. At the initial organizational meeting, Wilson had proposed that the township committees meet separately twice a year, in April and October, to transact the business of their local associations. Once a year, at the end of August or the beginning of September, all the township organizations would assemble to nominate a county ticket.[29] Because virtually any Republican voter could become an organization member simply by declaring himself so, the annual county meeting in effect was open to anyone. It was always held at Flemington, the county seat.[30]

The local chairmen, elected by the Republican organizations in each town, also served on the county committee of correspondence which met four times a year, and they were delegates to the state convention. Functioning on the local, county, and state levels, these township chairmen appeared to be the key men in the new organizations. In fact, however, while they exercised some administrative authority, real power, as in all other counties, lay with those few who exerted the greatest influence on the state level. Each annual county nominating meeting elected a chairman and a secretary for that meeting. It is instructive to note that while no chairman ever served twice in that capacity through 1812, James J. Wilson almost invariably was the secretary.[31]

28. Trenton *True American*, Apr. 4, July 25, 1803.
29. *Ibid.*, Jan. 3, 17, Sept. 5, 1803, Sept. 10, 1804, Feb. 18, Sept. 16, 1805, Sept. 8, 1806, Sept. 5, 1808, Aug. 5, Sept. 9, 1811, Aug. 17, 1812.
30. *Ibid.*, Apr. 9, 1804, Feb. 18, Sept. 16, 1805, Sept. 8, 1806, Sept. 5, 1808, Sept. 9, 1811, Aug. 17, 1812.
31. *Ibid.*, Jan. 3, 17, Sept. 5, Nov. 28, 1803, Sept. 10, 1804, Sept. 8, 1806, Sept. 5, 1808, Sept. 9, 1811.

In 1804, the county meeting was officially thrown open to all Republicans in the county, without need for formal party affiliation, although, in fact, that practice had already prevailed; townsmen to longer needed to be designated committeemen to take active roles in their towns. This change was not merely a concession to reality; perhaps it was also a recognition of the fact that the practice of identifying an individual as a party member before he was allowed to participate in the nominating process was abhorrent to many in Hunterdon County. At any rate, the changes wrought in 1804 modified party requirements by throwing open the organization to all Republicans, regardless of whether they formally affiliated or not.

The rank and file, thereafter, not only voted for nominees, they chose delegates to the state convention as well. From 1804 onward, township chairmen were not automatically designated as convention delegates; the delegates were chosen from the floor of the county meeting instead.[32] This alteration might well have reflected a fear on the part of the leadership that local chairmen would, through their myriad duties, grow too powerful. The change to elected convention delegates, while it appeared to be a concession to democratic practices, in fact helped to assure that only a few would retain authority at the state level. This conclusion would seem warranted by the role played by James J. Wilson in Hunterdon County.[33]

The county meeting had come a long way since its inception in 1801—half circle from a delegate convention to an open gathering. At the same time, however, the basic formality of party structure was kept intact, unlike the unstructured county machines in most North Jersey counties.

At the 1804 county meeting, all these changes were formally accepted. In addition, Wilson introduced a new, well-defined nominating procedure:

32. *Ibid.*, Sept. 10, 1804.
33. See also Carl E. Prince, "James J. Wilson: Party Leader, 1801-1824," N.J. Hist. Soc., *Proceedings*, 83 (1965), 24-39.

The Secretary shall take down the name of every person who shall be named to him by any member of this meeting for either of these offices [legislature or sheriff]; which list when completed, shall be read to the meeting.

The meeting shall then adjourn for one hour, to allow time for every member to provide himself with a ticket; which ticket shall be composed of persons whose names are on the list to be nominated. On convening again, the Secretary shall receive all tickets handed to him by Members of this meeting; after which the President shall call over the names of each . . . and the persons who shall have the highest number of votes as above shall be the candidates.

This nominating procedure was accepted and implemented by the more than two hundred men attending the county meeting.[34] No wonder that James Linn, onetime Republican congressman and an important party organizer in the county, could report, "We expect *Much* from the new association."[35]

Although the Federalists after 1802 encountered a long spell without a victory, they continued vigorously to contest each election.[36] Their efforts were of no avail. The firm guidance of James Linn and particularly James J. Wilson enabled the association to maintain its position in the face of serious Federalist challenges to its authority.

James Linn had been an anti-Federalist stalwart in New Jersey early in the 1790's. He served one term in Congress between 1799 and 1801, during which he moved from Somerset to Hunterdon County. Perhaps as a result of this move, he was not run for re-election by the state convention of 1800. Recovering from his disappointment, Linn acted decisively in Hunterdon politics in 1801 and thereafter. The results of his efforts appeared in the formation of the Republican party machine in Hunterdon County.[37]

34. Trenton *True American*, Sept. 10, 1804.
35. James Linn to Ebenezer Elmer, Jan. 3, 1803, Gratz Collection, Hist. Soc. of Pa.
36. See Table I, pp. 76-78. See also the Trenton *True American*, Oct. 1802, *passim.*
37. Joseph Bloomfield to Ebenezer Elmer, Aug. 25, 1801, Ely Collection,

Within a few years James J. Wilson came to share Linn's authority, and then, very slowly, he gained the lion's portion of it. He served his apprenticeship to the party by drawing up and publicizing the articles of association and acting as secretary thereafter at the county nominating meetings. By 1805, the Federalists, suspicious of his growing authority, had taken up the cry that Wilson "dictated" to the Republican county meeting "who should and who should not be voted for."[38] He became very much the envy of many other young Jeffersonians in New Jersey, who looked askance at his rapid rise.[39] An authoritative Republican critic sometime later reinforced the basis for the growing general suspicion of Wilson's motives. "Has not the wishes of the Democratic-Republicans of this County," he asked, "been frustrated by the ambitious and aristocratical intrigues of Mr. Wilson?"[40]

It was widely understood by about 1806 that, for all the democratic camouflage provided by the county Republican association, James J. Wilson was the man to be reckoned with in Hunterdon County politics. At the base of Wilson's authority from 1801 onward was the Trenton *True American*, a weekly that soon emerged as the leading Republican paper in the state. Its origins and early development offer a clear example of the close relationship between the party organization and the press in this formative period. Moreover, it was no accident that both Wilson's political power and the *True American's* prestige and importance grew apace. In Wilson's case as in that of William S. Pennington, his party leverage was derived in large measure from control of a potent communications and propaganda mechanism, and the associations that it forged.

N.J. Hist. Soc.; Trenton *True American*, Apr. 9, 1804; James Linn Correspondence, *passim*, Gratz Collection, Hist. Soc. of Pa.

38. *Trenton Federalist and New Jersey Gazette*, Sept. 9, 16, 1805; Trenton *True American*, Sept. 16, 1805, Oct. 13, 1806; Prince, "James J. Wilson: Party Leader, 1801-1824," N.J. Hist. Soc., *Proceedings*, 83 (1965), 24-39.

39. James J. Wilson to William Darlington, July 22, 1801, Darlington Papers, Lib. Cong.

40. Anon., *To the Republicans of the County of Hunterdon*, 5; Trenton *True American*, Sept. 16, 1805.

The launching of the Trenton *True American* in 1801 signaled the continuing Republican effort to improve the party's apparatus. The need for a newspaper in South and Central Jersey was one of the prime lessons party managers had learned from the hectic campaigns of 1800. They attributed the party's effectiveness in the northern counties in part to the Newark *Centinel of Freedom,* and, to a lesser extent, the Morristown *Genius of Liberty* and the Elizabethtown *New Jersey Journal.* Joseph Bloomfield, speaking for the Jeffersonian leadership, hoped that the proposed newspaper "will be supported by the Republicans in the Western Counties—not only by taking the paper but by detailing such facts and pieces to the people as will inform and Convince them . . . [of] Republican Principles."[41]

Indeed, the weekly proved to be a major instrument in bringing many of the South and Central Jersey counties to Republicanism. Bloomfield tapped two Republican printers to undertake the venture. Matthias Day had been associated with Shepard Kollock of the Elizabethtown *Journal* in the latter's early publishing ventures during and after the Revolution. Day's new partner was Jacob Mann who, young and inexperienced though he was, added necessary enthusiasm and capital to the operation. The partnership of Day and Mann was formed to print the *True American* at Trenton.[42]

Republicans exulted at this new evidence of party maturity. It was generally agreed that "a Republican printer here in Trenton . . . will be of great use in our Election next October for State Legislature."[43] The Federalists concurred. Some months after the *True American's* inception, a correspondent attributed mounting Republican success "to the persevering activity of certain leading men, and especially to the circula-

41. Joseph Bloomfield to Ebenezer Elmer, Dec. 28, 1800, Bloomfield Papers, N.J. Hist. Soc.; Mahlon Dickerson to Silas Dickerson, Feb. 18, 1801, Dickerson Letter Book, *ibid.*

42. *Ibid.* See also the Trenton *True American,* spring, summer, 1801, *passim.*

43. Moore Furman to Joseph Bloomfield, Jan. 5, 1801, in Historical Research Committee, New Jersey Society of Colonial Dames of America, eds.,

tion of certain papers favorable to that party."[44] The first number appeared in the early spring of 1801. Subscriptions were
coming in at an encouraging rate by June. The two partners,
casting about for additional help, settled upon James J. Wilson,
a youth of twenty-one. Born in Scotch Plains in 1780, he ap-
prenticed himself to the Elizabethtown *Journal* after a meager
country school education. In 1799, Wilson completed his apprenticeship and took a job as foreman of the Republican *Mirror of the Times* in Wilmington, Delaware, where he really
mastered the newspaper trade.[45]

Young Wilson was extremely ambitious. Within a few
months of his return to his native state he was able to capitalize
on an opportunity to become a partner. For some reason, old
Matthias Day wanted out; perhaps, Wilson intimated, the paper
was still not turning a profit by the summer of 1801, despite
a growing subscription list. In any event, Day stepped away
from the operation after just a few months of publication. Republican leaders, seeing their mouthpiece jeopardized, came to
the rescue. Wilson impressed party bigwigs favorably, and a
number of them either signed notes or put up the money necessary for Wilson to buy Day out. This is a striking piece of evidence of the tangible link between the Republican organization and its newspaper. His benefactors assured Wilson that the
money "shall be procured for [him] in time for the respective
payments."[46] One leader later reminded Wilson that "I was
one of the first to assist to establish the press you now are the
senior editor of."[47]

The Letters of Moore Furman, Deputy Quarter-Master General of New Jersey
in the Revolution (N.Y., 1912), 119. See also Joseph Bloomfield to Ebenezer
Elmer, Dec. 28, 1800, Bloomfield Papers, N.J. Hist. Soc.; James Linn to Ebenezer
Elmer, Dec. 29, 1801, Gratz Collection, Hist. Soc. of Pa.

44. New Brunswick *Guardian*, Sept. 17, 1801.

45. The Diary of William Darlington, with Reminiscences of an Earlier
Period, Entry 1800, Vol. I, N.-Y. Hist. Soc.; Trenton *True American*, Sept. 17,
1810; Prince, "James J. Wilson: Party Leader, 1801-1824," N.J. Hist. Soc.,
Proceedings, 83 (1965), 24-39.

46. James J. Wilson to William Darlington, June 28, 1801, Darlington Papers,
Lib. Cong.; Trenton *True American*, July 18, 1803.

47. *Trenton Federalist*, June 16, 1806.

The new editor immediately took hold. Early in 1802, he bought out Jacob Mann and replaced him with the much more "docile"—to use Wilson's own phrase—Lewis Blackwell. Wilson easily dominated Blackwell, and, with the material aid of the party, he slowly put the newspaper in the black.[48] As the paper's prestige grew, so did the reputation of its senior editor. Between 1801 and 1806, the struggling Wilson was aided by various dispensations of patronage, including positions as surrogate of Hunterdon County, clerk to the state Assembly, and printer for the state of New Jersey. As one wag put it, Wilson was "basking in the sun shine of public patronage."[49]

Wilson complained to his lifelong friend William Darlington, a Pennsylvania politician of some note, that he had "become an object of envy to some, for the influence I am supposed to possess, and for the offices I enjoy."[50] Even some of the editor's Republican colleagues had "heartburnings," as Wilson put it, over his rapid rise to power. His public position left him vulnerable to dissident Republican claims that he, like some other professed Republicans, was a "third party [quid] man."[51] Nevertheless, the *True American* and its editor continued to prosper, and with the aid of both, Hunterdon became the most reliable Republican stronghold in Central Jersey.

Burlington County

The same could not be said of Burlington County's role in South Jersey politics. However, the pressing party needs im-

48. James J. Wilson to William Darlington, Feb. 5, 1802, Jan. 10, 1803, Darlington Papers, Lib. Cong. Wilson claimed, in Jan. 1803, that the subscription list for the *True American* "has been for several months continually and rapidly increasing." No known circulation figures are available, however.

49. Newark *Centinel*, Sept. 17, 1805; Trenton *True American*, Nov. 23, 1812, July 12, 1813; Folsom *et al.*, comps, *Cyclopedia of New Jersey Biography*, I, 129; James J. Wilson to William Darlington, Nov. 6, 1804, Darlington Papers, Lib. Cong.; Anon., *To the Republicans of the County of Hunterdon*, 2-5, and *passim*.

50. James J. Wilson to William Darlington, Nov. 6, 1804, Darlington Papers, Lib. Cong.

51. *Ibid.*, Jan. 10, 1803, Nov. 15, 1804.

posed by a Federalist majority, well studded with Quaker support in Burlington County, resulted in an extensive Republican organization.[52] The highly formalized Democratic Republican Association of the County of Burlington, while it never won an election, was a fine example of the depth and clarity of which a local Republican group was capable. In the most Federalist county of the state, with its many Quaker inhabitants who remained loyal to the Hamiltonian cause, it was less surprising that the Republicans did not win than it was that they competed so faithfully; if the flesh was weak, the Republican spirit was willing, and, inspired by Governor Joseph Bloomfield, a resident of the county, the adherents of Jefferson never gave up their efforts to turn the Federalists out of office.

These efforts began to materialize in 1801, when Burlington Republicans emulated the party organization then developing in Essex County. Affirming the unity of leadership in the state, a convention of township delegates was introduced by Joseph Bloomfield, Thomas Newbold (later Republican congressman), and William Rossell (future first justice of the Supreme Court of New Jersey).[53] Between April and August, the groundwork was laid for a convention. It was officially convened by a Republican committee from Burlington Township and met at Mount Holly courthouse, implying the formation of other township delegations, probably at local public meetings. Despite these efforts there was not much of a contest in 1801.[54] Although the Republicans lost badly, the county machinery thus created remained intact in 1802, with a noticeable

52. The type of county organization—the democratic association—described here was duplicated in three of the four remaining South Jersey counties; Gloucester, Cumberland, and Cape May. Only Salem County never formed a democratic association.

53. Joseph Bloomfield to Ebenezer Elmer, Aug. 25, 1801, Ely Collection, N.J. Hist. Soc.; Joseph Bloomfield to Ebenezer Elmer, Apr. 20, 1801, Elmer Papers, Rutgers Univ. Lib.; Trenton *True American*, Aug. 25, Sept. 15, 1801.

54. Trenton *True American*, Aug. 18, 25, Sept. 15, Oct. 6, 13, 20, 1801; Joseph Bloomfield to Ebenezer Elmer, Aug. 25, Oct. 19, 1801, Ely Collection, N.J. Hist. Soc.; Silas Dickerson to Mahlon Dickerson, Nov. 4, 1801, Dickerson Letter Book, N.J. Hist. Soc.; Joseph Bloomfield to Ebenezer Tucker, Dec. 17, 1801, Albert Gallatin Papers, N.-Y. Hist. Soc.

improvement in the election results.[55] The gain inspired Burlington party men to greater efforts, and, early in 1803, they created a highly formalized and well structured countywide democratic association.[56]

Articles of association for the Democratic Republican Association of the County of Burlington were drafted and submitted for the approval of an organizational meeting, open to the public, that convened in February 1803 at Mount Holly. For the sake of appearances a constitutional committee of seven reported to the meeting. After a brief adjournment and some discussion a polished and complete constitution was ratified unanimously and without change. The meeting then elected as president of the association Thomas Newbold, who was among the earliest Republican organizers in the county and a close confidant of Governor Bloomfield. Executive authority in the association was vested in four county officers and seven members (one from each township) of a county committee of correspondence. The constitution provided also for an annual closed delegate convention to be held on the last Saturday in August of each year, at which officers were elected and other business transacted. Township meetings open to all local members were made mandatory; these were to convene each February to select local officers and township committees of correspondence of not less than six or more than eight members, thus duplicating locally the framework of the county apparatus. Township organizations, in fact, were in most ways exact replicas of the parent structure, if the constitution was an accurate guide. Finally, the governing document provided for the election in the townships of a delegate to the county convention

55. Trenton *True American*, Sept. 6, 1802.

56. The democratic association created in Burlington in 1803 was like that of Hunterdon County on paper, but it was, in reality, much more closely knit than even that integrated organization. Virtually identical organizations, built from the same blueprint as that employed in Burlington, appeared in Gloucester, Cumberland, and Cape May counties. It is clear that Joseph Bloomfield once again was the guiding force in shaping the structure of the new organization. See Joseph Bloomfield to Ebenezer Elmer, Apr. 20, 1801, Elmer Papers, Rutgers Univ. Lib.

whose presence, along with the local member of the county committee of correspondence, would insure that each town would have two representatives at the August conclave.[57]

The county committee of correspondence was an executive group empowered to meet at any time, make necessary decisions without recourse first to the body politic, and use the finances of the organization solely at its discretion. It was responsible for providing public notice of the annual convention, which was comprised of the four officers and seven members of the committee joined by seven additional township delegates. This group made nominations for the county offices at stake in the ensuing autumn elections and elected officers of the association for the coming year.[58] No more centralized formal structure existed in any county in the state, although informal centralization was in fact achieved in other counties by a relatively small number of activists who came to dominate the Republican organizations.

Local officers and committees ostensibly wielded similar local authority, but in practice their activities were curtailed. Local groups conducted Republican town meetings, guided electioneering efforts, and encouraged and supervised the locally oriented membership of the association; but township officers and committeemen were not empowered to act for the county association in any circumstances. This was the exclusive province of the county corresponding committee. Local officers, likewise, had no recourse to the treasury of the association. Officers and members at all levels were explicitly urged to employ their "utmost endeavors . . . to promote by [their] influence and exertions the election" of Republicans.[59]

The association was open to anyone professing Republican principles; the only disqualifying factor was membership in the Federalist party. A two-thirds vote of the township organization expelled a violator. Withdrawal from the association could be

57. Trenton *True American*, Jan. 24, Mar. 14, 1803, Aug. 20, 1804, Oct. 5, 1807.
58. *Ibid.*, Jan. 24, Feb. 14, Mar. 14, 1803.
59. *Ibid.*

effected simply by giving notice to the local chairman. The 1803 organizing assembly levied an initiation fee of fifty cents, and each member, charter or otherwise, signed the constitution. New members were added merely by their attending local meetings, signing the constitution, paying the initiation fee, and making payment of the annual dues of twenty-five cents. The dues were handled by the county treasurer and were allocated explicitly for the use of the county committee of correspondence.[60]

Although the Federalists by no means eschewed political action, they found the Burlington Democratic Association and others like it a distinct menace to everything they held dear. Among the many criticisms encountered, the following is typical: "These Associations exactly resemble the French Jacobin clubs. . . . They are permanent bodies, self-elected, extended over Counties and Townships. They have Presidents, Secretaries, and Committees . . . and bind themselves to pursue the objects of the Association, which are political. . . . Tho' not elected by the people at large, and not composing a tenth part of the citizens, they assume power even greater than that of the Legislature."[61]

A particular strength of the Burlington Association was that, despite its structural formality, it was able to improvise to meet existing conditions. It soon became clear, for instance, that the nominating convention, comprising the county committee of correspondence plus one delegate from each town, was too narrowly based to be even superficially democratic; Federalist criticisms of the apparatus soon found their mark. In an effort to overcome this structural flaw, the leadership of the association broadened political responsibility prior to the 1804 elections by inviting the public to participate in an open nominating meeting each August. The open county meeting, held in the afternoon, followed the regular annual association convention which gathered on the morning of the same day. Clear-

60. *Ibid.*
61. *Newark Gazette*, Oct. 4, 1803.

ly, the convention used its unity to advantage by instructing its followers to fall in behind the association's choices for spots on the ticket, and almost invariably, inasmuch as the association men constituted the largest bloc at the open meeting, they dominated the public proceedings.[62]

Although the association did not win a single election in the overwhelmingly Federalist county, it dominated Republican politics and was favored by the party's state hierarchy in patronage matters for more than a decade.[63] In a very meaningful way, the uniformly unsuccessful efforts of the association help to affirm the conclusion that this party organization, typical of South Jersey, was a remarkably able party vehicle, capable of retaining for a long period of time the loyalty and active participation of the minority of Jeffersonians in the county. That it did these things without winning an election, then, serves to highlight the depth and stability of the apparatus as well as the strength of its appeal.

Republicans early realized that success at the upper levels of party organization depended on enthusiastic participation below. The most able Federalist observer of the period, "Yorick," writing weekly for the New Brunswick *Guardian* in 1806 and 1807, reflected on the dangers that this passion for organization among Republicans seemed to create: "Township associations, county committees, state committees or conventions, and caucuses rise in gradation [and] have separately, particular operations to perform, and unitedly, constitute a body of forces, which regulate every movement in our political machine, and render the constitutional organs obedient to their commands."[64] That local party organization in particular was an evil Yorick doubted not: "These societies constitute a sort of government themselves. . . . These clubs and caucuses, which exercise

62. Trenton *True American*, Aug. 20, Sept. 3, 1804, Aug. 19, 1805, Sept. 22, 1806, Oct. 5, 1807, Sept. 5, 1808, Aug. 20, Sept. 10, 1810, Aug. 19, Sept. 9, 1811, Sept. 7, 1812, Aug. 16, 1814, Aug, 12, 1816.
63. *Ibid.*
64. New Brunswick *Guardian*, May 8, 1806.

usurped power and overrule our rulers, [are] incompatible with our constitution."[65] Federalists, lacking the local organizational strength of the Republicans, generally professed this view. But a good Jeffersonian found a ready answer: "We cannot . . . subscribe to the doctrine of some who say *that committees are of no use,* as a mutual interchange of sentiment expressed by committees chosen from each township, is certainly the best mode of concentrating the sense of the county, and in fact is the only proper mode of making judicious selections where there are rival parties in politics."[66]

Despite apparent differences regarding the role of party machinery, in other respects the parties were not so far apart. Even Yorick concluded that "the republican federalists and the republican democrats differ more about words than things, differ about minor points but agree on the main ones, differ as to means but not as to the end." In short, Yorick aptly noted, "Strange! all this difference should be Twixt tweedledum and tweedledee."[67]

65. *Ibid.,* Apr. 3, 1806.
66. Newark *Centinel,* Oct. 20, 1801.
67. New Brunswick *Guardian,* Mar. 6, 13, 1806.

IV

CAUCUS AND CONVENTION
1801-1806

CONCURRENT WITH THE BROADENING OF LOCAL PARTY APPARATUS
and leadership control, New Jersey party leaders introduced
a legislative caucus and institutionalized the state nominating
convention. Both agencies proved to be vital ingredients for
continued Republican success. Faced with the problems posed
by majority status for the first time as a result of the Republican legislative victory of 1801, the caucus provided an agency
able to filter and ultimately resolve most of the inevitable Republican conflicts that developed in the legislature. Meanwhile,
with party nominations to Congress made eminently more desirable by the promise of more Republican victories at the polls,
the convention likewise filled the role of mediator when the
time came to choose between conflicting powerful elements of
the party seeking the only at-large offices open to the state's
voters. The legislative caucus and the state nominating convention eventually became, along with the emergent leadership
and the county organizations, the cornerstones of the Republican party machine.

The trials that both the caucus and convention encountered in their formative years were complicated by the still

existing regional differences between East and West Jersey dating back to the colonial period. These differences, never far from the surface of New Jersey politics, may be found at the root of several of the most prominent post-1800 intraparty struggles. Regional difficulties, for example, were evident in the 1802 legislative set-to involving Speaker Silas Dickerson and his hostile Republican colleagues from the southern part of the state. Sectional jealousies were evident too in the active distrust of Governor Joseph Bloomfield by many party leaders from the northern areas. The same East-West Jersey cleavage was exploited by a faction in the 1804 state convention struggle for a seat in Congress between the aforementioned Dickerson of Sussex County in northern New Jersey, and James Sloan of Gloucester County to the southward. The caucus and the convention, in short, were both often hard put to resolve these internecine party differences. The fact that they did so was testimony to their strength and flexibility as components of the party machine.

Politics in the Legislature

In 1801, the Republicans captured the legislature, the last statewide Federalist stronghold. In that legislative canvass current local organizational efforts were rewarded when Republicans carried Hunterdon, Monmouth, Salem, and Cumberland, in addition to Essex, Morris, and Sussex. This victory initiated a significant period of adjustment for the new majority. While the party had operated as a minority, they experienced little difficulty in maintaining unity. There had been no patronage to divide and no opportunity to take the initiative in legislative matters. Success in 1801 carried with it the power to guide legislative affairs and appropriate the spoils. A prime desire of Republican legislators was to keep friction among themselves out of public view while they set about their legislative tasks.

And friction there was. From the outset, when the choices of a governor and Assembly speaker presented themselves, sectional Republican differences were made manifest. Apart from the usual leadership struggles and personal jealousies, trouble between East and West Jersey Republican interests, in various forms, haunted the party; it was a problem state Republicans resigned themselves to wrestling with perpetually.

The Jeffersonians wielded a majority of ten in the joint meeting of the legislature in 1801 and were able at last to take over the state's highest positions; Joseph Bloomfield was designated governor and Silas Dickerson speaker of the Assembly.[1] Bloomfield was a logical choice. The selection of the youthful Speaker, however, came as a surprise to Dickerson himself as well as to his Republican supporters and Federalist opponents. Aaron Kitchell had been considered the logical choice to succeed to the speaker's position, but Kitchell did not want it and, after declining, he placed his young protégé's name in nomination. This settled the matter and insured Dickerson's election. The latter recognized Kitchell's preeminent claim, admitting that he was only given the post at the former congressman's behest.[2] Kitchell, the scarred veteran of many political wars, had wisely seen fit to wait until the Republican legislative triumph hardened into Republican legislative organization before he once more placed himself on the firing line.

Mahlon Dickerson, who, like Kitchell, was wise in the ways of politics, saw the dangers Kitchell had seen in the speaker's position that the younger Dickerson had assumed. In the glory of the moment, the young and relatively inexperienced Silas overlooked the pitfalls of his new post, and Mahlon was troubled by his brother's too-rapid advancement. Silas Dickerson was just twenty-nine when he was elected in 1801. His brother wrote that the new Speaker had "done an imprudent thing in accepting the office . . . at [his] age." But it was done, and he could only caution Silas to "make the best of it. You will be careful to avail yourself of the friendship of Mr. Kitchell who

1. Newark *Centinel*, Oct. 27, Nov. 3, 1801.
2. Silas Dickerson to Mahlon Dickerson, Oct. 27, 28, 1801, Mahlon Dickerson to Silas Dickerson, Oct. 28, 1801, Dickerson Letter Book, N.J. Hist. Soc.

certainly ought to have been speaker. His experience and knowledge may be of the greatest service to you."[3] Silas, over-confident and naive, replied: "I am under the wing of Kitchell who is able to battle the best of them."[4] It was easy to see that power and position in the new legislature did not necessarily coincide. Mahlon Dickerson's fears for his brother's new role were soon borne out. Silas was caught squarely in the middle of a legislative party conflict early in 1802.

Because of weaknesses in New Jersey's political laws, the congressional canvasses in the even-numbered years were usually held several weeks after the state elections. The majority party, elected to the legislature in October, thus shaped the congressional election statute to its own needs for the national election in the following December. In the three congressional polls immediately prior to 1802, the Federalist majority had passed election acts which it thought best served its political interests. Many Republicans feared a Federalist triumph in the state elections of 1802 would result in a repetition of these manipulations. Republicans from South Jersey were especially anxious; they endeavored unsuccessfully to prevail upon the Republican legislature of 1801-1802 to plan simultaneous state and congressional polls in order to guarantee a general election for Congress.[5] A synchronized election would deny the Federalists an opportunity, even if they should win, to structure the congressional election to suit their purposes.

To the Republicans of South Jersey, a general or at-large election for Congress was a necessity. They needed the huge majorities piled up in North Jersey in order to elect congressmen running on a Republican ticket from their Federalist corner of the state. But the Republicans of northern New Jersey, with their overwhelming majorities in Sussex, Morris, and Es-

3. Mahlon Dickerson to Silas Dickerson, Oct. 28, 1801, *ibid.*
4. Silas Dickerson to Mahlon Dickerson, Oct. 27, 28, Nov. 10, 1801, *ibid.*
5. Joseph Bloomfield to "Dear Doctor" [Elmer], Jan. 25, 1802, Ebenezer Elmer to ?, Jan. 29, 1802, Ebenezer Elmer to David Moore, Jan. 24, 1803[2], Gratz Collection, Hist. Soc. of Pa.; Mahlon Dickerson to Silas Dickerson, Jan. 30, Mar. 29, Apr. 21, May 31, 1802, Silas Dickerson to Mahlon Dickerson, Feb. 12, 1802, Dickerson Letter Book, N.J. Hist. Soc.

sex, were assured of designating their representatives no matter what form the election took, and they were reluctant to make the change to simultaneous elections. One reason for their reluctance was that party leaders in North Jersey felt that the Republican hold on the state government was too tenuous; by passing an act that set both elections for the same time, they felt, they exposed the party to the charge of playing politics—thus offering the militant Federalists a ready-made campaign issue.[6]

The Republicans from the lower counties, failing to secure a simultaneous election law during the regular sessions of 1801, pressed for a special session of the legislature early in 1802 for the expressed purpose of passing the requisite statute.[7] The only man empowered to call a special session was the Speaker of the Assembly. Silas Dickerson's dilemma was painfully obvious; he was placed between two conflicting Republican camps. If he convoked a special session, Dickerson would antagonize many northern Republicans, including his mentor Aaron Kitchell and his own Sussex cohorts. If he did not, the youthful Speaker would feel the wrath of Joseph Bloomfield and a host of the Governor's South Jersey followers.

Pressure was applied. Governor Bloomfield organized a letter-writing campaign, asking all of the Republican legislators who favored a special session to write "confidentially" to Dickerson.[8] These Republicans also caucused in Trenton in February 1802 and declared that the end of May was a propitious time for such a session. Dickerson, who had to call the session, was not even notified of the caucus.[9]

The harried Dickerson was indignant that he had not even been consulted, let alone invited. Although more experienced

6. *Ibid.*
7. *Ibid.*
8. Joseph Bloomfield to "Dear Doctor" [Elmer], Jan. 25, 1802, Ebenezer Elmer to ?, Jan. 29, 1802, Gratz Collection, Hist. Soc. of Pa.
9. Ebenezer Elmer to David Moore, Jan. 24, 1803[2], Gratz Collection, Hist. Soc. of Pa.; Mahlon Dickerson to Silas Dickerson, Jan. 30, Mar. 29, Apr. 21, 1802, Silas Dickerson to Mahlon Dickerson, Feb. 12, 1802, Dickerson Letter Book, N.J. Hist. Soc.

politicians in both camps refused to commit themselves publicly while awaiting further developments, Silas angrily spurned the advice of his brother and addressed himself to the voters "upon the subject of *not* calling a special meeting of the Legislature." He published his diatribe in the Morristown *Genius of Liberty*, settling the matter and making enemies in South Jersey who would haunt him another day.[10]

The sequel to this dispute occurred after the October 1802 state canvass which returned a legislature evenly divided between Republicans and Federalists. South Jersey Republican leaders' fears were partially realized: this new body could not agree even on a congressional election law. So no provision was made to elect New Jersey's representatives in December, and the state was without congressmen in 1803.[11]

Silas Dickerson did not bear the brunt of intraparty criticism alone. For various reasons, his antagonist in the matter of calling a special session, Joseph Bloomfield, also shared his fate. Republicans were "very ready to censure [Bloomfield] for his [recommended] appointments" of Federalist lawyers to state posts.[12] The charge was true, but, in making it, party men overlooked the fact that there were few Jeffersonian lawyers who qualified for state judicial positions in 1801. When the office of chief justice of the state supreme court was vacated, therefore, the Governor wanted the legislature to appoint a moderate Federalist to the position. Even his closest ally in Republican circles, Ebenezer Elmer, observed to another party man that this was "just like him."[13] Bloomfield was continually un-

10. Ebenezer Elmer to David Moore, Mar. 24, 1803[2], Gratz Collection, Hist. Soc. of Pa.; Silas Dickerson to Mahlon Dickerson, Feb. 12, 1802, Mahlon Dickerson to Silas Dickerson, May 31, 1802, Dickerson Letter Book, N.J. Hist. Soc. Unfortunately, the text of Silas Dickerson's reply as it appeared in the Morristown *Genius of Liberty* is not available inasmuch as there is no known copy of that issue of the newspaper now extant.
11. See the Newark *Centinel* or the Trenton *True American*, Oct.-Dec., 1802. The subject is taken up in more detail later in this chapter.
12. Silas Dickerson to Mahlon Dickerson, Nov. 10, 1801, Mahlon Dickerson to Silas Dickerson, Nov. 28, 1801, Dickerson Letter Book, N.J. Hist. Soc.
13. Ebenezer Elmer to George Burgin, undated [1801], Emmet Collection, N.Y. Pub. Lib.; Joseph Bloomfield to Ebenezer Elmer, July 6, 1802, Ely Collection, N.J. Hist. Soc.

der suspicion because of his Federalist past and late conversion to Republicanism. When Bloomfield had occasion to visit his old Federalist cronies Jonathan Dayton and Aaron Ogden of Essex County, John Condit gossiped that "Federal *Flattery* and *Deception* has been fatal to many, I hope it will not be the case with him."[14] Even the much maligned Silas Dickerson observed that he wished "the Governor would act more from sentiments of his own and not place so much reliance on others."[15]

The Federalists too found the General an easy target. Despite Republican criticism that Bloomfield wanted to appoint Federalists to office, one Federalist queried whether "an anti-federal governor [will] be willing to commission a person for any office, who agrees not with him in his political sentiments?" Another critic likened Bloomfield to "Sancho Pansa because he was the greatest 'blockhead' among the Republicans." A third antagonist, alluding to Bloomfield's earlier Federalist leanings, dubbed him "a proper political weathercock."[16] The Governor was not insensitive to the jabs of his "friends" or enemies and promised, "whenever the Republicans give the least intimation of a desire of change, I shall instantly take the hint and retire."[17]

Bitterness and petty jealousy threatened to tear apart the party before it fairly established itself. With vast reserves of patronage and power suddenly opened to them by legislative victory, the Republicans sought the means with which to tighten party discipline. Better organization was necessary on another count; the Federalists, in a minority after 1801 (except

14. John Condit to Ebenezer Elmer, Sept. 29, 1802, Gratz Collection, Hist. Soc. of Pa.

15. Silas Dickerson to Mahlon Dickerson, Nov. 7, 1803, Dickerson Letter Book, N.J. Hist. Soc. Even as late as 1811, Bloomfield's motives were subject to severe and often bitter scrutiny. Despite his years of loyal adherence to the Republican cause, his sincerity continued to be doubted. Morris legislator David Thompson, Jr., wrote: "I did not suppose that any one expected him [Bloomfield] of belonging to the republican party from principle." Thompson to Samuel L. Southard, Oct. 4, 1811, Southard Papers, Princeton Univ. Lib.

16. New Brunswick *Guardian*, Sept. 17, 1801; *Newark Gazette*, Nov. 10, 1801, Nov. 9, 1802.

17. Joseph Bloomfield to Silas Dickerson, Mar. 19, 1804, Ely Collection, N.J. Hist. Soc.

for 1802 when the legislature was tied), were militant adversaries in defeat. Even personal friendships between Republicans and Federalists that had survived earlier factional divisions were broken off after 1801, indicating just how deeply party spirit penetrated the New Jersey legislature. Explosive party battles toughened the Republican legislators' resistance to Federalist forays aimed at dividing their ranks and reduced the divisive effects of Republican intraparty friction. The personal attacks and rank politicking by both sides that followed the 1801 Republican legislative victory thus tended to draw Republicans together.[18]

Initial hostilities between Republicans and Federalists broke out in the Assembly in November 1801, when Ebenezer Tucker, a party activist in Burlington County, induced some Republican legislators to attempt to impeach John Lacey, a Federalist justice of the peace in that county, for allegedly using his office flagrantly for political purposes. While most Republicans in the legislature felt that impeachment was unwarranted, they did not want to offend Tucker either; the Republicans resolved the matter by leaving Lacey in his office but at the same time resolving that "nevertheless [we] think it a duty . . . to express [our] high disapprobation of the official conduct of John Lacey." Tucker's effort naturally incurred the wrath of the Federalist minority. William Pierson, a volatile Federalist legislator, charged Tucker with being an "infamous rascal." Later, the Federalists even went so far as to oppose his appointment to a judgeship on the tenuous and personal grounds of "infidelity" to his wife, dubbing him the "stallion of Egg Harbour," so deeply rooted was their dislike.[19]

18. Party feuds often became personal. The embattled Federalists frequently lashed out at the Republicans on the floor of the Assembly, and vice-versa. Federalist legislator William Pierson, for example, initiated a personal controversy in the 1801 session when he referred to Speaker Silas Dickerson as a "foolscap." Mahlon Dickerson, usually mild-mannered, counseled on hearing of the affront: "My advice is to insult him in the same manner as he does you—give him a good beating. You are certainly able to do it." Mahlon Dickerson to Silas Dickerson, Feb. 13, 1801, Dickerson Letter Book, N.J. Hist. Soc.

19. Silas Dickerson to Mahlon Dickerson, Nov. 18, 1801, Nov. 26, 1803, *ibid.*; *Newark Gazette*, Dec. 1, 1801, Feb. 9, 1802.

Assembly Speaker Silas Dickerson moderated many strange debates from the speaker's chair, but none was so feverish as one he described in November 1801. This episode vividly brought home the charged atmosphere in which these men operated: "This makes war in our wig wam. Kitchel is now up. Frelinghuysen and Coxe have been up before him. Now Coxe is up again. Now Frelinghuysen no Kitchel—he has got wound up—he lathers them like fury. Frelinghuysen again—Kitchel again—Frelinghuysen with permission again—Pearson up—now Mr. Coxe—Pearson again—Committee by unanimous consent. The house is adjourned."[20] Little wonder that the young and inexperienced Dickerson lasted one short year in the speaker's chair.

A year did not improve the deportment of the legislators on either side. The canvass of 1802 resulted in a tie, with each party sending twenty-six members. John Condit, on hearing the result, doubted with many others whether a compromise was possible. Each party accused the other of abusing the election laws and casting illegal votes. Even so prejudiced a spectator as the former Speaker admitted "there was as much foul play on the one side as on the other." It was not surprising that the legislature did not set aside any elections, and the chambers remained tied.[21]

The lawmakers on both sides of the aisle stiffened their resistance. Neither side initially yielded its position long enough either to designate a governor, senator, or other officers or to pass a law providing for the election of congressmen. The Federalists offered to break the stalemate and divide the offices, one party electing a governor, the other a senator, and so forth. The Republicans turned them down cold and proceeded to make political capital of the offer, accusing the Federalists of

20. Silas Dickerson to Mahlon Dickerson, Nov. 26, 1801, Dickerson Letter Book, N.J. Hist. Soc.

21. John Condit to Ebenezer Elmer, Oct. 28, 1802, Gratz Collection, Hist. Soc. of Pa.; Newark *Centinel*, Nov. 2, 1802; Silas Dickerson to Mahlon Dickerson, Nov. 12, 1802, Dickerson Letter Book, N.J. Hist. Soc.; Assembly Minutes Papers, Nos. 1978, 1979, N.J. State Lib.

suggesting a corrupt bargain and threatening that these "propositions with the [Republican] answers will fly like wild fire through the United States."[22] A week later some Federalist legislators, frustrated and bitter, swore out a warrant for the arrest of James J. Wilson, one of their ranking tormentors. The editor of the *True American* was also clerk of the Assembly; he was charged with "divulging some of their [the legislature's] tenets" in the public press. Wilson was arraigned but was not held on such a trumped-up accusation. Although the incident was closed, the memory remained.[23]

It was not until 1804 that Governor Bloomfield could report after adjournment that "the Legislature harmonized in the late sitting better than . . . [in the] past and did not bring party into their common business." But if the two parties reached a tacit and temporary truce on the floor, they still acted the part of opposing parties outside the chamber. "Out of the House," Bloomfield disclosed, "the Republicans and Federalists lodged apart and did not visit more than actually necessary when in Committee business. . . . The line is . . . completely drawn."[24] The major factor in drawing that legislative dividing line, clearly, was the Republican caucus.

The Birth of the Legislative Caucus

The New Jersey legislative caucus developed out of a clear need for party unity. A caucus was not new to Republicans; in fact the device was one of the mainstays of Jeffersonian organization throughout much of the nation. It was employed by party men in the House of Representatives in the 1790's and remained in use among Republicans "irregularly" after 1801. State organizations were also caucus-prone. In Connecticut after 1800, a mixed caucus comprising "party leaders and mem-

22. Silas Dickerson to Mahlon Dickerson, Nov. 13, 1802, Dickerson Letter Book, N.J. Hist. Soc.
23. James J. Wilson to William Darlington, Nov. 18, 1802, Mar. 11, 1803, Darlington Papers, Lib. Cong.; Trenton *True American*, Nov. 1802.
24. Joseph Bloomfield to Ebenezer Elmer, Mar. 5, 1804, Miscellaneous Collection, N.-Y. Hist. Soc.

bers of the state legislature" dominated the state organization. The same, generally speaking, was true of Massachusetts, New Hampshire, and Rhode Island; in Vermont, although the Republican party was less highly organized than in other New England states, its caucus was more purely a legislative body. In the middle states, New York Republicans also adhered to a mixed legislative caucus as "the basic framework of the New York state-wide Republican organization." Warring statewide Republican factions in Pennsylvania weakened the existing caucus as well as statewide party machinery generally in the Keystone State. Unlike New Jersey's example, among the chief functions of these other state caucuses was the responsibility to nominate candidates for elective offices. Insofar as the New Jersey Republican legislative caucus did not involve itself in the nominating process, it appears to have been unique.[25]

It was natural in light of developments elsewhere that the harried Republican majority in New Jersey's legislature turned to the caucus in 1801. Not only were developments of a like nature taking place in other states, but also Aaron Kitchell, now in the chamber, had borne witness to the earlier potency of the caucus in congressional circles.

The success of the New Jersey caucus is measurable on three counts: first, it allowed the Republicans to dispense patronage with scarcely faltering unity; second, it provided solid party majorities on many sensitive issues; finally, by 1804 it succeeded in "drawing the line completely," as Governor Bloomfield put it, between the two parties.[26] In a day when most party alignments were still tentative, vigorous Federalist efforts in New Jersey usually met with a solid Republican front, whatever personal differences there were in the ranks.

25. Cunningham, *The Jeffersonian Republicans, 1789-1801*, 71, 82-91, 162-66, and *The Jeffersonian Republicans in Power, 1801-1809*, 99, 127, 133, 145-46, 148, 161-75.

26. Joseph Bloomfield to Ebenezer Elmer, Mar. 5, 1804, Miscellaneous Collection, N.-Y. Hist. Soc. For a description of Republican patronage policy and successes, see Carl E. Prince, "Patronage and a Party Machine: New Jersey Democratic-Republican Activists, 1801-1816," *Wm. and Mary Qtly.*, 3rd Ser., 21 (1964), 571-78.

By 1806, Republican legislative politics completely revolved around the caucus.

The genesis of the caucus was evident in the 1801 attempts to arrange a meeting of the new Republican legislative majority in Trenton before the session opened, "to give a tone to future operations [and] to [find] a system of united energy in support of the present administration of Mr. Jefferson."[27] This was the first opportunity for Republicans to show what they could do in the New Jersey legislature, and the caucus seemed a necessary means of achieving unity. The Republican lawmakers met, and, apparently, there followed two more gatherings in the next three weeks while the legislature was organizing.[28] However, apart from settling on who was to fill the offices of governor and speaker of the Assembly, little else was accomplished at these first caucuses. And even these two tasks proved difficult; we have noted the intrigue surrounding Dickerson's designation as speaker. Bloomfield, according to one reporter, was tapped as governor because he was a South Jerseyman and the Republicans could not agree on any others "after many meetings, altercations and buffettings."[29] Despite the initial weakness of the caucus, however, a precedent was established.

After the poll of 1802, the caucus really began to take hold. With the legislature deadlocked, lack of harmony became a luxury the Republicans could not afford. Although still fragile, the new caucus was stronger than its predecessor. The knowledge that one uncontrolled vote could upset the balance of legislative politics apparently insured the adherence of the Republican lawmakers most of the time. The Republicans regained a legislative majority in the 1803 elections, and the caucus thereupon matured into a major political force.[30]

27. Joseph Bloomfield to Ebenezer Elmer, Oct. 19, 1801, Ely Collection, N.J. Hist. Soc.
28. Silas Dickerson to Mahlon Dickerson, Nov. 8, 1801, Dickerson Letter Book, *ibid.*
29. *Newark Gazette*, Nov. 10, 1801.
30. John Condit to Ebenezer Elmer, Sept. 29, 1802, Gratz Collection, Hist. Soc. of Pa.; Newark *Centinel*, Oct. 25, Nov. 1, 1803.

The caucus, including all Republicans in both houses of the legislature, usually gathered at an inn in Trenton on an evening either just before each session convened or while it was sitting.[31] There is evidence that invited visitors often participated (they were always leading New Jersey Republicans) but only lawmakers voted in the proceedings. "His excellency" Joseph Bloomfield, not a legislator and, indeed, temporarily removed from the governorship in 1803 as a result of the lack of a Republican legislative majority, nevertheless participated in a patronage caucus in March of that year. Congressman James Sloan attended a caucus in 1805 to influence the appointment of the county clerk in Gloucester. A heated caucus controversy in 1806 was finally resolved when a "foreign emissary . . . appeared [and] was closeted with some of the weaker brethren."[32] The vote in caucus usually was taken openly so that each participant could note the position of his fellows. On occasion though, if the situation was delicate enough, the assembled caucus might decide to vote by secret ballot; objectors pointed out that this deviation tended to inhibit the frankness of the institution.[33]

Because no minutes were kept, many details of caucus organization remain obscure. On at least two occasions in

31. *Trenton Federalist*, Dec. 1, 1806; Diary of Mahlon Dickerson, Feb. 1, 1812, Rutgers Univ. Lib.

32. *Newark Gazette*, Mar. 15, 1803; *Trenton Federalist*, Nov. 11, 1805, Dec. 1, 1806; Edward Yard to Mahlon Dickerson, Nov. 7, 1814, Mahlon Dickerson Papers, N.J. Hist. Soc.; Diary of Mahlon Dickerson, Oct. 24, 1811, Rutgers Univ. Lib.; Trenton *True American*, Nov. 7, 1814.

33. David Thompson, Jr., to Samuel L. Southard, Nov. 15, 1814, Southard Papers, Princeton Univ. Lib. An example of such a situation occurred in the caucus of 1814, held for the purpose of choosing a United States Senator. Secret ballots were requested and a long and heated argument ensued as to the comparative advantages and disadvantages of this procedure. Because some candidates were themselves present and others were not, secret ballots were employed. This was the exception rather than the rule, however. There is evidence also that the caucus was susceptible to direct influence. A Republican innkeeper from Trenton, having played host to caucuses in his tavern for many years, advised Southard, who was fighting hard for a seat on the state supreme court, that "personal presence and intrigue has a wonderful influence. . . . If you could leave your family one or two days this week you could be judge. . . . All the political machinery will be in motion." Joseph Bonnell to Southard, Jan. 6 [?], 1816, *ibid*.

1804 Aaron Kitchell presided over the caucus although he was not then the assembly speaker.[34] This indicated that, with regard to the caucus at least, party position and official position did not necessarily coincide.

Sessions often lasted late, and frayed tempers frequently led to squabbles. In an 1803 gathering, "much debate was had on the question of Gen. Frelinghuysen's dismissal, and . . . the decision was ultimately postponed." In another caucus held the same year, Bloomfield was opposed as a gubernatorial candidate by a minority "as unfit and as a trimmer," although he was eventually carried. James Sloan's "revolutionary projects, it is said, were opposed by some . . . pretty warmly" in an 1805 conclave, "and Jemmy decamped without making any proselytes." Middlesex assemblyman Robert Lee "plagued the caucus" in 1811; harsh words were traded and that particular meeting dragged on late into the night. "The fire of faction," in short, often blazed, but nearly always the differences were resolved in caucus, removed from public scrutiny.[35]

The legislative caucus always operated on the basis of majority rule at its regularly scheduled semiannual meeting held prior to the joint meeting, and such other caucuses as were held from time to time. The unwritten procedure dictated that, if a majority of the Republican caucus agreed on an appointment, all Republican lawmakers from both houses were bound to vote for it in joint meeting. This rule was virtually inflexible with regard to patronage. Joseph Bloom-

34. Newark *Centinel*, Nov. 6, 1804; *Newark Gazette*, Nov. 30, 1804.

35. *Newark Gazette*, Mar. 15, 1803; New Brunswick *Guardian*, Sept. 15, 1803; *Trenton Federalist*, Nov. 11, 1805, Dec. 1, 1806; Diary of Mahlon Dickerson, Oct. 31, 1811, Feb. 1, 1812, Rutgers Univ. Lib. Sometimes arguments arose from differences more basic than personal friction among Republicans. In the 1816 legislature, for example, the old North-South Jersey cleavage, typical of the earlier years of party formation, reappeared. The South Jerseymen, it was reported, "would not go into caucus." It was feared that instead they would caucus by themselves as they had in the dispute over the 1802 election act, before the general party caucus was firmly established. One South Jerseyman admonished: "There will be a caucus. . . . The easterners [northerners] must be invited." Cooler heads prevailed and the difficulties were resolved—in caucus. Joseph Bonnell to Samuel L. Southard, Jan. 6 [?], 1816, Southard Papers, Princeton Univ. Lib.

field, in the caucus of 1803, was designated the Republican gubernatorial candidate by a one-vote margin. He received every Republican ballot in the joint meeting.[36] While it was not always so close, we know for certain that virtually the same situation recurred in the gubernatorial polls of 1801, 1811, and 1817, and in elections of a United States senator in 1814, 1817, and 1820.[37] The same was true, it is patently evident, for all state offices.[38] The Federalists were introduced early to the pressure the Republican caucus was capable of exerting on its members. After the 1801 Republican legislative victory, the joint meeting convened to elect a governor. The choice was between Bloomfield and Richard Stockton, and, according to a Federalist report, the packed gallery expected the latter to win. "But these bystanders were not in the secret, they had not attended the caucuses, and dark meetings in which were hatched this shocking resolution to dishonor and degrade the first office in the government." Bloomfield won every Republican vote and was elected governor.[39] While lapses in caucus discipline occurred from time to time, they were generally greeted with party condemnation.

The caucus' early years did not see the rush for jobs controlled with the scientific precision that was to mark the later period. Occasionally Republican office-seekers successfully bucked the new caucus, gaining positions in opposition to the Republican majority in that body. Most of the time,

36. New Brunswick *Guardian*, Sept. 15, 1803.

37. Joseph Bloomfield to Ebenezer Elmer, Oct. 19, 1801, Ely Collection, N.J. Hist. Soc.; J. F. Blackwell to Samuel L. Southard, Jan. 9, 1818, David Thompson, Jr., to Southard, Nov. 15, 1814, Mahlon Dickerson to Southard, Jan. 10, 1817, Silas Condit to Southard, Jan. 24, 1817, Southard Papers, Princeton Univ. Lib.; Diary of Mahlon Dickerson, Oct. 24, 1811, Rutgers Univ. Lib.; Trenton *True American*, Sept. 22, 1817; Edward Yard to Mahlon Dickerson, Nov. 7, 1814, Mahlon Dickerson Papers, N.J. Hist. Soc. Many of the examples cited above are elaborated upon in chapters five and seven. A full discussion of the caucus' patronage functions may be found in chapter eight.

38. One need only consult the *Minutes and Proceedings of the Joint Meeting* for any year after 1802 to note how effectively the caucus dispensed lesser offices. On appointment after appointment, Republican members voted as a bloc, with very few exceptions. See also Prince, "Patronage and a Party Machine," *Wm. and Mary Qtly.*, 3rd Ser., 21 (1964), 571-78.

39. Newark *Gazette*, Nov. 10, 1801.

subsequent party disapproval made such occasions Pyrrhic victories, and they became fewer and fewer with the passing years. Peter Gordon, for example, received a lucrative state appointment in 1802 without caucus backing. William Rossell and William S. Pennington were both appointed to the state supreme court in 1805 over James Linn, the caucus candidate. Joseph McIlvaine, Governor Bloomfield's nephew and ward, was the recipient of a high militia post despite determined caucus opposition.[40] By 1803, these were the exceptions that proved the rule. More than 95 per cent of the time caucus decisions were adhered to on matters relating to the distribution of jobs, as the roll-call votes in the legislative journals for the joint meetings in the years following 1801 indicate. It is reasonable to conclude that such unity could not have been achieved without prior caucus decisions.[41]

The development of the caucus immeasurably aided the tendency among lawmakers to identify and vote as a party on matters other than patronage. Republican fidelity in the chamber was apparent in dealing with many politically sensitive problems. Votes on key issues affirmed the presence of the caucus in many areas of legislative activity. Excepting patronage votes, the upper house (Legislative Council) balloted as a party on roll-call votes 55 per cent of the time from 1801 to 1805 (see Table II).[42] In a year-by-year sampling of the period, the Council of 1803 displayed the greatest tendency to adhere to party

40. Trenton *True American*, Sept. 22, 1817.
41. *Minutes and Proceedings of the Joint Meeting*, 1801-1806. In practice, during either a joint meeting or a regular session, Republicans who had been opposed to a measure or appointment agreed upon in caucus were permitted to fail to indicate their preference when the vote was taken by collective ayes and nays, and their vote was not needed for passage. If it came to the point where, upon challenge by the Federalists, their vote was needed, it was given according to the determination of the caucus. The effect was the same; Federalists only challenged voice votes when they wanted individual Republican members to commit themselves on an issue. Inasmuch as most appointments were made by a roll-call vote, it was difficult for Republican legislators to "duck" a vote in patronage matters. For a description of this practice, see the *Trenton Federalist*, Mar. 17, 1806.
42. Analysis of the *Minutes and Proceedings of the Joint Meeting*, 1801-1805.

TABLE II
Party Voting in the Legislative Council, 1801-1805*

Year	Total Roll Calls	Party Vote	Non-party Vote	Percentage Party Vote
1801	16	8	8	50%
1802	14	6	8	43%
1803	21	15	6	71%
1804	14	6	8	43%
1805	26	15	11	58%
Total	91	50	41	55%

*Figures drawn from roll-call votes only, excluding votes in joint meeting on patronage matters. Party votes were determined by the following method: if two or more Republicans dissented from the Republican majority on a question, that question was ruled out as a party vote. The Council was chosen for these years because it offered a stable body. Of the 13 members, the Republican delegation varied in these years between 7 and 9 members.
Source: Journal[s] of the Proceedings of the Legislative Council of the State of New Jersey (various places, various times).

lines. The Republican members voted together 71 per cent of the time. In the remaining four years of the period, the Republican councilors fell in their constancy to party principles, voting from 43 per cent to 58 per cent of the time as a bloc. The great jump in the 1803 figure can probably be explained in terms of the experience of the preceding year, when many sensitive issues that were postponed in 1802 because of the equal legislative division were brought to a vote in 1803. The Council's record of adherence to party demands, although imperfect, was proof that tangible and sustained legislative party ties existed.

The caucus expanded its authority to include issues other than patronage soon after getting its bearings. In November 1804, the Republican members from both houses met to find ways and means to combat new evidence of Federalist organization.[43] The irascible James Sloan attended an 1805 caucus to preach "a political sermon in favour of abolishing common

43. Newark Centinel, Nov. 6, 1804.

TABLE III
Breakdown by Issues in the Legislative Council, 1801-1805

Type of Issue	Total Roll Calls	Party Vote	Non-party Vote	Percentage Party Vote
Judicial-Legal	17	14	3	82%
Financial-Tax	10	6	4	60%
Slavery	5	3	2	60%
Roads and Acts of Incorporation	20	10	10	50%
Public Debtors	6	3	3	50%
Miscellaneous	33	14	19	42%

Source: *Journal[s] of the Proceedings of the Legislative Council of the State of New Jersey* (various places, various times).

law." "Jemmy," it seems, didn't much like lawyers.[44] These additional convocations occurred with increasing frequency after 1803; they were not held according to any fixed schedule, but apparently as the times demanded. Many sensitive issues bear the stamp of party regularity, indicating that Republican legislators convened often to discuss a wide range of matters.[45]

Bills of a judicial or legal nature that came before the Council consistently called forth party unity. These included laws regulating legal fees and the practice of law, bills affecting the size and structure of the state's judiciary, and changes in the legal code of the state. Inasmuch as the Republicans had long denounced the "tyranny of lawyers" in New Jersey and had enlisted the support of the "virtuous farmers" against legal leeches, legislative acts that touched on this area became vital party matters. Thus, of the bills coming before the Council for a roll-call vote, judicial and legal acts were by far the most important to the Republicans, excluding patronage. They voted as a party no less than 82 per cent of the time on such acts (see Table III). Other questions also appealed to the

44. *Trenton Federalist*, Nov. 11, 1805. See also the *Newark Gazette*, Dec. 1, 1801, Feb. 9, 1802; New Brunswick *Guardian*, Apr. 18, May 2, Oct. 24, 1805.
45. See Tables II and III, this chapter.

Republicans' sense of party unity. Tax measures and bills appropriating money for the state government to meet expenses, nearly always an election issue, caused the party to vote as a unit 60 per cent of the time. The same figure held on votes affecting the status of slavery in the state. In an area of the nation where abolitionist sentiment and organization was strong, the Republicans generally favored abolition or manumission laws of various kinds. Such other issues as turnpike and incorporation bills, and bills affecting debtors, drew the party together 50 per cent of the time. It may be concluded that, generally, party regularity in the Council was steady if not astounding. Counted in terms of the Republicans' stated beliefs, the degree of party regularity was more impressive.

Informal contacts strengthened the Republican *esprit de corps*, and thus the caucus. While the lawmakers were in Trenton, their favorite after-hours haunt was the office and living quarters of the *True American*. It was, according to their then unattached host James J. Wilson, a "general rendezvous for all the Jacobin members, or a large portion of them."[46] Batchelor's Hall, as the domicile was designated, was inhabited by the editors and their staff of two, all unmarried. Here, according to Wilson, "Republican equality in its highest pitch of perfection" was practiced, and "conversation and company was wholly and purely Republican."[47]

Not all Republicans liked the caucus, however. Some never accustomed themselves to its secrecy and influence. A Republican senator, for example, complained from Washington late in the era: "What a wretched, humbling state of things has existed in our state for years past. From the *Executive* to the *Constable*, there is scarcely an appointment made without bargaining or corruption!"[48] Another lifelong Republican, out of the legislature for the first time in quite a while, carped

46. James J. Wilson to William Darlington, Nov. 26, 1801, Darlington Papers, Lib. Cong.

47. Wilson to Darlington, Aug. 20, 1802, *ibid.*

48. George Holcombe to Samuel L. Southard, Oct. 17, 1825, Southard Papers, Princeton Univ. Lib.

that since he no longer "belong[ed] to the managing committee" he could not tell who was going to be governor. He described the caucus, after long personal experience, as "that invisible impossible body that directs all our political movements and appointments."[49] The Republican editor of the New Brunswick *Fredonian* revealed in 1820 that, until then, "none had been able to break the chain of political bondage under which it [the legislature] has been held."[50]

The Federalists, not having themselves created a permanent legislative counterpart of their own in this period, soon learned to despise the Republican caucus. "Yorick," one of the most effective Federalist critics, queried in the columns of the *Guardian* in 1805: "Who are the people" Republicans continually allude to? "The people," commented Yorick caustically, "are your committeemen, and caucus-men, and convention men." "Well," he went on to say on another occasion, "he is a legislator and swears to support the constitution. He gets into caucus; and then votes just as the caucus directs him. Why not alter the oath, and swear to vote and act as *caucus* shall order?"[51] A Federalist member of the Council was equally bitter after the 1806 joint meeting: "Argument, reasoning avail Nothing. . . . The questions which come before it [the joint meeting] have already been decided. Whether this is done out of doors or elsewhere I do not undertake to say."[52] A Republican much later emphasized the firmness with which the first rule of party responsibility was enforced: "When they [the legislators] went into caucus they were bound by what the majority did."[53]

The Federalists, in an effort to incite a public reaction in 1805 to the spreading authority of the caucus, attempted to convey an image of total involvement and intrigue with re-

49. Silas Condit to Samuel L. Southard, Jan. 24, 1817, *ibid.*
50. James F. Randolph to Samuel L. Southard, Nov. 9, 1820, *ibid.*
51. New Brunswick *Guardian*, Aug. 8, 29, 1805.
52. *Trenton Federalist*, Mar. 17, 1806.
53. J. F. Blackwell to Samuel L. Southard, Jan. 9, 1818, Southard Papers, Princeton Univ. Lib.

gard to it. The *Federalist* disclosed that the caucus could make appointments "as thick as hops," and, furthermore, do it secretly in dark places. "Caucus men coop themselves up in the back cabin of the ship," a Federalist tale revealed, "put out the lights, and do all the business privately, and in the dark, without suffering any person to see or hear them. . . . Nothing can be done on board ship without caucus."[54] The *Guardian* two weeks later reinforced this image of totality with the following anecdote: "A weak and well meaning man lately asked another of the same party, what *caucus* had agreed upon at Trenton? Why replied the latter, *caucus* have agreed, that you shall lose your nose. D - - n caucus; why must I lose my nose? Hush, hush; it is all for the good of the party; and besides, you must never inquire into the reason of what caucus orders or does, for that would be contrary to republicanism. So be quiet; and lose your nose, as it becomes a good patriot."[55]

The already disproportionate power of the legislature, as compared to the authority wielded by the governor, was further exaggerated by the caucus. That astute Federalist commentator Yorick exposed this new dimension of government-by-caucus: "Some persons, indeed, suppose, that when a caucus of legislators dictate . . . to a governor the removal and appointment of surrogates, they . . . usurp authority [and flaunt] independence and conscience." And he bitingly leveled his fire at the incumbent Governor Joseph Bloomfield: "See him prostrating his dignity; [he is] shamefully led by usurping caucuses, clubs who govern your state."[56] At a time when the governor's power was severely limited by the Constitution of 1776 anyway, the caucus' authority and range were immense and, possibly, a threat to the freedoms the Republicans ideologically were pledged to "restore" after years of Federalist suzerainty.

54. *Trenton Federalist*, Dec. 2, 1805.
55. New Brunswick *Guardian*, Dec. 19, 1805.
56. *Ibid.*, Mar. 20, 1804, Aug. 8, Oct. 3, 1805, and *passim*.

Politics and the State Convention

At the same time that the Republicans were achieving legislative unity, the state convention was maturing into another cornerstone of the Republican party apparatus. It grew into a real clearing house for Republican disagreements over ticket-making for national canvasses. Nomination conflicts that might have riven the party were almost always settled at the biennial convention. Because of this innovation, the Federalists usually faced a solid front at the general elections as well as in the legislature.

The convention did not meet in 1802 because the legislature was tied and no provision had been made to hold congressional elections. For one year New Jersey was unrepresented in Congress. It was not until 1803 that a convention similar to that of 1800 was finally summoned. This convention was heralded by an unsigned notice in the Republican papers, but it is safe to assume that those responsible for the previous gathering—notably Bloomfield, Kitchell, Elmer, and Condit— were also instrumental in convoking this one.[57] Most of the counties selected delegates at open meetings. In Hunterdon County, an exception to the rule, the chairmen of the township committees acted as emissaries.[58]

On November 23, representatives from every county but Cape May gathered at Matthew's Inn near the state house in Trenton. Silas Dickerson was designated chairman and James J. Wilson clerk. Although many more venerable (and perhaps wiser) men were present, the chairman was a young man of thirty and the clerk only twenty-three. Machiavellian logic in part determined this choice. The chairman's position usually was a thankless one, but Dickerson, who liked to collect titles and the appearance of authority, allowed his desire for the limelight once again to get the better of him. He accepted the responsibility and thus limited his personal effectiveness

57. Trenton *True American*, Nov. 7, 1803.
58. *Ibid.*, Nov. 7, 1803; Newark *Centinel*, Nov. 8, 1803.

and political mobility by filling a void deliberately vacated by others more knowing than the Sussex legislator.[59]

In nominating a ticket to stand for the Republican party, the convention stipulated that each county had one vote for each of the six places on the congressional ballot, regardless of the number of men from each county in attendance.[60] There is little doubt that such dicta were for public consumption and little more than veneer. County, regional, and personal interests had to be served. According to the newspapers the formal floor vote went off without a hitch—too smoothly, in fact. The real decisions were not made on the floor but either before the delegates convened or privately during the convention; in any event, nominations were made out of the public eye.[61] The Republican newspapers conveyed to their readers the impression that everything had been accomplished openly and freely in the best tradition of the democratic process.[62]

After the selection of the ticket it was ratified by the convention meeting as a whole, and the delegates selected a committee to report back to the convention a "suitable" address. The meeting ended, according to this address, "with union and exertion prevail[ing] among those in support of the ticket."[63] The address, the Federalists alleged, had been drafted by James J. Wilson, the "gibbetman" of the convention and already in 1803 "the Dictator" in New Jersey politics.[64] The nominees with the highest number of convention votes were James Mott of Monmouth, Ebenezer Elmer of Cumberland, Henry South-

59. Mahlon Dickerson to Silas Dickerson, Jan. 15, 1804, Silas Dickerson to Mahlon Dickerson, Nov. 27, 1803, Dickerson Letter Book, N.J. Hist. Soc.

60. Trenton *True American*, Nov. 28, 1803; Silas Dickerson to Mahlon Dickerson, Jan. 22, 1804, Dickerson Letter Book, N.J. Hist. Soc.; *To the Republican Electors of New Jersey*, Nov. 23, 1803, N.J. Political Broadsides Collection, Rutgers Univ. Lib.; Newark *Centinel*, Nov. 22, 1803.

61. Newark *Centinel*, Dec. 6, 1803; Trenton *True American*, Nov. 28, Dec. 26, 1803; Mahlon Dickerson to Silas Dickerson, Jan. 15, Mar. 18, 1804, Silas Dickerson to Mahlon Dickerson, Nov. 27, 1803, Dickerson Letter Book, N.J. Hist. Soc.

62. Newark *Centinel*, Nov. 29, Dec. 6, 1803; Trenton *True American*, Nov. 28, 1803.

63. *Ibid.*

64. *Trenton Federalist*, Apr. 8, 1805.

ard of Somerset, William Helms of Sussex, James Sloan of Gloucester, and Adam Boyd of Bergen County. Only the latter two were candidates for the first time, and they were familiar to Republicans, for each had actively served the party for some years.[65]

On the surface, things came off smoothly. The candidates were chosen "unanimously" on a motion from the floor and there appeared to be no untoward disagreements among the delegates. But the participants from both North and South Jersey carried home tales of favoritism and intrigue, and rumors spread alleging that the Republicans were falling "victim to the rage of factious party." Essex and Morris counties, pillars of Republican strength, were unrepresented on the ticket, and proved lethargic in their "electioneering" preparations. The newspapers implored the voters of these counties to "enliven and invigorate the inactive," and rally behind the Jeffersonian standard.[66] Continuing rumors resurrected memories of the old North-South Jersey cleavage. It was reported to Silas Dickerson that "Elmer and Sloan have a strong prejudice against the delegates from the upper Counties." It was bandied about that these southern nominees were particularly incensed at Dickerson himself, because they thought the chairman wanted to be a candidate and was on that account opposed to Elmer and Sloan.[67] Dickerson's refusal to call a special session of the legislature in 1802 apparently still troubled some South Jerseymen.

According to Dickerson, the rumor was only half true. He had nothing against Elmer, but Dickerson disclosed that "Sloan I do not like—he appears to me to be too anxious for any office."[68] Sloan was nominated anyway. That Silas wanted the nod from the party there can be little doubt. He was at the height of his popularity in Sussex County and a dangerous

65. Newark *Centinel*, Nov. 29, Dec. 6, 1803; Trenton *True American*, Nov. 28, 1803.

66. *Ibid*.

67. Mahlon Dickerson to Silas Dickerson, Jan. 15, 1804, Dickerson Letter Book, N.J. Hist. Soc.

68. Silas Dickerson to Mahlon Dickerson, Nov. 27, 1803, *ibid*.

foe. It was probably in order to preclude any move to name him at the convention that he was made chairman, which neutral post he could not desert short of resignation and open office-seeking. The ex-Speaker of the Assembly was incensed at Sloan's apparent enmity and characteristically refused to let the matter drop. He continued to denounce the Quaker politician to Republican colleagues. Backbiting only made the legislator more enemies, his brother wrote in disgust from Philadelphia, and "as to Sloan, I would not advise you to write or speak much of him."[69]

Perpetual, if private, bickering among the Republican elite gave little comfort to the Federalists. They were defeated soundly in the congressional elections of 1803. Federalist resistance to the Republican ticket was scattered and ineffective. Knowing they had little chance to win, the Federalists rested on their dignity and refused to contest the poll. The Republicans piled up a ten-to-one majority that testified to the advantages of running a broadly based and widely supported ticket. Voter response was assured by a concerted propaganda campaign on behalf of the candidates, who offered a wide range of geographic representation and known Jeffersonian leanings to the electorate.[70] The strong convention machinery in this instance was able to rise above the personal feuding of key men.

The congressmen elected in 1803 served only one year before their interim terms expired. Dickerson and Sloan, the same men who provoked friction at the previous convention again spearheaded intraparty controversy in 1804. Their differences reflected the mounting coolness between Republican politicos from North and South Jersey. These disagreements came dangerously near the surface when, on June 29, 1804, almost four months before the scheduled state convention, Republicans from five southern counties met in an unusual

69. Silas Dickerson to Mahlon Dickerson, Nov. 27, 1803, Mar. 11, 1804, Mahlon Dickerson to Silas Dickerson, Mar. 18, 1804, *ibid.*

70. Trenton *True American*, Dec. 26, 1803; Newark *Centinel*, Dec. 20, 27, 1803.

regional conference ostensibly to decide on a date and place for the convention, which, by prior agreement, was to be held in the southern part of the state. In reality, the South Jersey-men gathered in order to present a united front against the more numerous forces of North Jersey. James Sloan particularly played devil's advocate in order to secure for himself a seat in Congress. He summoned the meeting—although this fact was not reported to the public—to unite his South Jersey supporters behind his candidacy. In fact, Sloan inaugurated an effort to make his renomination a sensitive point of departure—almost a matter of honor—to South Jerseymen. The five counties represented—Burlington, Gloucester, Cumberland, Cape May, and Salem—designated a committee to meet with their northern brothers to settle on a time and place for the proposed convention. The latter reason was the one offered by the Republican newspapers to justify the meeting.[71]

The 1804 state convention gathered at Mill Hill in Burlington County on October 23. Its first order of business was to adopt unofficial Republican congressional districts for New Jersey that endured longer than the party itself. The Republicans divided the six congressional seats among the thirteen counties, two counties to each district, with one exception. The districts laid out were Morris and Sussex; Essex and Bergen; Middlesex and Monmouth; Hunterdon and Somerset; Gloucester and Burlington; and Salem, Cumberland, and Cape May counties. Sparsely settled Cape May, however, never sent a Jeffersonian Republican representative to Congress and for all practical purposes was left out of the division.[72]

In the convention of 1804 and its successors through 1826, each district's delegation designated its own nominee and presented his name to the assembled delegates for the entire body's approval. Very rarely, if ever, was such a choice rejected. In the event that a given district could not agree on one can-

71. Henry Southard to Ebenezer Elmer, June 19, 1804, Gratz Collection, Hist. Soc. of Pa.; Trenton *True American*, Aug. 27, 1804.

72. Trenton *True American*, Oct. 23, 1804; Newton *Sussex Register*, Oct. 23, 1820.

didate, the convention stepped in and arbitrated the trouble as quictly as it could. Only in extreme circumstances was it forced to a choice between two conflicting candidates. When this occurred, the decison was made by a majority of the entire convention.[73]

This scheme allowed few disagreements to reach the voters' attention, for all important decisions were regional in character. The candidates were chosen by the two county delegations in each district, meeting in a back room, so to speak. These candidates, if they were acceptable representatives, commonly served six to eight years. After this period, the convention usually honored the other county's choice. There were naturally some exceptions to this rule of thumb. A few congressmen served longer than the allotted eight years and others served less, for a variety of reasons.[74] Trials over congressional tenure presented one of the most recurrent problems the convention encountered over the years. The fact that the rules of this body were flexible enough to resolve most situations was a saving grace.[75]

73. *Ibid.* Some notable examples of the district method of nominating congressional candidates are described in the Samuel L. Southard Papers. See J. F. Randolph to Southard, Sept. 6, 1816, Henry Southard to Southard, Sept. 2, 1820, David Thompson, Jr., to Southard, Jan. 13, 1821, Ephraim Bateman to Southard, Aug. 7, 1822, Lewis Condict to Southard, July 28, 1826, Southard Papers, Princeton Univ. Lib.

74. *Ibid.* See also the Newton *Sussex Register*, Oct. 28, 1820; Trenton *True American*, Oct. 23, 1804; Newark *Centinel*, Sept. 19, 1820.

75. An example of the difficulties that might arise through districting occurred in Middlesex County in 1816. It was typical of local jealousies that cropped up at all times. James Fitz Randolph, in defending Middlesex County's Republican prerogatives, wrote angrily: "We prefer a claim as a *county*. . . . Surely if any advantage is supposed to accrue from the *locality* of a member [of Congress], Middlesex is entitled to her share of it. Or if it be a matter of mere *punctilious pride*, Middlesex has also a claim to be gratified. 'But Middlesex is Federal' it may be said, and therefore is not entitled to the same notice or distinction as Monmouth . . . . Such language *has been* used, and that too—by the *Monmouth candidate himself.* Perhaps, though, those who argue thus may consider Middlesex of more importance in a *general* election." Randolph to Samuel L. Southard, Sept. 6, 1816, Southard Papers, Princeton Univ. Lib. A similar situation arose in Salem County in 1822. Congressman Ephraim Bateman of Cumberland County, paired in the unofficial congressional districting with Salem, wrote: "I expected Salem would claim the Representative in the next election. It is natural enough for them to do so, especially as they

Despite the preventives operating to limit convention conflicts, it was not possible to stifle the ambition of Sloan and Dickerson. These two old antagonists were bent on gaining congressional seats in 1804 come what might. Perceptive Republican leaders smelled trouble early in the year. Speaking of the congressional and presidential elections coming up, Governor Bloomfield confided, "Nothing but dis-union among the Republicans will make them [the Federalists] have a chance of success." The Governor warned Dickerson that the success of the Republicans depended entirely on union.[76] Aaron Kitchell, whose ability to perceive the political mood of the state was sometimes uncanny, was "apprehensive that we shall not be able to harmonize [in the convention]." He was inclined to render the convention superfluous by passing a district election law, but realized that this also was dangerous inasmuch as it could not be done without opening a breach with Republicans from South Jersey.[77]

The need to "harmonize" at the 1804 convention was intensified by the approaching presidential canvass. Republicans were particularly anxious to demonstrate their supremacy because this was to be the state's first popular poll for president. The Republicans' failure to produce a victory for Jefferson in 1800 increased the incentive for an all-out effort in 1804. The Republican legislators scheduled the presidential contest to coincide with the biennial congressional elections. The state convention of 1804 thus was confronted with the dual task of nominating a slate of Jeffersonian electors and designating a congressional ticket.[78]

---

have the prevailing usage of the state on their side. If they can unite in a good man, perhaps it is best that they should be gratified." Bateman to Southard, Aug. 7, 1822, *ibid.*

76. Joseph Bloomfield to Ebenezer Elmer, Mar. 5, 1804, Miscellaneous Collection, N.-Y. Hist. Soc.; Joseph Bloomfield to Silas Dickerson, Mar. 19, 1804, Ely Collection, N.J. Hist. Soc.

77. Aaron Kitchell to Ebenezer Elmer, Feb. 22, 1804, Gratz Collection, Hist. Soc. of Pa.

78. Newark *Centinel*, Oct. 30, 1804; Silas Dickerson to Mahlon Dickerson, Oct. 24, 1804, Dickerson Letter Book, N.J. Hist. Soc.

A tense set of delegates convened at Mill Hill on October 23. Rumors were flying; it was reported that James Sloan threatened to bolt the convention and form his own ticket if he was not nominated. This was emphatically denied by the Gloucester Democratic Association, the dominant party group in that county—an organization ruled by Sloan with an iron hand. The delegates understandably preferred to have a denial from Sloan himself. James Sloan was by this time thoroughly disliked and distrusted by many ranking Republicans, including most Republican newspaper editors, Congressmen Elmer and Southard, Silas Dickerson, and Joseph Cooper, who was from Sloan's own county.[79] Though the Quaker political chieftain was not popular in North Jersey, a combination of luck, skillful maneuvering, threats, and appeals to South Jersey's sensitivity about North Jersey's alleged domination of the party organization gained him his coveted place on the congressional ticket. The Gloucester delegation voted for Sloan in his district. The other half of the district, Burlington County, stood resolutely by Joseph Cooper, Sloan's local arch-foe. The issue was beyond quiet arbitration and was forced to the convention floor where Sloan wanted it. There, it was alleged, "not more than two Counties [were] in favour of Sloan, yet by bartering this way and that he has succeeded."[80]

Sloan fought his way to a nomination through a combination of strong support at home and the convention's fear of an open Republican breach. Silas Dickerson, on the other hand, possessed neither Sloan's experience at political in-fighting nor the necessary support from his home county of Sussex. What he lacked in political acumen he compensated for with his engaging personality, drive, and ambition. He had made it his business to cultivate political friends ever since his elec-

79. Henry Southard to Ebenezer Elmer, June 19, 1804, Gratz Collection, Hist. Soc. of Pa.; Newark *Centinel,* Sept. 18, 1804; Silas Dickerson to Mahlon Dickerson, Nov. 27, 1803, Jan. 27, Mar. 11, 1804, Dickerson Letter Book, N.J. Hist. Soc.; *Trenton Federalist,* Aug. 26, Sept. 2, 1805, Apr. 14, 1806.

80. Henry Southard to Ebenezer Elmer, June 19, 1804, Gratz Collection, Hist. Soc. of Pa.; Trenton *True American,* Aug. 27, 1804; Silas Dickerson to Mahlon Dickerson, Oct. 24, 1804, Dickerson Letter Book, N.J. Hist. Soc.

tion as speaker in 1801. He enlisted his brother's aid in doing the same. As far back as October 1801, he had requested Mahlon to "keep up a correspondence with your friends in the lower part of Jersey and endeavor to make more. It may be an advantage to me some future day."[81] That day had come. Silas hoped that his friends to the south would offset the many enemies he had made from that region.

Earlier in the year, young Dickerson had sought the backing of the Sussex delegation for the congressional seat held by William Helms and failed to get it. He was not without support at the convention, however. At one time, he was told, seven counties favored him if he could bring his candidacy to the floor of the convention as Sloan had done. Without the backing of his home district, however, this plan came to naught. According to its own rules, the convention was not obliged to arbitrate unless there was disagreement within a district. There was no disagreement in Dickerson's district; it voted for Helms, and Silas could not get his bid to the floor where in an open fight his supporters could aid him. He complained bitterly afterward that the convention had done him out of a place on the ticket after a day and a half of "electioneering bartering selling and buying."[82]

The evening following adjournment, Dickerson was approached by the equally disgruntled Joseph Cooper, downed by Sloan in his attempt to gain a seat in the House. Cooper suggested bolting the party and forming a ticket of their own. Dickerson, in a quandary, wrote his brother: "He [Cooper] solicits me not to decline [and] that he will circulate [an] address through the State immediately if I will permit it. I told him that it would break into the ticket formed and perhaps be attended with disagreeable circumstances. . . . I am at a loss whether to leave town without saying anything or to make a public declination. . . . I am sorry I had not got out of

81. Silas Dickerson to Mahlon Dickerson, Oct. 4, 1801, Dickerson Letter Book, N.J. Hist. Soc.
82. *Ibid.*, June 22, Oct. 24, 1804.

town this morning and then they might have done what they pleased."[83] Torn between an intense sense of party loyalty and his ambition to sit in Congress, Dickerson must have spent an anxious night or two before making up his mind. With the help of Cooper and other dissident Republicans, he could have marshaled strong support and given the regulars a hard run. But Dickerson apparently decided not to bolt inasmuch as nothing more was heard of the project. Dickerson's decision, to a degree, affirmed the authoritative nature of convention nominations; it was a victory for party regularity and, by implication, for party machinery.

Nothing of this backstage scrambling appeared in the convention's address printed in the Republican newspapers. The Republican press, too, was part of the party's apparatus, and its reports held no hint of the rival factions present or the infighting that took place. The usual claim of unanimous Republican support building for the coming campaign was made, and the address called for vigorous activity to insure the victory of both the congressional and presidential tickets.[84]

With all threats to party unity dissolved at the convention, the discouraged Federalists introduced only token opposition; the minority party rarely competed in an at-large election if they could help it, preferring instead either countywide or district contests. The Jeffersonians went on to win the two national elections. The vote in both races coincided to a remarkable degree, indicating a continuity of the ticket voting that appeared first in 1796.[85]

The 1806 convention met in Trenton on September 17. Compared to its predecessor, this meeting was remarkably tame. The expected biennial movement to drop the unpopular but tenacious James Sloan from the ticket materialized and

83. *Ibid.*, Oct. 24, 1804.
84. Newark *Centinel*, Oct. 30, 1804; Trenton *True American*, Oct. 1804.
85. Newark *Centinel*, Dec. 4, 1804. The Republican congressional vote was 13,039-13,119. The presidential vote varied only slightly from 13,119 to 13,138. No Federalist candidate for either office garnered more than 19 votes. The absence of any competing Republican tickets in this election indicated the degree of party unity which the discouraged Federalists faced.

was quickly quelled. The Quaker was in the vanguard of the congressional assault on the alleged "tertium quid" John Randolph of Roanoke. Sloan's biting irony on the floor of Congress, Jerseymen believed, hurt the ostensible third-party movement, and Sloan's friends argued that it would prove embarrassing to the New Jersey Republicans' national posture to "throw James Sloan out of Congress by leaving his name off the ticket." Even the Federalists agreed that Sloan was run again "in order that John Randolph might have a competent opponent against him." He retained his seat much to the chagrin of his Republican adversaries.[86]

In a surprise move the convention dropped Ebenezer Elmer from the ticket, ostensibly because he was "not quite Jacobinic enough for the time." The Federalists, picking up this Republican comment, interpreted it to mean that Elmer was passed up because he was "too moderate a man—one that doesn't like persecution—this is his crime."[87] Besides Sloan, Henry Southard and William Helms were renominated. Newcomers to the slate were John Lambert of Hunterdon, Ezra Darby of Essex, and Thomas Newbold, now removed to Monmouth. The Republican address reiterated the theme that the ticket was selected democratically by duly authorized delegates.

The Federalists disagreed. "Combinations of men," they pointed out, "for several years past have governed the elections of New Jersey. . . . [They] vote for people to be put on nomination, as if they and they alone had the right of deciding who should and who should not be voted for by the people." Elections, according to the minority party, had become a "nullity" as a result of the Jeffersonians' well-structured organiza-

86. Mahlon Dickerson to Silas Dickerson, Oct. 6, 1806, Dickerson Letter Book, N.J. Hist. Soc.; Trenton *True American*, Sept. 8, 1806; Trenton *Federalist*, Sept. 22, 1806.

87. Silas Dickerson to Mahlon Dickerson, Oct. 12, 1806, Dickerson Letter Book, N.J. Hist. Soc.; *Trenton Federalist*, Sept. 22, 1806. Perhaps another reason for dropping Elmer from the congressional ticket was his defense of Aaron Burr in Congress. See Joseph Bloomfield to Ebenezer Elmer, Mar. 5, 1804, Miscellaneous Collection, N.-Y. Hist. Soc.; Ebenezer Elmer, *Address to the Citizens of New Jersey* (Elizabethtown, 1807), N.J. Pamphlets Collection, Rutgers Univ. Lib.

tion. To prove the point, the Republican slate was elected almost without opposition, although some apparently Federalist support was generated for the incumbent Republicans who were left off the convention ticket.[88]

The Federalist party made a much better showing in the 1806 state elections, which took place on a county level, and which they thus contested vigorously. They captured almost enough seats to balance the legislature. Bergen, Middlesex, Somerset, Burlington, and Cape May counties, in their entirety, went Federalist and minority contingents were returned from Gloucester, Cumberland, and Sussex counties.[89] The strong show of resistance was the only cloud on the Republicans' horizon, however, as the dominant party settled in to enjoy the prospect of a long period of uninterrupted authority.

The eventful years 1801-1806 brought the Republicans mastery of the politics of New Jersey. The party strengthened and spread its local organization, captured the state's congressional delegation and the legislature, and in 1804 capped its victories by casting the state's electoral vote for Thomas Jefferson. These successes were made possible by an effective party machine that succeeded in exciting the imagination and vigorous activity of New Jersey's electorate. The construction of party apparatus took imagination and a realization that internal difficulties were manageable only when rules were applied and precedents established to meet all of the foibles of an increasingly aware electorate. Republicans created devices also with an eye to forwarding agreement among the leaders, thus assuring union at the top in county and state. The legislative caucus, in one sphere, and the state nominating convention, in another, answered both needs admirably.

88. Trenton *True American*, Oct. 6, 20, 27, 1806; Newark *Centinel*, Oct. 14, 21, 1806; *Trenton Federalist*, Sept. 29, 1806.
89. *Ibid.*

V

THE PARTY IN TRANSITION
1807-1812

———•—•———

CHALLENGED BY EXTENSIVE IF UNEVEN FEDERALIST PRESSURE EX-erted from without and significant tensions within Republican ranks, the depth and cohesive qualities of existing party machinery were severely tested in the years 1807-1812. Generally speaking, the Republican apparatus responded well. Local party organizations developed along the lines indicated in their fledgling period, but not without absorbing the strains born of rapid change, continuing leadership conflicts, and, often, consequent structural uncertainty. Indeed, while mounting grass-roots sophistication was in evidence prior to the War of 1812, it was not necessarily synonymous with party stability. Moreover, a new set of party managers on the state level helped to facilitate the general transition occurring in the Republican structure. Finally, the Republican legislative caucus confirmed its leadership in party circles as a result of its adaptability and secrecy. These developments and others discussed in the succeeding chapter helped to mold the party into a more highly institutionalized political mechanism.

[131]

Local Party Organization

The Federalists, taking advantage of unpopular Jeffersonian diplomatic policies after 1806, continued resolutely to provide strong resistance in a majority of counties. In elections for the legislature, upon control of which party rewards depended, the Federalists could count upon majorities from Burlington and Cape May counties to the south, and Somerset and Middlesex (except for 1811) in the central region of New Jersey.[1] Growing Republican inroads in Bergen County after 1809 were offset by emergent Federalist strength in Gloucester; as the former became increasingly Republican, the latter moved into the Federalist camp. Monmouth occasionally strayed from the Republican ranks also.[2] In general, then, throughout the pre-war period Federalists could be counted upon to provide contests in most counties, even if in New Jersey they chose occasionally not to challenge the Republicans at some national elections.

Essex County was one of the counties in which the Federalists rarely competed in the years before the War of 1812. In the absence of a two-party system the local Republican situation deteriorated to the point where the most exciting local contests were among Republicans. Indeed, for several years prior to 1807 legislative seats were sought by more Republicans than there were openings.[3] Republican miseries reached a new high in the latter year as a result of a bitter election battle growing out of an attempt to remove the county courthouse from Newark to Elizabethtown; this constituted a struggle tailor-made to perpetuate the existing regional feud in the county, and provide headaches aplenty for Republican regulars everywhere in New Jersey.[4]

1. Trenton *True American*, Oct. 19, 1807, Aug. 16, Oct. 24, 1808, Oct. 23, 1809, Oct. 15, 22, 1810, Oct. 28, 1811, Oct. 19, 1812, Oct. 18, 1813, Oct. 24, 1814, Oct. 16, 23, 1815, Oct. 21, 1816; Newark *Centinel*, Oct. 1807-16, *passim*. See also Table I, pp. 76-78.

2. *Ibid.*

3. Newark *Centinel*, Oct. 16, 1804, Oct. 15, 1805, Oct. 21, 1806, Oct. 20, 1807.

4. *Ibid.*, Oct. 21, 1806-Feb. 24, 1807, *passim*.

At the beginning of 1806, Essex freeholders had decided to replace the small, outmoded courthouse in Newark. This determination precipitated a bitter fight. Newarkers naturally wanted their town to retain its status as the county seat, but the inhabitants of Elizabethtown saw in the proposed change a chance to bid for the same advantage. The ensuing "court-house canvass" of February 1807 was significant on two counts: the poll aggravated existing regional intraparty animosities within the county, and it gave rise to turbulent electioneering the likes of which had not been seen since 1789. Indeed, the courthouse election surpassed the Junto effort of 1789 in that both sides employed existing Republican party machinery and methods unknown in the earlier contest.

Newark Republicans (there were few others in that town) introduced one of the earliest and most complete neighborhood committee systems known to New Jersey. It was no exaggeration when one observer predicted that the contest "promises to be the most warm, active, and perhaps disputed election ever witnessed in the county."[5] Almost two months before the poll, interested Newarkers met to discuss the situation. From their number a standing committee of twenty was chosen "with full powers to use all reasonable and legal means to secure the election." The committee agreed to meet every succeeding Monday night to implement their plans. Committeemen during the week visited "the different parts of the county, friendly to the object for which this committee was appointed, and endeavor[ed] to procure the aid and cooperation of the citizens at the ensuing election." Committees were also appointed in the outlying areas of the county by the Newark men, and they too attended the Monday night sessions in Newark.[6]

When the smoke cleared, Newark had won. The winning side turned out an unbelievable majority of 7,666 against a

5. *Ibid.*, Feb. 10, 1807. See also the Elizabethtown *N.J. Journal*, Oct. 1806-Feb. 1807, for the Elizabethtown side of the story.
6. Newark *Centinel*, Jan. 6, Feb. 3, 17, 1807.

disproportionately large Elizabethtown contingent of 6,181, yielding an impossible voter-participation count of 279 per cent of the legally "eligible" voters of the county. Obviously women and perhaps Negroes voted freely in this election.[7] No one doubted that the courthouse election "was the most warm and spirited ever held in the county." One bemused participant added: "When the tenth of February arrived, every man stood ready at his post, prepared for the combat; every town and village was divided into districts, and men especially appointed to see the electors to the poll." If evidence of corruption abounded, as both sides freely charged, the courthouse still remained in Newark.[8]

The Newark victory and the nature of the contest exacerbated the Newark-Elizabethtown party rivalry. In ensuing years other differences cropped up, causing these old wounds to fester anew. In 1810, intraparty competition eventuated "between the friends and opposers of a tax on Bank Stock [an issue discussed in its statewide context in the next chapter]."[9] The following year a Republican clash for the sheriff's office split the party along the old sectional line of cleavage.[10]

7. *Ibid.* Clearly, gross irregularities were common in the 1807 Essex election—including, we may assume, a good deal of ballot box stuffing as well as female voting. I think also that it is valid to conclude, generally speaking, that female suffrage was important in New Jersey in every way except numerically. While this conclusion, given present evidence, is impossible to prove or disprove, no more than a few dozen women voted in any given election—except for some notable special situations, e.g., the courthouse canvass of 1807. Strong inferential proof that comparatively few women voted is indicated by the fact that, although female balloting was clearly and specifically forbidden by law *after* 1807 (as a result of the Essex travesty), there was no appreciable break in the rhythm of the rising vote totals of the state. That is, voting in the counties continued to reflect a growth consistent with both the rising population and mounting party sophistication. See for confirmation Table I, pp. 76-78. It seems to me, then, that the statistics offered in the voting tables are a reasonable reflection of the true state of voter participation in New Jersey. Like all statistics, however, they should be used with care. For a description of female suffrage in New Jersey in this period, see Turner, "Women's Suffrage in New Jersey," *Smith College Studies in History,* 1 (1916), 182-85, and *passim.*

8. Newark *Centinel,* Feb. 3, 17, 24, Apr. 21, 1807.

9. Trenton *True American,* Oct. 22, 1810; Newark *Centinel,* Sept. 11, 18, 1810.

10. Newark *Centinel,* Oct. 8, 1811; Trenton *True American,* Oct. 14, 1811.

Essex politics, then, too often degenerated into a Republican donnybrook.

The free-for-all in Essex was not easily borne by Republican leaders throughout the state, but initially in this era they consoled themselves with the knowledge that only Republicans were elected to office. When even this became doubtful as a result of the pressures of impending war and consequent increasing Federalist efforts in the state and county, Essex Republicans came together temporarily in 1812 to repulse a Federalist threat.[11] But the rapprochement was ephemeral; the compromise that wrought it never got to the roots of the trouble—shifting and uninstitutionalized party apparatus and regional jealousies. Both of these failings reappeared after 1812 to haunt the Republican interest.

The struggle to maintain Republican unity was only somewhat more successful in Sussex County, New Jersey's northernmost enclave. Continuing strong Federalist resistance dictated the need in that county for a well-structured apparatus. Republican leaders, therefore, were forced to keep one eye on the Federalists, even as they warily watched each other. Thus they continued to experiment with and modify their local apparatus to meet the opposition challenge, while at the same time competing Republican elements sought to tilt the intraparty balance of power in their favor.

Although the earlier quid scare in Sussex eased temporarily in 1807 after the untimely accidental death of the controversial Silas Dickerson, political prosperity (see Table I) was as great a burden for Sussex Republicans as it was for Essex men. By 1809 an advanced case of what was still called quidism reappeared and plagued the local Republican element until the war. The recurring attacks of suspicion among men of the same political stripe began anew when in 1809 and 1810 a number of Jeffersonians, unhappy with the open nominating meeting, aired their grievances publicly.

11. Newark *Centinel*, Oct. 6, 13, 20, 1812.

A later complaint might well have summarized the critics' feelings in 1809-1810. Nominating meetings were always held at Newton during August (Circuit) Court, and this practice, many party men claimed, discriminated against the farmers who were perforce tending their crops at that time of year. The traditional meeting as a result favored "the most prominent characters of the county [who] must necessarily be on the spot [Newton] on other business." The open meeting gave these prominent men, particularly lawyers, an undue advantage in party councils, for most of them were at Newton anyway and were able to participate actively in selecting candidates, whereas many farmers were unable to do so. A delegate convention, as well as a shift in time, it was felt, would wipe out this inequity.[12]

After mere complaints by the offended faction proved unavailing in 1809, Republicans—acting in the name of democratic practices—the following year had recourse to more drastic measures. A "Division Ticket" was formed by Republican dissidents and Federalists, combining both Republican and Federalist candidates in equal numbers. The Republican supporters of the ticket, however, withdrew their backing well before the election of 1810 when the regular party leadership bowed to some of the aggrieved Republicans' demands and inaugurated a countywide delegate convention in place of the by now traditional open county meeting. Each town was represented by two or more delegates, but it was still held during August Court, as in the past.[13] The one major concession, appeasing the Republican mavericks, was enough to bring about the withdrawal of Republican support, causing the division ticket to collapse. The Federalists must have placed their full weight behind the combined slate, for when it crumbled before the election there were no other Federalist entries in the

12. *Ibid.*, Sept. 26, 1815. See also *ibid.*, Nov. 5, 1811, and the Trenton *True American*, Nov. 4, 1811, for substantiation of the fact that this issue was the same one that provoked Republicans from 1809 to 1811.
13. Trenton *True American*, July 30, 1810; Newark *Centinel*, July 13, 1810.

field; for the first and only time, the Sussex Republicans were virtually unopposed.[14]

Republican party regulars apparently decided that the division movement was a passing threat, for in 1811 they reverted to form and resumed the practice of holding an open nominating meeting at Newton. They failed even to move the meeting up to early autumn, a change that ostensibly would have allowed more farmers to attend. Discontented Republican farmers once again joined with the Federalists to form another division ticket. Inasmuch as the previous effort had quickly been called off, many Republicans felt this one was also a bluff. As the election drew closer, however, it became clear that the insurgents were not feinting, for the division ticket was not withdrawn. Although it lost, the combined effort drew enough votes (1,668 to 810) to frighten the Republican regulars into seeking some reconciliation with the mavericks.[15]

In an unusual display of accommodation, the regular Republicans and insurgents agreed to meet after the 1811 election to discuss their differences. This effort to achieve unity pointed up the innate strength of the Sussex Republican organization. The peace gathering was held at Newton at the end of October, and all Republicans were invited to attend: "After a friendly discussion on the subject of the late division, which has unfortunately taken place between the men who in more trying times rallied under the same standard the meeting appeared to be fully impressed with the belief that an opportunity of a mutual and friendly interchange of sentiment would lead to a reconciliation of all men of the same political opinion." The meeting resolved to "discuss and decide on every subject where there is an honest difference of sentiment, and particularly whether the ticket in the future shall be agreed on before or after the first Monday in September

14. Newark *Centinel,* Oct. 9, 16, 23, 1810; Trenton *True American,* Oct. 15, 22, 1810.

15. Newark *Centinel,* Oct. 15, Nov. 5, 1811; Trenton *True American,* Sept. 9, Nov. 4, 1811.

annually."[16] The last provision, so pointedly emphasized, reinforces the conclusion that at least part of the trouble between the factions was the arrangement and time of the annual county nominating meeting.

The 1812 meeting, in fact, was held in September instead of August, a concession to the insurgents. The format of the meeting remained open, mollifying the regulars.[17] It should be noted that this new compromise was a reversal of the one that failed in 1810. The meeting of reconciliation the Republicans held in 1811 also addressed itself to strengthening the existing local machinery. Although the towns usually guided electioneering, the 1811 Republican post-election gathering provided for the formation of a county committee of correspondence. This constituted an innovation, presumably created to oversee preparations for the canvass of 1812 (and perhaps subtly to head off any last-minute factionalism).[18] The Republican breach was in this way temporarily healed and the Sussex party organization strengthened, helping to extend for a time Republican suzerainty in the county.[19]

Middlesex County in central New Jersey was one of the most durable Federalist strongholds in the state. Except for the canvass of 1811, the followers of Hamilton won every election through 1817. The Republicans took over permanently only after that date. Yet, despite repeated Republican failures, party men in Middlesex constructed and maintained one of the better political organizations in New Jersey. Annual losses did not demoralize party machinery or undermine Republican enthusiasm. The Middlesex Republican contingent challenged every election after 1802. The canvass of 1803 offered the first sign that Middlesex Republicans had formed a county organization. The peripheral (for Middlesex politics) *Centinel of Freedom* revealed prior to that poll that the Republicans had "come

16. Newark *Centinel*, Nov. 5, 1811; Trenton *True American*, Nov. 4, 1811.
17. Newark *Centinel*, Sept. 15, 1812.
18. *Ibid.*
19. See Table I, pp. 76-78.

out systematically, and made a formidable appearance."[20] A year later the first known delegate convention met. Although it was weak at first, it developed within a few years into an effective party vehicle. Vote totals in the county bear out this conclusion.[21]

The delegate nominating convention became an annual institution in Middlesex County politics by about 1807. Thereafter, delegates gathered in New Brunswick at the end of August or the beginning of September, after the towns had been notified to send Republican representatives.[22] Two delegates were sent from each of the eight towns in the county; they were usually elected at open township meetings. These sixteen men comprised the convention.[23] In addition to forming a county ticket, the delegates were charged with the responsibility for appointing from their number the standing county committee and delegates to the state convention.[24]

The nominating procedures of the convention were institutionalized soon after its founding. The eight towns were

20. Newark *Centinel*, Sept. 12, 1803.

21. Republican voter returns indicate that Republican organization took a sharp turn upward in 1803, and again in 1806. See Table I, pp. 76-78. See also the Newark *Centinel*, Sept. 25, Oct. 2, 9, 16, 1804, Oct. 1-29, 1805, Oct. 7-21, 1806; Trenton *True American*, Oct. 7-21, 1805, Sept. 28-Oct. 19, 1806.

22. Newark *Centinel*, Sept. 25, 1804, Oct. 3, 1809, Sept. 1, 1812, Sept. 3, 1816, Sept. 2, 1817, Sept. 14, 1819; New Brunswick *Fredonian*, Aug. 14, 1811, Sept. 1, 1821, and Aug.-Sept., 1811-22, *passim*; Trenton *True American*, Sept. 24, 1804, Aug. 29, 1808, Aug. 12, Sept. 9, 1811, Aug. 10, 1812, Aug. 31, 1813, Aug. 16, 1814, Oct. 2, 1815, Sept. 23, 1816, July 27, 1818, Aug. 23, Sept. 3, 1819, Sept. 9, 23, 30, Aug. 11, 1821. Usually, the presiding officer varied from convention to convention.

23. Trenton *True American*, Sept. 30, 1820. Although most towns held open meetings to choose delegates, apparently not all did each year. Woodbridge party men, ever protecting things Republican, resolved in 1819 that they "Shall not henceforth act with any delegates from other Townships, but those chosen at meetings held pursuant to public notice previously given." They generously added: "To ensure a fair, free and full representation of all the Townships in our future conventions, a committee of fifteen of our respectable Republican citizens shall be appointed to communicate with, and if necessary, to visit all other Townships of this county, between this and July next, and urge upon them the necessity of regular Township meetings to choose delegates to attend the county convention." *Ibid.*, Nov. 1, 1819. The newspaper citations previously noted (nn. 21-22) indicate that most towns did convene open meetings prior to the county convention.

24. See above, nn. 21-22.

paired to nominate a would-be legislator in alternate years. Delegates from the town whose turn it was through customary courtesy usually submitted a name for the approval of the sixteen men in the convention. The would-be nominee received that body's imprimatur, presumably without difficulty. To preserve formality, the sixteen delegates each cast a secret ballot, voting for one man in each paired township district. If the township delegates were uninstructed and could not agree or if more than one candidate was nominated from a town, the candidate from that locale with the highest number of convention votes was placed on the ticket. If the paired towns broke over representation, the same solution was applied. If there was no controversy, only one name for each pair of towns would be submitted to the convention as a whole, and approval was automatic.[25]

Township party machinery flowed naturally from the series of local meetings necessary to elect delegates to the county convention. Woodbridge, described later, claimed the best local organization and provided an outstanding example of grass-roots party machinery in New Jersey Republican politics. Other Middlesex towns from time to time also developed extraordinarily strong local parties. Even prior to the advent of the county convention, South Brunswick party men held township meetings. On at least one occasion, they established "a standing committee for said township, one in each of the several Neighbourhoods in the township, to preserve our electoral Rights."[26]

25. Trenton *True American*, Sept. 23, 30, 1820. A controversy aired in 1820 indicated the customary course of action in dealing with nominations. An irate correspondent wrote the *True American* that the town of North Brunswick was entitled to a man on the ballot in 1820. In this instance, some delegates from *other* towns did not like the nominee of the North Brunswick representatives and, in violation of existing practice, suggested another possible candidate from North Brunswick. "The claims of North Brunswick to a candidate were not only not denied," the angry writer declared, "but thus openly acknowledged; yet the unanimous wish of the township . . . [expressed by the North Brunswick delegates] was contemptuously disregarded—the privilege always hitherto granted, of selecting was denied [North Brunswick delegates]."

26. *Ibid.*, Sept. 19, 1803.

New Brunswick enhanced its party apparatus in 1809 by transforming its delegation to the county convention into a standing committee. The committee strengthened party response in the city by holding an inauguration day dinner on March 4, 1809, in honor of James Madison's accession to the presidency. Apparently the affair was successful enough to warrant annual repetition. Republicans gathered at the same time two years later for a sumptuous dinner and an evening of speeches; by this time, local party men had formalized the proceedings by making it a yearly convocation of the "Democratic Corresponding Society of New Brunswick." The society remained to rally party men through the crisis occasioned by the War of 1812.[27]

Party leaders in New Jersey long felt that the absence of a Jeffersonian newspaper in Middlesex was a primary cause of the repeated defeats the Republican interest suffered there. Republican managers twice encouraged attempts to establish a weekly in the county, but efforts in 1809 and 1810 both failed. Finally, in 1811, the New Brunswick *Fredonian* was launched under the auspices of members of the Fitz Randolph family. The results were immediately apparent in the growing strength of the county organization and an increase in the Republican party vote. The *Fredonian's* editors were offered lucrative patronage appointments to help them overcome operating losses and remain a permanent auxiliary to existing Republican machinery. The *Centinel* summed up the optimism felt at the newspaper's establishment: "If the republicans of that county [Middlesex] generously patronize the *Fredonian* . . . we have no hesitation in believing that such will be the diffusion of truth and correct sentiments among the people in that county, as in every county of the state, where republican papers are generally circulated." Increasing subscriptions to the paper from Middlesex, the *Centinel* concluded,

27. *Ibid.*, Feb. 20, 1809, Mar. 11, 1811, Mar. 23, July 9, 1812; Newark *Centinel*, Mar. 10, 1812.

promised "that federalism has fallen, to rise no more."[28]

Although the Republicans won the county in 1811, the *Fredonian's* first year of publication, the Newark newspaper's prediction was too optimistic; it was not until 1817 that the county Republicans could boast of a second victory, and only thereafter did the Federalist challenge diminish.[29] Middlesex's Republican interest, although consistently in the minority, generally succeeded in developing a party structure both deep and stable—something that could not be said of its more advantaged neighbors to the north.

A Changing Leadership

The construction of a solid county organization or the delivery of a significant countywide Republican plurality at election time—the two did not always go hand in hand—sometimes singled out the responsible county manager as a potential mover and shaker at the state level of the Republican organization. In the years 1807-1812 some powerful county pilots moved into a growing leadership vacuum materializing at the top; changes in leadership were especially in evidence in these years as many party captains who helped found the organization in the 1790's for one reason or another departed the political scene. Aaron Kitchell resigned his seat in the Senate in 1808 because of ill health and ceased thereafter to busy himself with state politics. Governor Bloomfield returned to military service when the War of 1812 commenced. Silas Dickerson died, and James Sloan and Ebenezer Elmer lost their influence in their local organizations between 1807 and 1809. By 1812, then, many of the original party managers had disappeared from the political scene.[30]

28. Newark *Centinel*, Oct. 3, 1809, Oct. 15, 1811, Sept. 1, 1812; Trenton *True American*, Feb. 20, 1809, Feb. 5, 1810, Mar. 11, 1811, Mar. 23, July 9, 1812.
29. See Table I, pp. 76-78.
30. Aaron Kitchell's disappearance from New Jersey party councils by about 1808 can be verified in H. D. Kitchel, *Robert Kitchel and His Descendants*, 76-78; Folsom, *et al.*, comps., *Cyclopedia of New Jersey Biography*, I, 141. For Bloomfield's return to active army service, see *Biographical Encyclopaedia of New Jersey*, 273; Elmer, *The Constitution and Government of New Jersey*, 124.

New faces appeared. William S. Pennington, long a power in Essex politics, slowly built a following throughout the remainder of the state. In 1810 it was rumored that "Pennington is to be Governor . . . [for] Bloomfield, if all things work right . . . is to go with the condemned ware."[31] The announcement was premature, but indicative of the changes occurring. The vote in the 1810 caucus for governor bore witness to Pennington's growing stature in the party.[32] He continued to add to his strength outside Essex County after 1810. Woodbridge Republicans in 1811, for instance, resolved that "as he [Pennington] is worthy of, so may he soon be called to the highest office of this state."[33] He finally did become governor in 1813, despite the opposition of some South Jerseymen. Pennington's prestige as a party leader suffered a serious blow in 1814, however, in his caucus struggle with James J. Wilson over a Senate seat. The latter proved to be a powerful opponent.

James J. Wilson inherited the mantle of party leadership from Aaron Kitchell. Just as the Morris blacksmith was a cut above other party leaders in the exercise of power in his heyday, so did Wilson later exert more authority in party matters than other highly placed Republicans. Wilson's awareness of his growing role was evident in his actions with regard to the bank issue of 1810-1811. His intemperate utterances and apparent feeling for power indicated that, by 1809, Wilson con-

James Sloan's demise in New Jersey politics around 1808-9 is detailed in the *Trenton Federalist*, Sept. 28, 1807; Trenton *True American*, Sept. 5, 1808, Mar. 20, Sept. 13, 1809. Ebenezer Elmer wrote his own valedictory in his *Address to the Citizens of New Jersey* (Elizabethtown, 1807), N.J. Pamphlets Collection, Rutgers Univ. Lib. See also Silas Dickerson to Mahlon Dickerson, Oct. 12, 1806, Dickerson Letter Book, N.J. Hist. Soc. Silas Dickerson died in Jan. 1807, when the tails of his greatcoat caught in his new water-driven nail-making machine; he was killed before he could be freed. See clippings cut from the Morristown *Genius of Liberty* (undated), describing his death in detail, in the Dickerson Letter Book, N.J. Hist. Soc.

31. *Trenton Federalist*, Sept. 17, 1810; Trenton *True American*, Oct. 1, 1810.

32. Pennington received fifteen caucus votes for governor before going down to defeat. Trenton *True American*, Oct. 1, 1810; Diary of Mahlon Dickerson, Oct. 24, 1810, Rutgers Univ. Lib.; Newark *Centinel*, Mar. 27, Apr. 10, 1810.

33. New Brunswick *Fredonian*, Oct. 16, 1811; Trenton *True American*, July 22, 1811.

sidered himself a force to be reckoned with in party circles. The *True American*, after all, was by 1808 the first Republican newspaper in the state and it was a strong foundation for political leadership.[34]

Wilson's was a personality that created friction. Unlike Kitchell, he was always outspoken and given to extremes.[35] However, he possessed a feeling for party politics and the uses of political power when these were comparatively new elements insofar as political parties were concerned. One characteristic evident early in Wilson's career was his willingness to use his position to best advantage for himself. In 1810, a critic noted, "Wilson sat in the Assembly [to which he had been elected in 1809] and held the office of Adjutant General of Militia at the same time, in direct violation of the [state] constitution." Because of his position in the legislature, "he can influence that body, and even vote for his own salary as Adjutant General." A year later, he used his legislative influence to gain an appointment to the presidency of the State Bank at Trenton—a bank he had been most instrumental in creating. By 1812, it was rumored, he sought to "seat himself in the Governor's chair." An anonymous pamphlet bitterly attacking Wilson in 1812 queried: "How many offices does he now hold and [is] not yet content? . . . His restless and aspiring disposition are too notorious to be questioned." Wilson, in short, had "become

34. James J. Wilson to William Darlington, Jan. 10, 1803, and *passim*, Darlington Papers, Lib. Cong.; Newark *Centinel*, Mar. 27, Apr. 10, 1810. See also Prince, "James J. Wilson: Party Leader, 1801-1824," N.J. Hist. Soc., *Proceedings*, 83 (1965), 24-39.

35. Various incidents in his long career reflected this characteristic. See the account of his run-in with Federalist toughs in 1803 in the Trenton *True American*, July 18, 1803. For his position with regard to the bank issue, see the Newark *Centinel*, Mar. 27, Apr. 10, 1810. For the antagonism he engendered when he ran for the United States Senate, see Edward Yard to Mahlon Dickerson, Nov. 7, 1814, Mahlon Dickerson Papers, N. J. Hist. Soc.; James J. Wilson to William Darlington, Nov. 8, 1814, Darlington Papers, Lib. Cong.; David Thompson, Jr., to Samuel L. Southard, Nov. 15, 1814, Southard Papers, Princeton Univ. Lib. Perhaps his role in Hunterdon County politics best set off his character and personality. See the Trenton *True American*, Aug. 24, 1818, Sept. 22, Oct. 13, 1817; Anon., *To the Republicans of the County of Hunterdon*.

the most influential and powerful individual in the State."[36] Another writer much later remembered that "Mr. Wilson," in conjunction with a few others, "controlled [the party's] management in the State." A former editorial associate of Wilson described him as "the great man of Trenton," a not unjust designation, for the editor sometimes assumed that role.[37]

Perhaps Wilson's rise to power had not made him "the Dictator of New Jersey,"[38] but he did exercise a remarkable leadership over the party he was alleged to control. His newspaper set the pace for party propaganda and was used more than once as an instrument of vengeance. Wilson personally exercised a strong hold over the caucus. This became apparent in 1815, as we shall see, when he was finally elected to the Senate. It was noticeable also in the numerous appointments tendered him over the years by the legislature. Wilson's dynamic qualities subordinated others to his will. His political ingenuity made his leadership essential. He helped to organize and guide his party from above on both the local and state levels, in much the same way as it is done today. His career, in fact, was a pointed example of relatively modern party management. Although flaws in his character, including a lust for power, do not lend themselves to adulation, one must admire James J. Wilson's grasp of political realities and opportunities, when to capitalize on them meant to explore yet uncharted political byways. Wilson was one of a relatively small number of realists who contributed vitally to America's emergent party system. Although his fame did not outlive him, even in his own state, he left his mark on New Jersey Republican politics in the first quarter of the nineteenth century.

36. Anon., *To the Republicans of the County of Hunterdon,* 7-8, 14, 16; *Trenton Federalist,* Feb. 22, 1808; New Brunswick *Guardian,* Oct. 8, 1812; Trenton *True American,* Oct. 1, 1810, Aug. 17, 1812. Probably because of such criticism, Wilson resigned his bank presidency in the summer of 1812.

37. Elmer, *The Constitution and Government of New Jersey,* 211-12; J. F. Blackwell to Samuel L. Southard, Jan. 9, 1818, Southard Papers, Princeton Univ. Lib.

38. Anon., *To the Republicans of the County of Hunterdon,* 6-9.

In many ways, Wilson personified the results of the altera-
tions occurring in party machinery in the period discussed—
changes deriving not only from the transition of leadership,
but also from the crucible of war, the changing nature of the
opposition, and the dominant role of the caucus.

Wilson personified too, in a small way, the versatility which
characterized the Republican leadership over the years. He
and most other Republican top men did not at all mirror the
stereotype of the virtuous farmer leading the uprising against
aristocratic and mercantile Federalism; in New Jersey, in fact,
that stereotype wilts under scrutiny. A sampling of thirty-three
county leaders, representing twelve counties (all but Cape
May) is extremely revealing in this connection.[39]

A breakdown of the county leaders by occupation discloses
that among the thirty-three, there were seven doctors, six
merchants, four printers, four lawyers, two blacksmiths, an
innkeeper, a minister, a day laborer, and a sometime scrivener
who was also a farmer. There were only six county leaders
who were exclusively farmers.[40] This was an interesting re-

39. The sampling attempted to ascertain the occupations, religion, age,
service in the Revolution, and place of birth of the thirty-three men from
the county organizations. It was not possible to uncover full information about
all thirty-three; for many, only partial data was available. The statistics, then,
depending on the category, vary downward from 33 samplings for the occupational category to a low of 23 samplings of religious affiliations. All thirty-three
had in common at least five years of active party leadership in their respective
counties between 1800 and 1817. All were powerful figures for at least that
long, and hence were potent also on the state level. The thirty-three were
Essex: John Condit, Shepard Kollock, William S. Pennington; Bergen: Adam
Boyd, Solomon Froeligh; Morris: Lewis Condict, Mahlon Dickerson, Aaron
Kitchell; Sussex: John Armstrong, Silas Dickerson, John Linn; Hunterdon:
John Lambert, James Linn, James J. Wilson; Middlesex: Robert Lee, James
Fitz Randolph; Somerset: Henry Southard, Hugh M'Eowen; Monmouth:
James Mott, Jehu Patterson; Gloucester: Ezra Baker, Joseph Cooper, Thomas
Hendry, James Sloan; Burlington: Joseph Bloomfield, Thomas Newbold,
Ebenezer Tucker, Stephen Ustick; Cumberland: Ephraim Bateman, George
Burgin, Ebenezer Elmer; Salem: Daniel Garrison, Jacob Hufty. Major sources
employed in the sampling include: Folsom, *et al.*, comps., *Cyclopedia of New
Jersey Biography*; *Biographical Encyclopaedia of New Jersey*; *Biographical
Directory of the American Congress, 1774-1961* (Washington, D.C., 1961).
Genealogical sources too numerous to mention were consulted also. In most
instances they provided only fragmentary information.

40. These occupational categories are not mutually exclusive; many party

flection on the leadership of the party that claimed singularly to derive from that dominant agrarian element of early nineteenth-century America. A good deal of class mobility is reflected in the occupational range of the county leaders, verifying the assumption that the party, like the society of which it was a part, was essentially classless in an economic sense after 1800.

The religious affiliations of only twenty-three of the group were ascertained. This sampling is enough to disclose that by far the greatest number of party leaders were Presbyterians. Thirteen of the twenty-three were of that denomination, most of them from northern and central New Jersey. Of the thirteen Presbyterians, only two (both from Cumberland County) were from South Jersey. The others were from Essex, Morris, Sussex, and Hunterdon counties. Of the remaining ten leaders, three were Episcopalian or Anglican (two from Salem, one from Burlington), two were Baptists (Hunterdon and Monmouth), two were Quakers (Gloucester and Burlington), two were Dutch Reformed (Bergen), and one was a Methodist (Burlington). Significantly, in the majority of cases this distribution reflected the preponderant religious beliefs in the leaders' respective counties.

The birthdates of twenty-seven were determined. Of these, eight were sixty years old or older in 1810, a median year for the purposes of the sampling. Eight more were between fifty

---

leaders, reflecting the environment of which they were a part, partook of many economic activities, often at the same time. Thus, of the categories enumerated above, the following distinctions apply: (a) one merchant (William S. Pennington) after 1800 read law and became a lawyer, to capitalize on his party's political success. Another merchant, owning land, was also a sometime farmer. Still another merchant (John Armstrong) concurrently served his community as a surveyor, practiced a little farming, and even dabbled in iron manufacturing; (b) one lawyer was an iron manufacturer of note (Mahlon Dickerson); (c) the day laborer (Henry Southard) eventually saved enough money to buy a farm of his own. He became quite prosperous; his son, following in his father's political footsteps, eventually served in President Monroe's cabinet; (d) one of the blacksmiths (Aaron Kitchell) in time became a gentleman farmer. In all cases, the original category for each of the above, enumerated in the text, can be considered the county leader's prime occupation apart from politics.

and fifty-nine years old. Four party leaders in 1810 were in their forties, three in their thirties, and four more under thirty. Twenty-seven of thirty known Republican party leaders were born in New Jersey; the other three were native Americans also, although they were born outside the state. Of sixteen Republican county leaders old enough to have fought in the Revolution (born prior to 1760), only one was not in some way a tested patriot veteran of that struggle. Of the fifteen who did participate, eleven served with the Continentals. Four were either militiamen who saw action or known rebel supporters who suffered at the hands of the British. Clearly, only the most severely hedged socio-economic generalizations can be applied to the Republican leadership that matured in the Era of Good Feelings.

The Caucus and Legislative Politics

A mark of that leadership was the influence which the individual party manager wielded in the legislative caucus. The caucus built on its strong beginnings in the pre-1806 period to rise to the top of the party machinery in the succeeding years. If a weakness in its public image prevented the convention from doing the same (a development dealt with in the next chapter), no sign of weakness was evident in the operation of the caucus after 1806. Indeed, the caucus increasingly manifested a healthy appetite for party power in this era. Although party voting in the Legislative Council taken as a whole remained unimpressive between 1807 and 1811, some issues continued to stand out as important party issues—principally through caucus efforts.

Some issues before the Legislative Council between 1807 and 1811 remained sensitive to party considerations.[41] Party voting in the Council generally, however, even in the formative years 1801-1805, when the Republicans strove to consoli-

41. The incidence of party voting in the Council was sampled for the years 1801-1805 in chapter four. The same criteria employed in the earlier survey were utilized in the current one. See Tables II and III, pp. 114-15.

TABLE IV
Party Voting in the Legislative Council, 1807-1811*

Year	Total Roll Calls	Party Vote	Non-party Vote	Percentage Party Vote
1807	17	6	11	35%
1808	24	11	13	46%
1809	18	9	9	50%
1810	3	1	2	33%
1811	68	31	37	46%
Total	130	58	72	45%

*Figures drawn from roll-call votes only, excluding votes in joint meeting on patronage matters. Party votes were determined by the following method: if two or more Republicans dissented from the Republican majority on a question, that question was ruled out as a party vote. The Council was chosen for these years because it offered a stable body. Of the 13 members, the Republican delegation varied in these years between 7 and 9 members.
Source: *Journal[s]* of the Proceedings of the Legislative Council of the State of New Jersey (various places, various times).

TABLE V
Breakdown by Issues in the Legislative Council, 1807-1811

Type of Issue	Total Roll Calls	Party Vote	Non-party Vote	Percentage Party Vote 1807-1811	Percentage Party Vote 1801-1805
Judicial-Legal	14	7	7	50%	82%
Financial-Tax	24	16	8	67%	60%
Slavery	3	3	0	100%	60%
Roads and Acts of Incorporation	39	11	28	28%	50%
Public Debtors	12	6	6	50%	50%
Miscellaneous	38	15	23	39%	42%

Source: *Journal[s]* of the Proceedings of the Legislative Council of the State of New Jersey (various places, various times).

date their position, did not appear to be unduly significant. In the earlier period, Republican councilors voted as a unit 55 per cent of the time; between 1807 and 1811, when the party was firmly entrenched in power, its usually comfortable majority position was reflected in a decline in discipline. Republican members of the Council adhered to party lines only

45 per cent of the time on all roll-call votes (see Tables IV and V this chapter).

Between 1801 and 1805 the greatest incidence of party voting in the Council was on judicial and legal bills—laws regulating legal fees and the practice of law, statutes affecting the size and structure of the state's judiciary, and bills altering the legal code of the state. In the early period (1801-1805), when there were few lawyers in the Republican ranks, the party tended to denounce lawyers and their alleged tyranny over the law during the Federalist era. Republicans in the Council had voted along party lines 82 per cent of the time on bills touching on this sensitive party area prior to 1806. Very early in the Republican reign, then, this was far and away the primary party issue in the legislature, apart from patronage. By 1807, however, some changes had occurred in New Jersey. First, with the Federalists long out of power, the Republicans no longer could blame them for encouraging legal tyranny through control of both the lawmaking process and the administration of the law. Moreover, the number of lawyers within the Republican party had increased, for men with Republican leanings were encouraged to study law to be eligible for public appointments that awaited them when they became members of the bar.[42] The decline of Republican sensitivity and the rise of lawyers through the ranks of party preferment were mirrored in the demise of judicial and legal bills as the chief party issue

42. The case of William S. Pennington is classic. A merchant who as an adult studied law and was admitted to the bar, he chose this path because there were so few Republican lawyers in New Jersey in 1801 to fill judicial positions. See the description of Pennington, chapter three. Another example was that of Samuel L. Southard, whose father, Congressman Henry Southard, encouraged him to study law and settle in New Jersey (he was living in Virginia at the time) because of the opportunities open to him in his native state. See the papers of Samuel L. Southard, *passim*, 1808-1817, Princeton Univ. Lib. Finally, Mahlon Dickerson, a native Jerseyman and a lawyer, returned to the state in 1808 from Philadelphia to enter politics. His legal background and connections made it possible for him to rise to the state supreme court, the governorship, and the United States Senate during the Republican period. See chapter two. An increasing number of Republicans were found, therefore, to fill judicial offices. By 1812, four of the thirty-three leading Republicans were lawyers; only two other occupations or professions were

before the Legislative Council; between 1807 and 1811, Republican councilors voted only 50 per cent of the time as a unit on these bills, a decline of 32 per cent from the earlier period.

On the other hand, the Republican ideological commitments to government economy, equitable taxation with an eye to the farmer, and a long-standing dislike of Hamiltonian spending and taxing remained as strong as ever. Indeed, the state bank issue of 1810-1812 as well as the tax on private bank stock imposed by the Republicans seemed to bear out the persistence of these commitments. The continuing Republican appeal to Thomas Jefferson's "virtuous farmer" was very much in evidence as a standing party obligation during this period of party consolidation. Consequently, Republican councilors voted as a party 67 per cent of the time on all roll-call votes pertaining to taxes, money appropriations, and state governmental expenses. Party sensitivity to financial and tax measures increased 7 per cent over the earlier period.

Slavery as a political issue declined in importance after the enactment of the 1804 law providing for gradual emancipation. There were only three roll-call ballots relating to the status of slavery between 1807 and 1811 in contrast to the five votes between 1801 and 1805 touching on the slave question. Republicans favored anything that hastened abolition, voting all three times as a party in the later period on bills relating to slavery. Numerically, the 100 per cent party response compared favorably to the earlier 60 per cent figure, branding slavery a consistent party issue. That it was only an occasional issue, compared with others, reduced the significance of the party's attitude toward it.

The years 1807-1811 coincided with the heyday of turnpike construction in the state. The number of turnpike and bridge bills and related legislation rose sharply from the earlier period. Road bills, consequently, dominated the legislative

more highly represented among party leaders. It no longer behooved Republicans, therefore, to make an issue of the profession.

acts of incorporation. The incidence of roll-call votes on in-corporation bills nearly doubled after 1806. Party response to acts of incorporation was even more unimpressive after 1807 than it was after 1801. Councilors voted as a party for such legislation 50 per cent of the time in the early period. Republican adherence dropped significantly to 28 per cent in the later era. The clear implication was that Council members voted increasingly according to regional interests rather than party affiliation on such legislation. Farmers as well as commercial interests wanted good roads and bridges. On the other hand, since most acts of incorporation affected North Jersey where the great preponderance of turnpikes and bridges were built in the Republican period, many South Jerseymen, regardless of party affiliation, could be counted on to vote against many of these bills enhancing North Jersey's economic potential, while their brethren from the north would vote for them.[43]

The Council's position with regard to public debtors remained unchanged. Republicans balloted together 50 per cent of the time after 1806, as they had in the earlier period. No other clear issues stood out in the Council. All other roll calls between 1807 and 1811, taken together, brought the party together only 39 per cent of the time, an insignificant drop of 3 per cent from roll-call votes on miscellaneous acts for the years 1801-1805.

The vitality of the caucus was much more in evidence when a different set of criteria is applied to it. Whereas leadership struggles within the party were often resolved in the state convention prior to 1807, after that date such skirmishes most

43. For a fine description of the turnpike era in New Jersey, consult Wheaton J. Lane, *From Indian Trail to Iron Horse: Travel and Transportation in New Jersey, 1620-1860* (Princeton, 1939). Further evidence of the absence of party lines on such pragmatic economic issues as road building and incorporation appeared in the action of Somerset County's parties in 1816; Federalists and Republicans united to oppose further incorporation laws by the legislature. Both parties merged and ran one ticket dedicated to this end. Trenton *True American*, Sept. 23, 1816.

often occurred in the caucus. From the institution's inception at the start of the nineteenth century, important party leaders were invited to participate in caucus discussions, although they had no vote. The governor, for example, although not a legislator, was a regular participant. The caucus in this way always represented the true leadership of the party. Moreover, each county leader easily influenced his legislative followers even if he chose not to attend the caucus in person. The shift of real intraparty authority from convention to caucus was most evident in the politicking surrounding the appointment of governor and senator, the two most important positions requiring legislative confirmation. While Republicans could not always agree initially in making these selections materially affecting party leadership, the caucus eventually almost always resolved all differences.

In a contest for a United States Senate seat in 1808, the Republican caucus candidate was John Lambert of Hunterdon County. He received twenty-six votes in joint meeting on the first ballot, one short of a majority. Ebenezer Elmer, whose supporters were still miffed over his omission from the 1806 congressional slate, garnered four votes. When the Federalists voted as a unit, however, casting all of their twenty-three votes for John Doughty, one Elmer vote defected to Lambert and the caucus choice was honored.[44]

In the prewar period, before Joseph Bloomfield was recalled to active service in 1812, the governor's office remained a major bone of contention between long-standing competing regional factions in the caucus. North Jersey Republicans were unhappy with Bloomfield's long tenure and sought repeatedly and unsuccessfully to replace him, while party men from South

44. Trenton *True American*, Nov. 7, 1808. While caucus activities for the choice of governor and senator are singled out for examination, the caucus' authority, as it is made clear in chapter eight, extended to virtually all appointive offices in the state. In 1807, for example, a caucus was held "for the purpose of deciding who should be Clark of the Supreme Court. . . . At this meeting it was agreed that whoever had a majority of the votes present, should be supported in joint meeting by the whole body of the democrats in the Legislature." In caucus, William Hyer garnered 18 votes, and two

Jersey clung tenaciously to the General, more, perhaps, as a symbol of their status in the party than out of any affection. Despite deep and continuing disagreement, the caucus imposed its majority will each time the designation of governor threatened to bring party chaos. The *Trenton Federalist* disclosed in 1809 "that the eastern and western democrats divided as to the person who should succeed the present governor. Neither, it seems wanted him continued, but each party determined not to resign its favourite man. Thus situated it was finally concluded to let the old governor go in once more." The names of William S. Pennington of Essex County and William Rossell of Burlington County were withdrawn from caucus consideration, and Bloomfield was re-elected.[45]

The struggle came to a head in 1811, for Pennington was once again brought forward by northern party men. "However, whatever the eastern democrats may say or wish about judge Pennington," a Federalist editorial concluded, "it is pretty well ascertained now, that West Jersey democracy is as fully determined that he shall never be governor." The caucus divided thirty votes between Bloomfield and Pennington on its first ballot. Another caucus candidate, Rossell, was in the desirable position of holding three balance-of-power votes. These three South Jersey ballots went to Bloomfield, giving the General a caucus victory by the close margin of eighteen to fifteen. When the joint meeting convened, Bloomfield received all thirty-three Republican votes. His election was made unanimous by the Federalists in the face of an undivided Republican bloc.[46]

The suzerainty of the Republican caucus inevitably eroded

---

other candidates split 12 votes. Hyer received all the Republican votes in joint meeting. *Trenton Federalist*, Nov. 30, 1807. For a more detailed description of the workings of the caucus in a senatorial election see chapter seven.

45. *Trenton Federalist*, Oct. 30, 1809.

46. *Ibid.*, July 29, Aug. 5, Oct. 21, 28, 1811; New Brunswick *Guardian*, Oct. 31, 1811; *Minutes and Proceedings of the Joint Meeting*, 1811; Trenton *True American*, Nov. 13, 1811; Diary of Mahlon Dickerson, Oct. 24, 1811, Rutgers Univ. Lib.

legislative democracy, discipline. and morale. Legislative sessions frequently were anticlimactic: "The shrugs, and motions and gestures and looks, which passed between the Emperor and the outstanding conscripts, while scarcely a word was uttered in the house," a Federalist report of an 1811 legislative session noted, "gave the whole proceeding more the appearance of a Pantomime than any thing ever before exhibited in this sort of a Play-house." Another description, this time of a joint meeting, disclosed that most members "were much of the time outside the bar at the fires engaged in private conversation, while the chairman went on with the list, and two or three members saying yes or no." The onlooker concluded: "This, to be sure, was of little moment, for the business had undoubtedly been arranged before in the caucus."[47]

The Federalists, after many bludgeonings, learned eventually to offer only token gestures of opposition. "The proceedings of the joint meeting [of 1811] passed off without much contention or heat," chronicled one Federalist lawmaker. "A few federal characters were permitted, here and there, to slip in, but very few were offered." A Federalist legislator, a year later, withdrew the name of a nominee because he was "informed that the caucus had determined he should not be appointed."[48] Clearly, then, the caucus directly transformed and perverted the legislative process.

In many respects also the caucus replaced the state convention at the apex of Republican party apparatus between 1806 and 1810. In the formative period prior to 1807, when the Republican party was becoming stabilized, the more inclusive and public character of the state convention suited the party's needs. It was especially apt as a popular device to draw voters into the party's activities, and it served well as a

---

47. *Trenton Federalist*, Jan. 21, Feb. 25, 1811, Feb. 10, 1812. "Emperor" refers to James J. Wilson, who was by this time the most influential Republican in the state, and a member of the legislature. See the discussion of Wilson in this chapter, and in Prince, "James J. Wilson: Party Leader, 1801-1824," N.J. Hist. Soc., *Proceedings*, 83 (1965), 24-39.

48. *Trenton Federalist*, Jan. 21, Feb. 25, 1811, Feb. 10, 1812.

Republican court of highest appeal when and where it was most needed—at general elections and at the state level of leadership. The caucus grew in importance, however, as party continuity became a certainty; after 1806, with the Republican machine operating smoothly, party needs under these new and more stable conditions changed. The caucus provided a more adequate cover for leadership activities. Even if a given Republican leader was not in the legislature, some of his followers were. Therefore, the caucus was representative enough, after it had gained stature and permanency, to embrace all areas of party authority. Also, the caucus could meet almost at will; the convention, of course, could not.

The evidence indicates that, before 1807, the most significant party battles were waged at the state convention. The dispute between Silas Dickerson and James Sloan in the convention of 1804 involved issues far greater than a mere attempt to gain a nomination on the one hand and efforts to thwart it on the other. Adherence to party discipline was involved as well as larger regional differences. By the same token, the caucus struggle for the governor's chair between William S. Pennington and Joseph Bloomfield through 1811 involved issues and philosophies that transcended the relative positions of the two combatants. The same adherence to party decisions and a similar regional struggle lay at the root of the difficulties. Needless to say, both conflicts involved deep personal ambitions. The difference between the two incidents was that the first was fought out at the state convention in 1804, and the second was settled in the legislative caucus in 1811. The setting had changed; large party issues were decided in the caucus as the party matured, and not in the convention.[49]

Both these elements of party machinery continued to serve well, however, and both remained important in their respective spheres of influence. The caucus was as much the court of last resort after 1806 as the convention had been before that

49. This conclusion is reinforced by a party struggle in the caucus between James J. Wilson and Mahlon Dickerson in 1814, described in chapter seven.

date. In New Jersey at this time, the epithet "king caucus" would indeed have some merit if applied to areas of party leadership other than the nominating procedure.

A highly professional and well organized Republican party dominated New Jersey politics in the half decade or so before the War of 1812. A fair measure of this was, simply, that under great pressure, the party usually gained strength rather than fell apart. If adaptability was not universally characteristic of local machinery, the major component of the party organization was blessed with that attribute. The caucus and the leadership adjusted as conditions in the state changed under the stress of the approaching war. Even locally, Middlesex and Sussex party organizations usually responded quickly to the changing needs of the era. Only Essex's Republican interest did not conform to this generalization—and, it should be noted, perhaps it alone did not have to. The caucus' ability to mask disagreement and the party leadership's deftness in maintaining continuity in its ranks even as the erosions of time took their toll demonstrated the institutionalization that marked the state's Republican party as a professional and stable organization. Indeed, it had to be professional and stable to withstand the pressures to which it would be subjected in the prewar years.

VI

ISSUES AND ELECTIONS
1807-1812

———•———

WHILE MOUNTING PUBLIC CRITICISM SAPPED MANY OF THE DY-
namic leadership qualities inherent in the state nominating
convention, it still provided an important democratic screen
for the party's choice of congressional candidates, and a major
platform for the Republican view of leading issues of the day.
Inasmuch as these two features together constituted a *sine
qua non* for the Republicans' public image, the convention retained an important—if reduced—place in the party apparatus. In short, it never lost its cosmetic value to the party.
And outlets for the propagation of the party view on many
issues, most connected with American foreign policy, were
vitally needed in the years 1807-1812. The controversial aspects
of that policy helped to regenerate Federalist enthusiasm and
support; taken together with the state banking scheme—an
equally controversial local issue—the Republicans found themselves on the defensive for the first time since the 1790's. National elections for Congress and president in New Jersey
especially were affected by these issues. The vigor of the Federalist party was in large measure restored, and the increasing
tendency toward a one-party situation evident in the state in
the years 1801-1806 was reversed.

Pre-war Issues, Politics, and the State Convention

While other issues intruded, by 1808 foreign difficulties pre-empted the concern of most politically aware Jerseymen. Republican activists were forced increasingly to defend the national administration's often unpopular conduct of foreign affairs—particularly, of course, Jefferson's Embargo. Following hard upon the encounter in 1807 between the British ship *Leopard* and the American *Chesapeake*, an inflammatory incident brought on by the impressment of American seamen, the Embargo assured that foreign issues would, taken as a whole, remain an obsessively recurrent theme in New Jersey politics, as elsewhere in the nation. Local Federalists' unrelenting assaults on the Jefferson administration forced the Republicans onto the defensive.[1] As the minority party hammered away at presidential policies, Republican answers became increasingly partisan. The majority, for example, promised that it would not "speedily forget the treasonable part federalists have acted since the laying of the embargo."[2]

The Republicans, linking New Jersey Federalists to British policy, were in turn arraigned for their servitude to "French influence." As the issues were publicized, popular Republican attitudes in the state crystallized. Perhaps the most cogent expression of local party feelings was summed up in a Fourth of July toast Republicans drank in 1808, at the outset of the national campaign: "On war with the two nations, France and England—let us forget recent injuries of the former, and call to mind former kindnesses, and if we must apply to the sword, let it be with the latter."[3] As the campaign of 1808 moved into high gear, then, Republican efforts were complicated by a growing need to defend the actions of the outgoing administration; party men increasingly found that instead of leveling

1. *Trenton Federalist*, Sept. 14, Oct. 5, 1807, Jan. 18, Sept. 5, 1808, Oct. 2, 9, Nov. 27, 1809.

2. Newark *Centinel*, Sept. 22, 1807, Aug. 9, Sept. 6, 1808, Sept. 5, 19, 1809; Trenton *True American*, July 18, Oct. 3, 1808, Sept. 10, 1810, Sept. 9, 1811; Fee, *Transition*, 160-68, and *passim*.

3. Trenton *True American*, July 18, Oct. 3, 1808.

their broadsides at the Federalists, they were defending the President and his secretary of state and heir-apparent, James Madison.

Local Republican difficulties were compounded in 1808, moreover, by a growing uneasiness about the public role of the state nominating convention. The convention's prestige was jeopardized by an incident that compromised its democratic facade. Ezra Darby, congressman for the unofficial district embracing Essex and Bergen counties, died at the end of 1807. An interim poll to fill the vacated seat was scheduled for the beginning of 1808. The unexpected canvass required some hurried arrangements by the Republicans. There was no announced party procedure for such a contingency, so James Mott, chairman of the 1806 convention, authorized the Essex and Bergen delegations to that body to select a party nominee. While in fact this procedure had been quietly employed at all conventions, it had never before transpired so openly and without a formally constituted convention. The spectacle of a handful of men publicly designating a congressman apparently shocked many party men. There was no effort at pretense; no local delegate nominating meetings were held, and no one was consulted. Adam Boyd, handpicked candidate of the local leadership, easily won the interim election in the absence of any organized opposition.[4]

However, a hard-core group of constituents were disgruntled by the fact that Ebenezer Elmer did not receive the endorsement of the regular party machine. Supporters had hoped to restore Elmer to the House seat he had been turned out of by the 1806 convention. According to one Federalist, the ex-congressman had no cause to complain. Prior to 1806, he had been "dubbed 'member of Congress for this state' by about 30 or 40 persons, who as 'good republicans' stiled themselves a convention of the Representatives of New Jersey." Elmer

---

4. *Ibid.*, Feb. 15, 1808; Newark *Centinel*, Feb. 16, 1808. Adam Boyd gathered 7,318 votes to Aaron Ogden's 884 and Ebenezer Elmer's 336. The latter's vote may well have been a form of Republican protest, for Elmer was a Republican who had been turned out of Congress by the convention in 1806.

had been elected to Congress in the past, according to this biting observer, only in the sense that "Bonaparte was elected Emperor." Therefore, when the 1806 convention "used [its] election rod and whipped him aside," Elmer had simply received his just deserts. Adam Boyd, after all, was as legitimate a candidate as Elmer had been in better times, "just as the interest, caprice or whim of some 18 or 20 men will dictate."[5] Nevertheless, the Federalists, aided by Elmer's followers, invoked devastating criticism of the convention system, thereby making effective political capital of the incident.

Elmer's rejection by the convention touched a raw Republican nerve. Despite apologies for and defenses of the convention's utility, the long-term prestige of the institution suffered. The *True American* particularly expended many words defending the convention's "innocent and useful" purpose. "We believe," Wilson noted, "the practice [of making nominations] is not abused. . . . Should abuse of it creep in, the People will check it by rejecting the nominations so made."[6] But nominations by the party machine were not so easily rejected, as unhappy supporters of Ebenezer Elmer had learned in the interim election of 1808.

The regular 1808 state convention, therefore, met at Trenton under a cloud. James Linn of Hunterdon chaired the unexciting proceedings. Congressional and presidential slates were drafted for the concurrent state and national elections scheduled for November 1 and 2. The customary address was a model of passivity, alluding only obliquely to the possibility of diminished public confidence. After briefly reiterating the party's position on outstanding national issues, it explained carefully the rationale behind the two tickets: "On making this selection, you will observe that we have kept in view the accommodation of every part of the state, as the means of preserving union and harmony in the Republican interest."[7]

5. *Trenton Federalist*, Aug. 10, 1807, Feb. 29, Sept. 26, 1808.

6. Trenton *True American*, Mar. 21, 28, 1808; Newark *Centinel*, Feb. 16, 1808.

7. Trenton *True American*, Sept. 26, 1808; Newark *Centinel*, Sept. 27, Oct.

Presidential politicking, meanwhile, was well underway in New Jersey by the end of 1807. The Republican legislative majority itself opened the way to disagreement in the state when it passed a resolution asserting that "the nation have a claim to the services of their most enlightened and experienced statesman," and called upon Jefferson to reconsider his decision not to seek a third term.[8] When it was made clear that the President would not run again, a boom materialized for George Clinton, much to the chagrin of most regular party leaders in New Jersey who had fallen quickly into step behind James Madison, the designate of the congressional caucus.

The *True American* early publicized out-of-state endorsements for Clinton, taking New Jersey's pulse in order to determine a safe course of action. There seemed to be a few takers among the state's party leaders, for a ground swell for Clinton of New York persisted until the week of the election, judging by the many references to him in the papers. James J. Wilson, nevertheless, reported in the spring of 1808 that "the Republicans of this state, so far as we are informed, have long looked to Mr. Madison as the successor of Mr. Jefferson— they had united in him before the Republican Members of Congress, after a conference on the question [had] recommended him to their suffrage."[9] In light of earlier expressions of the New Jersey Republican legislative bloc, this statement was patently untrue, but Wilson was pressed by the demands of political expediency; during the summer of 1808, Republicans feared a split in their ranks despite the *True American* editor's best efforts. The *Centinel* also exhorted Republicans not to abandon Madison, for to do so, it warned, was to "throw yourselves into the phalanx of your worst enemies."[10]

The leader of the Clinton movement in New Jersey was

4, 1808. No correspondence or other private sources touch on this convention or later ones discussed in this chapter. The only extant information was that found in the newspapers.

8. *Trenton Federalist*, Dec. 7, 1807.

9. Trenton *True American*, Dec. 28, 1807, May 23, 1808.

10. Newark *Centinel*, July 25, Oct. 2, 1808.

Congressman James Sloan. He alone openly endorsed Clinton in a public letter to the citizens of New Jersey, proposing the New Yorker for president and James Monroe for vice-president. This public appeal, in April 1808, contained an attack on the congressional caucus, one of several assaults that together hastened its demise.[11] He reiterated his position at the annual nominating meeting of the Gloucester Democratic Association in August, attempting unsuccessfully to persuade his local followers to join him in denouncing the candidacy of James Madison.[12] The *True American* helped to freeze Sloan's efforts when it disclosed the findings of its own straw poll; "In truth, after a diligent enquiry of the numerous Republicans from the various parts of the state we have found *but one individual* (Mr. Sloan) unfriendly to Madison's election."[13]

Isolated as Sloan was made to appear, he apparently excited enthusiasm among enough Republicans to create some consternation in the ranks of Madison's supporters. Woodbridge Republicans appointed a committee to travel to New York to ascertain from George Clinton his receptivity to the vice-presidential nomination. In another of his private polls, the editor of the *True American* revealed that "certain it is that they [Clintonians] have no solid foundation to build on; and we much doubt whether in the state eight men (our number of Electors) could be found." Wilson admitted that his purpose in printing this denial was to answer rumors that Clinton was widely championed in New Jersey. Late in the campaign, the *True American* was still publishing correspondence discrediting the much maligned aspirant from New York. One writer vowed that Clinton was too old for the presidency; indeed, he had entered his "second childhood."[14]

The regular party endorsement eventually drowned out any echoes of existing grass-roots Republican feeling for Clin-

11. *Trenton Federalist*, May 2, 1808.
12. Trenton *True American*, Sept. 5, 1808.
13. *Ibid.*, May 23, 1808.
14. Newark *Centinel*, Nov. 1, 1808; Trenton *True American*, May 23, Oct. 24, Nov. 7, 1808.

ton. Even his candidacy for vice-president came in for criticism. The charge that he was too old persisted. Others backed in his stead for the second position included John Langdon, John Quincy Adams, Elbridge Gerry, or some other "easterner."[15] In the months before the canvass, the local parties went to work to create Madison sentiment. Ten county meetings endorsed the Virginian's candidacy. The *True American* disclosed that "the meetings of Morris, Monmouth and Cape May did not take up the subject at all but equal unanimity and zeal are known to exist [for Madison]."[16]

The Federalist resurgence compounded Republican difficulties. Encouraged by Federalist gains in New England, the minority party seriously contested both the presidential and congressional races, mounting campaigns in at least eleven New Jersey counties.[17] The congressional and presidential slates offered by the Republican convention in 1808 won a difficult victory over a stubborn Federalist interest.[18] Mounting controversy over American foreign policy undoubtedly contributed heavily to the rise in Federalist morale.

Political tempers grew warmer as the war approached. The growing concern over the Federalist resurgence Republicans felt by 1810 was expressed in the latter's increasing willingness to allege Federalist treason among their many political sallies: "Surrounded as we are by domestic traitors—threatened by war with the most powerful maritime nation on earth . . . it is certainly an improper season now to . . . be divided." Such indictments were usually punctuated with the ultimate accusation: "The Federal party [has] deserted the American standard and cause and placed themselves under British ban-

15. Trenton *True American*, Oct. 24, 1808.

16. *Ibid.*, Aug. 29, Sept. 5, 26, Oct. 3, 24, 1808.

17. *Trenton Federalist*, Aug.-Oct., 1808, *passim*. See also the Newark *Centinel*, Nov. 22, 1808.

18. Trenton *True American*, Sept. 26, Oct. 3, 24, Nov. 1808; Newark *Centinel*, Nov. 22, 1808. The total vote cast was 33,300. The Republican vote was 18,705, and 71.8 per cent of the vote turned out.

ners."[19] Implicit in this propaganda line was the Republican conviction that English violations far outstripped French transgressions. As English impressment and exercise of authority on the high seas increased, and Napoleonic motives were obscured, this attitude hardened. In the 1810 campaign, the Republican press compared Napoleonic decrees to British Orders-in-Council, and found the latter to be far more dangerous to the maintenance of American sovereignty.[20]

Politics in this period, while dominated by frequent reference to foreign entanglements, did not ignore local problems. Particularly significant were the successful Republican efforts, first, to tax privately owned bank stock and, later, to create state banks. The issue aroused deep antagonisms in New Jersey around 1810, for it reawakened old ideological distinctions between the two parties reminiscent of the conflicts surrounding Alexander Hamilton's programs in the 1790's. Some Republicans sought to correct what they conceived to be a Federalist abuse of the state's private banking system. In 1807, a bill authorizing the state to subscribe to private bank stock had failed to pass the legislature. Two years later, an act taxing bank stock also failed; neither effort aroused much attention among rank and file Republicans. Both times, as many Republicans voted against the measure as balloted for it. As yet, the bank question had not become a party issue.[21]

The moving force behind these early efforts was James J. Wilson. He apparently convinced enough Republican leaders of the efficacy of his proposals to force the issue to the surface of Republican politics; banking regulation became a party goal early in 1810. Most Republican legislators thereafter sought to correct the speculative aspects of banking, first by imposing a tax on private bank stock and, ultimately, by creat-

19. Newark *Centinel*, Sept. 5, 19, 1809; Trenton *True American*, Sept. 10, 1810; Fee, *Transition*, 160-68, and *passim*.
20. Trenton *True American*, Sept. 10-24, 1810, Sept. 9, 1811; Newark *Centinel*, Sept. 4, 1810, Aug. 20, 1811; Fee, *Transition*, 160-68, and *passim*.
21. *Minutes and Proceedings of the Legislative Council*, 1807, 1809, *passim*; Trenton *Federalist*, Oct. 2, Nov. 20, 1809.

ing state banks in key cities and towns, making banking for all practical purposes a state-regulated enterprise. Wilson, however, did not convert all Republicans to the idea. Some of his own party feared along with most Federalists that legislation taxing bank stock and creating state banks would make all banks, private and public, so many engines of patronage and political footballs.[22]

In the legislative sessions of 1810, two major Republican defections occurred, despite—and perhaps partly because of—Wilson's best efforts. The Essex legislative delegation, with one exception (Councilor Charles Clark), voted with the Federalists against a bill taxing bank stock, causing the bill to fail. The Essex renegades were chided by the *Centinel* and eventually dropped from the ticket in the autumn elections of 1810.[23] Another serious impasse developed during a second attempt in 1810, when John Scudder, a Republican legislator from Monmouth County, voted against a repetition of earlier bank tax bills, causing it also to go down to defeat, this time by one vote. The frustrated editor of the *True American* promptly and publicly accused Scudder of accepting a Federalist bribe. The *Centinel*, although itself in favor of the bank tax, nevertheless widened the breach in the party by pinning on Wilson "a great portion of the odium" for splitting the party. Rejecting a warning to curb his temper, Wilson pressed home his assault on Scudder—and by now the *Centinel* as well—in a biting letter to the editor of the Newark newspaper.[24]

Despite the dangerous differences he was arousing, Wilson continued to force the issue. The *Centinel's* editor, William Tuttle, overlooked his personal pique against Wilson and

22. Fee, *Transition*, 160-68; *Minutes and Proceedings of the Legislative Council*, and *Minutes and Proceedings of the Legislative Assembly*, 1810; Newark *Centinel*, Sept. 18, Oct. 9, 1810. For confirmation of Wilson's active role as the author of the banking reforms, see Anon., *To the Republicans of the County of Hunterdon*, 9-16.

23. Newark *Centinel*, Sept. 18, Oct. 9, 1810. There was found no known expressed relationship, incidentally, between the New Jersey bank issue and the expiring charter of the First Bank of the United States.

24. *Ibid.*, Mar. 27, Apr. 10, 1810; Trenton *True American*, Feb.-Apr., 1810, *passim*.

allowed the *Centinel* to join with the *True American* in pushing the bank issue to the fore in the election campaign of 1810. Enough pressure was applied to Republican candidates (the fate of the old Essex representatives was an example) to insure passage of a bill taxing bank stock when the new legislature convened with its usual Republican majority at the end of 1810.[25] A sequel to the bank tax bill was a second bill creating six state banks in leading cities and towns. It was passed at the beginning of 1812 and completed the renovation of the state's banking structure.[26] Wilson had been elected to the legislature in 1810, and had the satisfaction of voting for both bills.

The entire banking question, in the course of events, was thrown into the political maelstrom. Federalists capitalized on Republican differences, hoping to defeat measures that they believed to be contrary to good government and free enterprise. Moreover, the Federalists correctly alleged, the "great rage" for state banks among New Jersey Republicans was motivated by "the office hunters [who] want places, and therefore new banks are lustily called for."[27]

Republican attacks on Federalist "aristocracy" in connection with that party's defense of the old banking system, however, carried the day. The two leading newspapers, the *Centinel* and the *True American*, joined, for example, in the campaign of 1810 to lay low the Federalist opposition. In so doing they revived briefly the original ideological differences between the two parties. The *True American* assaulted "gentlemen" who wished to avoid payment of the bank stock tax, although they could well afford it. A few comparatively rich men, mainly Federalists, it was charged, owned the bank stock.[28]

25. *Minutes and Proceedings of the Legislative Council,* and *Minutes and Proceedings of the Legislative Assembly,* 1810, 1811; *Trenton Federalist,* Aug. 26, 1811; Newark *Centinel,* Sept. 18, Oct. 9, and Nov.-Dec., 1810, *passim.*

26. *Minutes and Proceedings of the Legislative Council,* and *Minutes and Proceedings of the Legislative Assembly,* 1811, 1812; *Trenton Federalist,* Jan. 20, Feb. 3, 1812.

27. *Trenton Federalist,* Aug. 26, Dec. 9, 1811; Anon., *To the Republicans of the County of Hunterdon,* 9-16.

28. For examples of Republican propaganda of an ideological nature per-

In view of the explosive nature of national diplomatic issues in 1810, it was perhaps, after all, fortunate for the Republicans that, because of the banking issue, they could pin on the Federalists in New Jersey the old and dreaded aristocratic label. For if all attention in the state had been focused on American foreign affairs, the elections of 1810 might have proved considerably less comfortable for the majority party. The congressional election of 1810 was scheduled to run simultaneously with the legislative poll in October. The Federalists, still seeking the right political combination, offered no legislative tickets in six overwhelmingly Republican counties, hoping that the lack of opposition would make the Republicans complacent in these counties and cut down the number of votes cast for congressional candidates. They campaigned vigorously, however, in counties where Federalism remained strong. At the same time, they tried to capitalize on existing dissatisfaction with the nominating convention. Federalist papers learned that the Republicans planned to drop some incumbents from their congressional ticket, shunting them aside, the Federalists said, as "condemned stuff." "The people are, on the 19th of Sept., to be blessed with a new batch of patriots with certificates on their backs under the seal of the democratic convention."[29] The men behind that convention were forced to meet this challenge.

James J. Wilson, as was so often the case, fired the opening Republican salvo in defense of the Republican nominating machinery. Uncharacteristically, the *True American* offered only a lame justification for the expected changes in the congressional alignment: "If they [the congressmen to be dropped] are not re-elected, it is not because they are distrusted or condemned—it is because they have done a long tour of duty, and it is thought to be time to relieve them." Few congressmen, indeed, ever sought such "relief," and so the convention itself,

taining to the bank issue, see the Trenton *True American*, Sept. 3, 24, Oct. 1, 1810, Oct. 7, and *passim*, 1811; Newark *Centinel*, Sept. 18, Oct. 9, 1810.

29. Trenton *True American*, Sept. 10, 24, 1810; *Trenton Federalist*, Sept. 17, 1810; Newark *Centinel*, Sept. 25, 1810.

meeting in Trenton on September 19, 1810, felt the need to explain further via its address: "The principle of rotation in office has not been forgotten; and men have been selected who have the confidence of the districts in which they reside and where they are best known."[30] The shadow cast by the 1808 proceedings, it is clear, had not disappeared by 1810.

The convention's difficulties were augmented by the Middlesex County Republican meeting, which, in complete violation of all existing procedures, nominated an entire congressional slate for the consideration of the state's delegates. As if to heighten the grandeur of their departure from established party traditions, five of the six designated by Middlesex Republicans hailed from the central counties of the state, one was from Bergen County, and no one represented the southern portion of New Jersey. The dilemma, according to one Federalist, occasioned at the convention "such whispering and caucusing, such plucking of coats and shaking of hands, such manoevreing and electioneering, such meeting of delegates and confrerees [until] by 12 o'clock a ticket had been arrived at."[31] The designated candidate for Middlesex, James Morgan, whom the delegation from that county was particularly committed to support, was named to the convention ticket—in part, at least, as a sop to the recalcitrant Middlesex delegates.

The Republican leaders' concern with such deviation was apparent in the address, which pointedly admitted to "having a due regard to the local interest of different parts of the state" in designating a ticket. A Federalist offered his congratulations: "Fellow-Citizens, how thankful you ought to be to those . . . who volunteer their services in saving you the perplexing difficulty of choosing your own candidates." The election, ac-

30. Trenton *True American*, Sept. 10, 24, 1810; *Trenton Federalist*, Sept. 10, 17, 24, 1810; Newark *Centinel*, Sept. 25, 1810. The 1810 congressional ticket included Jacob Hufty, Thomas Newbold, Adam Boyd, Lewis Condict, George C. Maxwell, and James Morgan. The last three named were running for the first time, replacing Henry Southard, James Sloan, and William Helms.

31. Trenton *True American*, Sept. 10, 24, 1810; *Trenton Federalist*, Sept. 10, 17, 24, 1810; Newark *Centinel*, Sept. 25, 1810.

cording to the same source, was as good as over—"the Convention has willed it."[32]

The desire to protect the fading democratic image of the convention was evidenced by an increase in the average number of delegates attending. Up to 1810, three or four from each county sufficed, but in 1810 the average mounted to five or six.[33] The expected Federalist resistance proved negligible, despite the convention's problems. The strategy of campaigning only in selected counties perhaps dulled the overall Federalist effort, and the Republican congressional ticket swept to victory.[34]

Mounting Pressures and Defeat

The Federalists would not prove so obliging again for some time to come. As diplomatic tensions eventuating in the War of 1812 mounted, so did the political stresses caused by the regeneration of a vigorous two-party system in New Jersey. Appeals to national honor and defenses of the national administration, as a result, reached a peak in the campaigns of 1812, when the Republican party found itself in its most precarious position in a dozen years.

One Republican observer reported that "perhaps party politics and party dissentions never ran higher . . . than at the present time." In both the state and the national elections the Republican interest was labeled the "war party," and expressions of support for Madison's foreign policy were tinged with the quiet desperation of a party facing wholesale desertions at the polls. Nevertheless, Republicans in New Jersey responded energetically to the allegation that they were the party of war. "American federalists" were asked to separate from "Tory federalists"; British influence was denounced. Reviewing "peace

32. *Trenton Federalist*, Sept. 24, 1810; Trenton *True American*, Sept. 10, 17, 24, 1810.
33. Trenton *True American* and Newark *Centinel*, Aug.-Sept., 1810, *passim*. See reports of the county meetings.
34. MS Minutes of the New Jersey Privy Council, Oct. 30, 1810, II, 69, N.J. State Lib. The vote was 13,734 for the leading Republican candidate to a meager 523 for the top Federalist.

party" charges, Republicans denied that Britain desired peace with America and that "Produce [was] rotting in our Hands." To the credit of the Republican party, the press asserted, revenue was accruing to the American government from prizes taken through privateering; the national debt had been reduced by the Republican regime; America, after all, was fighting a war of honor to preserve American dignity and integrity; finally, voters were reminded of the hated acts of impressment, prime examples of British tyranny.[35]

The Republican campaign in the summer and fall of 1812 was hampered by the need to explain the anti-war votes the previous June of three Republican congressmen and one Republican senator from New Jersey. Congressmen Adam Boyd, Thomas Newbold, and Jacob Hufty, and Senator John Lambert all stood with the Federalists against the declaration of war. The Republican attitude toward the renegade members of the House, vulnerable because they were up for re-election, was exemplified by a resolution adopted at a South Jersey rally: "On a question of such magnitude, as that of war or submission, it is the indispensible duty of public agents, to attend to the will of the majority of their constituents, and as the representatives in Congress from this state were divided on that great question, they shall hear from the people of New Jersey at the next congressional election."[36] A toast drunk by Middlesex Republicans to Senator John Condit pointedly reminded the participants of Lambert's lapse: the toast named Condit "the man who voted in favor of war rather than submission to the injuries heaped upon us by Great Britain. He has met the wishes of his constituents."[37] Remonstrances like these, however, did not go very far toward explaining the congressional lapse that occasioned them.

After war commenced, and during the election campaign,

35. Newark *Centinel*, Aug. 25, Oct. 13, 1812.
36. Trenton *True American*, Aug. 3, 1812; Newark *Centinel*, Sept. 22, 1812.
37. New Brunswick *Fredonian*, July 16, 1812; Newark *Centinel*, Aug. 3, Sept. 22, Oct. 13, 1812; Trenton *True American*, Aug. 17, 1812, and *passim*; Trenton *True American Supplement*, Aug. 3, 1812.

many in New Jersey responded to the wave of expansionist sentiment for an American conquest of Canada. The Republicans in the state, naturally, often touched on this theme. Even before the declaration of war, the *Centinel* proclaimed that "procrastination is too much the order of the day. . . . Why are not troops . . . raised: Why are they not on the march to the Canadas?" One party man, riding a nationalistic crest in the summer of 1812, toasted the "Flag of the U.S. on the walls of Quebec." A second Republican offered relief to "the frontier inhabitants . . . the conquest of Canada shall soon terminate your troubles." Still another ardent supporter turned expansionism to political advantage: "Why would the federalists clamour against invading Canada now, more than they did in the revolutionary war, when Washington applauded the expedition. . . . If we conquer Canada it is not to make the Canadians slaves, but freemen." Some Republicans professed high hopes for General Bloomfield, recalled in 1812 to active service: "When in the camp, on the march, or under the walls of Quebec, may he never want the genuine character of a Jersey Blue." Bloomfield, however, marched little, and did not get any closer to Quebec than Poughkeepsie, New York.[38]

Preoccupation with the outbreak of war in 1812 did not completely drown out the echoes of the bank issue. One Republican during the campaign effectively tied the foreign and local problems into one neat package: "Foreign commerce and the [old] banking system—Twin sisters, twin monsters, and twin destroyers of the rights of man." Assaults on aristocratic and undemocratic Federalist poses were also prominent through

38. Newark *Centinel*, Mar. 10, July 23, Nov. 3, 1812; Trenton *True American*, Aug. 3, 1812. The Federalists were aware of the potential appeal of this issue and rejected it as a justification for war. See, for example, the *Trenton Federalist*, May 14, Oct. 5, 1812. Bloomfield was not exactly esteemed as a general by the Madison administration, hence the limitations on his command. Henry Dearborn to James Madison, Feb. 14, 1813, Madison Papers, Lib. Cong. His appointment was originally made with the hope that, given his earlier record of military service and his reputation as a man politic enough to placate diverse elements, he would help to ease political tensions in the army. James Madison to James Monroe, Aug. 15, 1813, James Monroe Papers, Lib. Cong.

1812.[39] Republicans much later recalled that "by laying a tax on Bank Stock, they [the Republican party] relieved your farms, your cattle, etc., from their burthens. By creating the State Banks, they at once accommodated the community."[40]

Republican efforts to gain the initiative in the campaign of 1812, intensive though they were, for the most part were too little and too late. Astutely designating themselves "peacemen," Federalist leaders held a "Peace Convention" embracing delegates from all parts of the state to nominate a Federalist congressional ticket and a slate of presidential electors. They went all out to break the Republican hold on New Jersey.[41]

Republicans, branded "the party of war," mounted an offensive of their own. They hoped, despite the evidence at hand, to elect six congressmen and a ticket of Madison electors. The party took appropriate precautionary steps to meet the unusual political conditions created by the recent entry into war with England. The Burlington Democratic Association suggested that an extraordinary state convention gather early in July to offset the Federalist convocation meeting at the end of June 1812. Party men from nearly every county, responding enthusiastically in spite of short notice, attended the Republican gathering at the Mount Holly Inn in Burlington on July 10. Nearly one hundred delegates appeared, including most of the leading Republicans; only Sussex and Cape May counties, at the two geographic extremes of the state, were not represented.[42] The Republicans were much encouraged by this display of enthusiasm. A committee of one delegate from each county present drafted a public address. The assembled delegates, before adjourning, arranged for the usual autumn convention to nominate presidential and congressional slates.

39. Trenton *True American*, Aug. 3, Oct. 12, 1812.
40. *Ibid.*, Sept. 11, 1815.
41. See both the Trenton *True American* and the *Trenton Federalist*, 1812, *passim*, and the Newark *Centinel*, June 9, 23, and *passim*, 1812.
42. Diary of Mahlon Dickerson, July 10, 1812, Rutgers Univ. Lib.; Notes from the Diary of Isaac Andruss, 1812-1828, July 10, 1812, N.J. Hist. Soc.; Newark *Centinel*, June 9-July 28, 1812; Trenton *True American*, July 12-26, 1812; New Brunswick *Fredonian*, July 16, 1812.

Admittedly, the growing Federalist challenge within and without the state drew the Republicans together, for, at least temporarily, "the greatest unanimity prevailed."[43]

In 1812, the Federalists, however, did not have to depend on internecine warfare in the Republican party. Catching their opponents napping, the aggressive "peace men" illustrated both their determination and their "nonpartisan" policy by including on their congressional ticket the three Republican congressmen who had voted against the declaration of war in 1812. In vain, Republicans waited for the three men—Adam Boyd, Jacob Hufty, and Thomas Newbold—to decline and denounce such obvious Federalist politicking. But these incumbents assented, as some Republicans expressed it, "to become the foot balls of the federalists." In anger—and frustration—party men swore that the congressmen's names were "ever to be blotted out of the tablet of Republicanism."[44]

The Republican state convention, planned at the July 10 meeting, assembled on October 20 at the Bloomsbury Hotel just outside of Trenton. In another attempt to demonstrate the democratic nature of the institution, it was publicized as the largest convention ever held by New Jersey Republicans. Delegates poured in by the score; the Hunterdon and Essex delegations being the largest. The arrivals were not disappointed by their welcome. They were wined, dined, and paraded; the First Light Infantry Company of Trenton, Captain James J. Wilson commanding, entertained with a parade drill and then, at three o'clock in the afternoon, dinner was served, with the party footing the bill.[45] The editor of the *Trenton Federalist* commented wryly on the parade: "Some thought they [delegates

43. *Ibid.* See particularly the reports and address of the convention in the Newark *Centinel*, July 14, 21, 28, 1812.

44. Newark *Centinel*, Sept. 22, 1812; Trenton *True American*, Sept. 26, Oct. 3, 1812; New Brunswick *Guardian*, June 11, 18, 25, 1812.

45. Trenton *True American*, Aug. 24, Sept. 14, 28, Oct. 5, 26, 1812; Newark *Centinel*, Aug. 25, Sept. 22, Oct. 6, Nov. 3, 1812. The gala trappings, the extra day given over to entertainment, and the inordinately large number of delegates were all added this one time in an obvious attempt to stir an embattled party.

and militia] were going off, post haste, to Canada."[46]

The next day the convention settled down to the business at hand. A committee of two members from each county, twenty-six in all, was appointed to confer and report congressional and presidential tickets to the convention for its consideration. The nominating procedure was not new but was merely an adaptation of the earlier form when just a few delegates from each county were present at the convention. That the district system of nominations was still intact was indicated by the choice of two from each county. Also, a committee of six was selected to draft an address. With these initial steps taken, Chairman Aaron Munn of Essex adjourned the body for an hour to allow the committees to do their work. After the convention reconvened, the tickets were quickly accepted. The delegates resolved to "use all lawful and honorable exertions in support of the ticket[s]," and the address was read aloud. It belabored most of the issues facing the nation, attacked the internal Federalist menace in this time of crisis, and justified the War of 1812. The convention adjourned, and the delegates went home to seek out Republican support for the imminent state election and the subsequent national canvass.[47]

Presidential politicking, meanwhile, was very much in evidence through the summer and autumn of 1812. Like the state's Republican hierarchy, the national administration—particularly the President—encountered a good deal of adverse feeling. The Federalists encouraged dissatisfaction with Madison by deluging the state with anti-Madison, anti-war, and anti-Republican campaign literature, much of it originating outside of New Jersey. At the same time, the hopeful minority

46. *Trenton Federalist*, Oct. 26, 1812.

47. Trenton *True American*, Oct. 26, 1812; Newark *Centinel*, Oct. 27, 1812. The congressional ticket included Lewis Condict, James Morgan, Henry Southard, Thomas Ward, Thomas Hendry, and Isaiah Shinn. Only Condict and Morgan were holdovers from the previous Congress; Southard was returned to the ticket after an absence of two years.

unwound an initially hesitant campaign on behalf of Governor DeWitt Clinton of New York.

New Jersey's Federalists, in effect, settled reluctantly on Clinton as their most realistic choice. "If a man of the Washington school cannot be brought forward with any success," the *Trenton Federalist* apprised its readers in justifying its endorsement of the Republican Governor of New York, "take DeWitt Clinton. . . . Take any sensible and honest American, not a Virginian of the present ruling party, and we shall do better." The New Brunswick *Guardian* agreed that Clinton "may not be altogether the man of [our] choice; but all circumstances viewed for the best interest of the country, [we] will unite in him."[48]

Two tracts supporting DeWitt Clinton that were particularly well circulated in New Jersey were an *Address of the Committee of the City of New York* and *The Republican Crisis*. The former was moderate, the *True American* commented editorially, but "we do not believe . . . that they [the writers] will convince one Republican of the necessity, expediency or propriety of a change of President at this time; nor make one friend to the candidate whom they hold up to supercede Mr. Madison." The second pamphlet, entitled, appropriately enough, *The Republican Crisis*, proved far less impersonal. It appeared to make the rounds in New Jersey with some effect, for James J. Wilson chastised bitterly this assault on Madison: "This pamphlet exhibits such a destitution of candor, truth, and even decency, that it must disgust every man of common information and honesty who reads it."[49]

The Federalists undoubtedly campaigned locally for legislative office by introducing the presidential issue, for the anti-Madison literature was widely distributed *before the state elections*, scheduled earlier than the national poll in New

48. *Trenton Federalist*, Aug. 10, 1812; New Brunswick *Guardian*, Aug. 19, 1812. Both of these Federalist papers industriously—and much more warmly—supported Clinton throughout the fall of 1812.

49. Trenton *True American*, Aug. 31, 1812. Copies of the pamphlets themselves were not uncovered.

Jersey. A growing coolness toward the President's foreign policy was evident in the state, and the minority party played heavily upon this advantage. Many who voted for local Federalist tickets in close counties may have suspected that the "peace men," if they won a majority of seats in the legislature, might call off the scheduled popular vote for presidential electors and select Clintonian electors themselves. So the Federalists, hopeful of finally upsetting the Republican hegemony in the state, redoubled their assaults on the President and the national administration as the state campaign progressed. The *Centinel* warned Republican party men "to see how industrious they [the Federalists] are in spreading pamphlets to allure and deceive you."[50]

That the Federalist campaign for Clinton was successful in aiding local Federalist candidates there can be little doubt. "Those persons near unto us, and elsewhere in this country, who are spreading pamphlets among us in order to sow the seeds of discord and create confusion . . . should be considered as British spies and the worst of Tories," commented the Newark Republican sheet. The antagonists of the incumbent administration, prior to the legislative poll, concentrated their efforts in those "counties in which the strength of parties hitherto have been nearly balanced." These areas "have been literally deluged with inflammatory pamphlets, handbills and papers."[51]

A much more significant barometer of grass-roots dissatisfaction with Madison may be found in a comparison with the 1808 Republican support for the President. In 1808, ten Republican county meetings made it a point to endorse Madison. Four years later, only two—gatherings in Salem and Burlington—did so. The two state conventions of 1812 heartily endorsed the incumbent, but both were controlled by Republican professionals whose prestige often depended on federal appointments.[52]

50. Newark *Centinel*, Sept. 15, 22, Oct. 20, 1812.
51. *Ibid.*
52. Trenton *True American*, July 12, 19, Aug. 31, Sept. 7, 14, Oct. 5, 26,

To combat this antipathy, a letter to New Jersey citizens from the President himself was extensively circulated throughout the state. The letter, obviously written for the relief of the embattled New Jersey Republican party, was an answer to the expression of continued support sent to the President by the extraordinary state convention of July 10. "No part of the American people," Madison wrote, "had a more meritorious share [in building the nation] than the people of New Jersey. From none, therefore, may more reasonably be expected, a patriotic zeal in maintaining by the sword, the unquestionable and unalienable rights, acquired by it."[53] New Jersey Republicans industriously circulated other campaign literature, and, in a variety of ways, proselytized for their cause. Handbills were very much in evidence. One, written and printed by James J. Wilson, and another, written by William Rossell, were "circulated with great industry, especially in the southern counties." According to one indignant Federalist, the Republicans far exceeded the bounds of propriety: "Riders were employed to circulate handbills, newspapers and pamphlets throughout the state. . . . In addition to these false reports were fabricated and industriously circulated. . . . Menacing notes and verbal threats were addressed to individuals of the federalist party, warning them not to exert themselves at the polls."[54]

The Republicans also countered anti-Madison feelings by denigrating Clinton. Madison's adherents quoted extensive-

1812; Newark *Centinel*, July 14-28, Oct. 27, 1812. For the importance of federal patronage to party leaders and the extent to which state conventions were dominated by officeholders, see chapter eight. Another indicator of the decline of Madison's popularity in New Jersey may be found in the fact that following his initial election in 1808, several New Jersey groups celebrated his inauguration as they had Jefferson's in the past, but there was no evidence of this in 1812-13. See James Madison to Thomas T. Kinney, Mar. 18, 1809, and to Thomas Yarnow, Mar. 18, 1809, Madison Papers, Lib. Cong. Even Madison realized prior to the 1812 elections that "New Jersey is doubtful at least." Madison to Jefferson, Oct. 14, 1812, in Gaillard Hunt, ed., *The Writings of James Madison*, 8 vols. (N.Y., 1906), VI, 227ff.

53. Newark *Centinel*, Aug. 11, 1812; Trenton *True American*, Aug. 10, 17, 24, 1812; James Madison to ?, July 25, 1812, Madison Papers, Lib. Cong.

54. *Trenton Federalist*, Oct. 5, 1812; New Brunswick *Guardian*, Jan. 7, 1813.

ly earlier New Jersey Federalist attacks on the Governor of New York written when they had considered him a Republican. Invariably, the quotes were followed by some variation of the query "how can the Federalists of New Jersey support such a Republican?"[55] However, the Republican campaign for Madison, despite the deluge of printed matter, uncharacteristically never got off the ground. Enthusiasm was lacking, and many Republicans, before the scheduled national elections, saw the handwriting on the wall: "Let it never be told in Gath," one discouraged party man wrote, "or published in Askelon, that at this important crisis of national affairs the people of New Jersey have elected federal members of Congress, and federal electors of President."[56] By the time this lament was printed, the Federalists had already won a majority in the legislature, foreshadowing the further blows to Republicanism in New Jersey that were to follow.

Just a week before the scheduled general elections for presidential electors and congressmen, the Federalist majority in the legislature negated all campaign efforts for President by altering the election law, assigning the choice of electors to the legislature, and setting forth a district canvass for representatives. As a final insult, the Federalists dropped from their congressional ticket two of the three "peace" Republicans they had previously designated, leaving only Jacob Hufty to run with five Federalists on the "Peace Ticket."[57]

After assuring the choice of Clinton electors, the victorious Federalists outrageously gerrymandered New Jersey in an effort to drive most of the Republican delegation out of Congress. The state was carved into three districts, the first comprising the counties of Bergen, Sussex, Essex, and Morris, the second containing Middlesex, Monmouth, Somerset, and Hunterdon counties, and the third including Gloucester, Cape May, Cumberland, Burlington, and Salem counties. Each dis-

55. See, for example, the Trenton *True American*, Oct. 5, 1812.
56. Newark *Centinel*, Oct. 27, 1812.
57. *Ibid.*, Oct. 27, Nov. 3, Dec. 1, 15, 22, 1812; Trenton *True American*, Oct. 26, Nov. 23, 30, Dec. 7, 1812.

trict was allotted two representatives. Republican complaints that the first district, which held the bulk of the Republican strength, had 18,000 people more than the third, availed them nothing. That it was indeed a "great and unwarrantable infringement of the principles of equal representation" was not denied, nor was it rectified.[58]

The Republicans adapted to the situation as best they could. In the predominantly Republican first district, the party held a district convention at Morristown at which each of the four counties in the district was represented. The two North Jersey nominees selected at the state convention in October were again named the standard-bearers from the new district.[59] The second district promised a close race. The Federalists, with a legislative victory behind them, were much better organized than their opponents who were demoralized by the task of revamping their machinery to fit the new situation. Attempts to assemble a district meeting were only partially successful. In a convention which was not representative of the entire district, the two candidates chosen at Trenton again were nominated. Preparations for the election, however, were localized, hasty, and inadequate.[60] In the third district, there was no contest. After finally rounding up delegates from the five counties, the Republicans decided not to nominate any congressional candidates, for "no object presents itself at the ensuing election as worthy of our arduous conflict." The Republicans in South Jersey were completely cowed. After issuing a few ineffective resolutions and condemning Federalist "Usurpation," the meeting adjourned, reserving only "the most unquestionable right to complain," which Republicans did, long and loud.[61]

58. Trenton *True American*, Nov. 23, 1812; Newark *Centinel*, Nov. 3, Dec. 22, 1812.

59. Newark *Centinel*, Dec. 1, 15, 1812; Trenton *True American*, Dec. 7, 1812. The two nominees were Thomas Ward and Lewis Condict.

60. Trenton *True American*, Dec. 7, 1812, Jan. 4, 1813; Bernard Smith to Samuel L. Southard, Dec. 9, 1812, Southard Papers, Princeton Univ. Lib. The nominees were James Morgan and Henry Southard.

61. Trenton *True American*, Jan. 11, 1813.

The Federalists captured the two lower districts, electing three of their number and the maverick Jacob Hufty. The Republicans managed to return only Thomas Ward and Lewis Condict, candidates from the first district.[62]

Discouraged, failing to deliver the state's eight electoral votes to Madison, and placed in the unaccustomed role of a minority party, the Republicans indeed reached a low point in their fortunes. Certainly the political future looked bleak to Republicans looking ahead from the vantage point of 1812. Major components of the party machinery were immobilized, the party's image was under attack, and the voters had turned on the Republican party for the first time in more than a decade. The defeat of 1812, in short, seemed to put the Republican machine to its most severe test to date. That it was the New Jersey Federalists' last fling the Jeffersonians could not know.

62. *Ibid.*, Jan. 25, 1813; Newark *Centinel*, Jan. 26, 1813.

VII

THE DECLINE OF
PARTY ORGANIZATION
1813-1817

———•—•———

IT WAS IRONIC THAT WHILE THE REPUBLICANS SOON RECOUPED
all that they had lost in 1812, their victories were increasingly
accomplished with such ease that organizational decay set in.
Among the early indications that formal Federalist resistance
was dying was the declining pressure the opposition applied
to the long-standing diplomatic issues as the course of the war
changed. On the other hand, with the restoration of peace
Republican attempts to perpetuate ideological myths failed,
and party lines blurred still more. Local party organizations
reacted first to the easing of tensions, and they paced the gradual structural decay of the Republican party. By 1817 the
smudging of party lines had so progressed that local distinctions and party groupings were impossible to maintain in most
counties. Although it still met regularly, the convention, weakened by prewar assaults on its validity, was old hat by the
end of the conflict. By 1815 it attracted only cursory attention
from either party. Only the caucus, retaining its position as
the forum for the most important leadership decisions and

party battles, sustained the structural vigor so reminiscent of the entire party apparatus in the earlier years.

The Demise of Local Party Machinery

Between 1813 and 1817 the strong county organizations weakened and the weak ones fell apart. Examinations of party formations in Essex and Sussex in North Jersey, Hunterdon and Middlesex in Central Jersey, and Burlington in South Jersey accurately comprehend the causes and symptoms of local decomposition in some depth. Once again, the fate of the above county structures was generally shared by their neighbors.

In Essex, the county with both the greatest Republican majority and the weakest organization, the decline after 1812 was so complete that it ultimately posed a threat to the statewide Republican interest. After two years of difficulties, the 1815 county meeting disbanded without designating a Republican ticket. An opportunistic group of Republicans, led by Shepard Kollock and representing in force every town but Newark, promptly convened another meeting. Under Kollock's firm guidance this gathering named a slate that included himself and Samuel Pennington—an old antagonist and the Governor's brother. The selection of a Pennington on the ticket assured many votes from Newark and diminished the possibility of a revival of the original county meeting under Newark Republican auspices. The Penningtons, involved in 1814 and 1815 in a struggle with James J. Wilson for position in the state organization, were unwilling to create further difficulties for themselves at home and went along with Kollock's machinations.[1] With a Pennington and a Kollock running on the same slate, it easily swept the election, vindicating the political astuteness of the Elizabethtown editor. If the victory forecast a reconciliation between the rival regional groups, it had come

1. Newark *Centinel*, Sept. 26, Oct. 3, 10, 17, 1815; Edward Yard to Mahlon Dickerson, Nov. 7, 1814, Mahlon Dickerson Papers, N.J. Hist. Soc.; James J. Wilson to William Darlington, Nov. 8, 1814, Darlington Papers, Lib. Cong.

too late. The election of 1815 was complicated by the presence of numerous splinter tickets in the field, many overlapping one another.[2]

In the absence of a strong county organization in 1815, many individuals and factions took to publishing slates of their own. In a sense, party machinery and discipline in this weakly contested county reverted to a pre-1800 fragmented state of development. Shepard Kollock, with little to lose, used to advantage the decomposition of party machinery to gain control of what was left of the organization. Little wonder that William S. Pennington resigned the politically insecure governorship to take a federal judicial appointment when the opportunity offered itself at the end of 1815.[3]

The passing of William S. Pennington from the mainstream of Essex politics signaled the end of the county meeting as an Essex party institution. Republicans, to be sure, were called to meet at Camptown (Irvington) in September 1816, but before nominating legislative candidates, the meeting entered into an enlightening discussion of the changes that had occurred in Essex politics since the good old days. The need for a consensus, according to one participant, had been "removed by the dissolution of Federalism in this part of our State." An old-timer, attending his first meeting in years, found that things had changed quite a bit since his last appearance. He complained that "the county meetings were formerly composed of the most respectable farmers and townsmen in the county. . . . The whole appeared to be pursuing the public good, and intent on selecting such candidates as would best serve the county in its public councils." The critic was sorely disappointed that "there is . . . a great falling off in all respects" from a dimly remembered past, that, compared to the present, looked much better in retrospect than it really was. Many left the meeting in disgust, leaving it in the hands of "old Federalists and self-seeking politicians," who, in their eagerness,

2. Newark *Centinel*, Sept. 26, Oct. 3, 10, 17, 24, 1815.
3. *Ibid.*

"clearly discovered a disposition to promote the election of favourite candidates, instead of making an impartial selection." The Camptown convocation finally nominated a ticket amid complaints that "county meetings . . . are fast degenerating into scenes of management, intrigue and disorder—and are wholly uncalled for by the circumstances of the times."[4]

Shepard Kollock was outspokenly critical of the Camptown gathering. After it adjourned, he called a meeting of his own to nominate a complete slate. Numerous smaller meetings followed, endorsing his ticket. Kollock's slate easily defeated the county meeting ticket in the October elections, bringing the prestige of the open county gathering to a new low, even for Essex politics.[5] In 1817 the demoralized county meeting broke up without agreeing on a ticket; it never met thereafter except to name delegates to the state convention. At each election after 1816, numerous tickets appeared, supported occasionally by a section or group within the county but, in most instances, simply placed before the public by an individual "elector." County politics in Essex degenerated to a petty level, with a dozen little groups vying for the crumbs of office.[6]

Among those who remained active in Essex politics were a number of Federalists. While Federalism never gained a foothold organizationally, many of that party capitalized on Republican divisions in Essex to make inroads into the political control of the county after 1812; they gained in strength and significance as Republican machinery crumbled. Federalists existed in the county in the only way open to them—in the guise of Republicanism.

The Essex Federalists first took on the political coloration they were increasingly to assume in 1813. They knew better than to employ the term "Federalist," and instead their announcement of a county meeting invited "friends of all parties" to join in forming a ticket "most likely to promote measures

4. *Ibid.*, Sept. 17, 1816; Trenton *True American*, Sept. 17, 1816.
5. Newark *Centinel*, Sept. 24, Oct. 8, 15, 1816.
6. *Ibid.*, Sept. 23, 1817, Sept. 29, Oct. 12, 1818, Sept. 14, 1819, Oct. 3, 1820, Sept. 25, 1821, Oct. 1, 1822, Oct. 14, 1823.

which may speedily terminate the present war upon honorable terms." Few Federalist ballots were cast for the mixed slate that had been formed until "the seventh hour" when, as the polls were about to close, "a number of up-town embargo grumblers and peace men made a muster," hoping to catch the Republicans napping. They were not successful and the county remained Republican.[7]

The Federalists broke into the Republican monopoly at the polls for the first time in 1814. No less a man than Jonathan Dayton—former Federalist speaker of the House of Representatives, United States senator, Burr conspirator, and, for a score of years, a leading opponent of the Jeffersonians—was elected to the Assembly on the Republican ticket. He ran at the behest and with the blessings of Governor Pennington himself. Despite sustained criticism of this turn of events, Dayton proclaimed himself a Republican because of his stand in favor of the War of 1812. Even the faithful *Centinel* defended him against the outraged denunciations of many Essex Republicans.[8]

Much more significantly, Federalists after 1814 infiltrated to the very foundations of the county Republican organization or what was left of it. The jerry-built structure of that machine considerably eased their way. Many Federalists, claiming a Republican kinship that in the long run proved to be of dubious quality, attended the already tumultuous Essex County nominating meetings. Even before the end of the war, some

7. *Ibid.*, Sept. 14, Oct. 19, 1813. For indications of Republican recognition of this menace to their hegemony in Essex, see William S. Pennington to Jonathan Dayton, Aug. 15, 1814, Gratz Collection, Hist. Soc. of Pa.; Newark *Centinel*, June 9, 1812.

8. William S. Pennington to Jonathan Dayton, Aug. 15, 1814, Gratz Collection, Hist. Soc. of Pa.; David Thompson, Jr., to Samuel L. Southard, Mar. 8, 1816, Southard Papers, Princeton Univ. Lib.; Newark *Centinel*, Oct. 3, 1815, and autumn, 1814, *passim*. For Jonathan Dayton's career in New Jersey and national politics, see *Biographical Encyclopaedia of New Jersey*, 367-68; *Cyclopedia of New Jersey Biography*, I, 35-36; *United States Congress Biographical Directory*, 791; Jonathan Dayton Papers, Princeton Univ. Lib. Dayton also made at least one effort to ingratiate himself with the national administration. See Jonathan Dayton to James Monroe, Mar. 1, 1815, Monroe Papers, Lib. Cong.

local Republicans accurately predicted that, if these "old Feds" were allowed to participate, existing Republican machinery in the county could not survive. Nevertheless, Federalists were present in some numbers at the controversial county meeting of 1816. The *Centinel*, cautious for fear of provoking greater disunity, hinted that "not a few" of the participants "have but little claim to public confidence." Two of the minority, indeed, were appointed at the 1816 gathering to the nominating committee; Isaac H. Williamson, a "war Federalist," was nominated and subsequently elected to the legislature, just as Jonathan Dayton had been two years earlier. In the contest for sheriff, although both aspirants claimed to be Republicans, one accused the other, with some justice, of being a Jeffersonian in name only.[9] Some years later, a Republican retrospectively alluded to these developments, pointing out that the nation had entered "an era of good feelings in politics and party animosity has happily subsided."[10]

Within a few years of the Essex developments of 1816, Republicans from all over the state were taking note of the Essex Republicans' laxity with regard to Federalism.[11] One of many critics from South Jersey, for example, lashed Essex Republicans for playing a double game with the party: "We middle and western men begin to judge the tree by its fruits . . . and not by the political name which they bear. . . . They [middle and western Republicans] have weighed actions and name in the republican scale, and have . . . found the former amazingly wanting."[12] The Essex Republicans, stripped of all but the rudiments of their organization following the war, knowingly or unwittingly gave their Republican brethren in the hinter-

9. Newark *Centinel*, Sept. 17, Oct. 8, 1816, and *passim*.
10. *Ibid.*, Oct. 10, 1820.
11. J. F. Randolph to Samuel L. Southard, Nov. 6, 1817, Henry Southard to Southard, Feb. 19, 1818, David Thompson, Jr., to Southard, Feb. 23, 1818, Mar. 6, May 3, Aug. 4, 1819, William S. Pennington to Southard, Aug. 14, 1818, Southard to Pennington, Aug. 11, 1818, Southard Papers, Princeton Univ. Lib.; Henry Southard to Ebenezer Elmer, Jan. 25, 1819, Gratz Collection, Hist. Soc. of Pa.; Newark *Centinel*, Sept. 8, 1818; Trenton *True American*, Oct. 12, 1818.
12. Trenton *True American*, Oct. 12, Nov. 2, 1818; Newark *Centinel*, Sept. 8, 1818.

lands just cause for complaint. War Federalist Isaac H. Williamson, with the imprimatur of the Essex legislative contingent, was elected governor in 1817, to the chagrin of many long-time Republicans. As late as 1820, Essex Republicans elected an avowed Federalist to the Assembly. A Republican, objecting to that choice, proclaimed that "the Federal Counties stick to their men—they select federalists—and don't yield an inch but where they are compelled to do it." If the Federalists were through as a party, those remaining in Essex had not been told about it. Henry Southard, an old Republican war horse from Somerset County, commented on the Federalist resurgence: "There has been as much Intrigue carried on in the county of Essex as in any county in the state."[13]

Although the Essex Republican party was broken by constant internal division and subjected to the final indignity of Federalist infiltration, it never flagged when it came time to elect a favorite candidate to office. In the weeks preceding an election, active party members worked hard to aid the man of their choice. More often than not, the local activists helped to defeat another Republican, but this did not dim their enthusiasm or blight their ingenuity.

The use of printed tickets in Essex County was quite common. A Republican meeting in 1814 recommended to "the different townships the use of printed tickets with the Congressional Candidates thereon, and blanks left sufficient for adding the Members for Council and Assembly."[14] In 1817, "the mystery of electioneering," in the words of one disgruntled soul, was uncovered: "Tickets may be had on favourable terms, hot from the desk, to suit any candidate in the County."[15]

Personal appeals to the electorate by the candidates had also become accepted practice by 1817. Squire Burnett, Newark's perennial post-war candidate for sheriff and a master of

13. Henry Southard to Ebenezer Elmer, Jan. 25, 1819, Gratz Collection, Hist. Soc. of Pa.; Newark *Centinel*, Oct.-Nov., 1817, Sept. 19, Oct. 10, 1820; Trenton *True American*, Oct. 12, 1818.

14. Newark *Centinel*, Oct. 4, 1814.

15. *Ibid.*, Sept. 30, 1817.

the art of electioneering, was denounced for "pretending and giving . . . speeches." His handbills were well known "at almost every corner, post and tree in town." Burnett was tagged with the nickname of the "Spouter," in recognition of his propensity in that direction. One critic summed up Burnett's talents: "Is there a sign post in the County that has not been decorated with handbills for your information, or a bar room that has not trembled beneath the martial strides and re-echoed to the sonorous voice of the spouter aforesaid?"[16]

The collapse of the party's machinery after the War of 1812 did not dim the imaginations of vote seekers. Indeed, the earlier development of that machinery had helped to originate these electioneering practices. By 1821, charges of "side street deals" were bandied about in the newspapers. Candidates, drawing a lesson from a more formative period, built personal machines. They used their aides to "sound the bottom of their strength in the county, by which means they are enabled to know the probable result of the Elections before they take place; and if their Election appears doubtful, they can decline in time to help secure the election of their favourite." This practice was known in Essex as "playing into each others hands." Friends of the candidate attended "the polls of other townships for the purpose of soliciting the votes of the honest and unsuspecting class of the community in favor of their favourite candidate."[17]

Essex County offered the clearest example of the political tribulations of a one-party county. Disputes between towns and regions within the county and clashes between leading Republican politicians resulted in the early demoralization of party machinery as well as Federalist infiltration of the crumbling organization. Yet Essex was the earliest and always the greatest Republican stronghold. Time and again, it provided large Republican pluralities to aid the state ticket. Its party men also introduced important innovations in the techniques of

16. *Ibid.*, Oct. 8, 1816, Sept. 30, 1817, Oct. 12, 1819.
17. *Ibid.*, Oct. 16, Nov. 20, 1821.

winning elections. In this sense, while party machinery may have disintegrated, the efforts to construct that machine were not wasted.

Old disagreements revived anew, combining with new sources of unrest, contributed to the appearance of much the same malady in Sussex County's Republican organization that plagued the Essex interest. Nominating meetings after 1812 reverted to the days of August Court in Sussex, providing a basis for disagreement once again.[18] In 1815, mounting dissatisfaction with the county meeting was once again brought sharply into focus. The 1815 election campaign opened with a concerted Federalist attack on the "caucus system." It drew sympathy from many disgruntled Republicans who ignored Republican regulars' warnings to avoid participating in a "federal jockey race," thus subjecting the county meeting—the bastion of Republicanism, it was alleged—to a "stamp of infamy." At the root of existing Republican disaffection was, once again, the disillusionment of some Republican farmers with "men of influence" who were purported to control the party machinery—especially at August Court. Any "who could get their names upon this caucus ticket," one unhappy Republican disclosed, "think themselves elected as safely and surely as if the election were passed . . . and truly they may, calculating on past experience, for the caucus ticket has uniformly succeeded these fifteen years past."[19]

The remedy, according to a number of Republicans in 1815, was to form a "combination ticket" like the earlier division slate. This was done. One regular organization Republican implored the Republican candidates on the combination ticket to resign their candidacies and not "become a foundation stone to a schism that may burst asunder the strong ties of Republican feeling." The *Centinel* perceived editorially that the effort was motivated by the obvious opportunism of "the friends of

18. Newark *Centinel*, Aug. 31, 1813; Trenton *True American*, Aug. 9, 1814.
19. Newton *Sussex Register*, Sept. 25, 1815, Oct. 6, 1823; Newark *Centinel*, Sept. 26, 1815.

peace."[20] Despite many dire predictions, the maverick slate remained in the field; one of its number, a Republican, captured the sheriff's office, providing encouragement to "quid" supporters, as they were still called.[21]

The Republican break persisted in 1816, and this time the entire regular Republican ticket went down to defeat. Two Federalists were elected to the legislature on the combination ticket. A similar loss occurred in 1817.[22] The epitaph for the party organization was written in 1818; the *True American* noted that "no county ticket has been regularly agreed on; and it is probable federalists will obtain one or more members." The object lesson was clear: "put down caucuses, and the door is thrown open to Federalists."[23] If the Federalists were through nationally and lacked even statewide cohesion in New Jersey, it was nevertheless clear that they were busily changing the rules of party warfare in some counties.[24]

Centrally located Hunterdon County's Republican party, still ruled with an iron hand by James J. Wilson, also experienced its share of difficulties during the war and post-war periods. Because that county organization was so solidly structured and unequivocally led, however, it was able to survive intact pressures similar to those so effectively applied to local interests in North Jersey. Once again, at the root of the internal dissensions that gave rise to these stresses was the understanding that the Federalist threat was fading, and that Republicans could thus afford the luxury of organizational laxity that inevitably led to familial unrest.

The first major assault against the Wilson machine was mounted in 1813. A number of Republicans tried to restore the long discarded county delegate nominating convention in order to prevent "artful intriguers [Wilson, *et al.*], supported

20. Newark *Centinel*, Sept. 19, 26, 1815.
21. *Ibid.*, Oct. 24, 1815.
22. *Ibid.*, Oct. 22, 1816; Newton *Sussex Register*, Sept. 29, 1817.
23. Trenton *True American*, Oct. 12, 1818.
24. For a description of Federalist party machinery and tactics in the states in this period, see Shaw Livermore, Jr., *The Twilight of Federalism: The Disintegration of the Federalist Party, 1815-1830* (Princeton, 1962).

by strong pecuniary resources" from bringing their adherents to the now traditional and institutionalized open county meeting at Flemington at their own expense, thereby insuring a majority for the machine. The attempt failed, and the county nominating meeting remained true to the form inaugurated in 1804.[25]

Another attack on the county machine was launched in 1817. Justification for this effort rested on the fact that Federalist competition in Hunterdon had temporarily abated in 1816. Typical of Republican attitudes prevalent in other New Jersey counties at this time, many party men lamented that, inasmuch as "the power of Federalism is annihilated . . . Republicans [should be] restored to their liberty of choice." Wilson defended the county organization, pointing out that "we cannot consent to abandon a system which has saved us in seasons of imminent danger."[26] Senator Wilson proved strong enough once again to stem the attack, although similar assaults were scuttling other Republican county organizations at this time. The Independents of 1817, as they styled themselves, made "great exertions" with the help of the Federalists, who "pretty generally joined them."[27] Although the merged enemies of the organization made the strongest bid yet to unseat it, they went down to defeat. Wilson himself had no small part in ending the challenge, and he exacted his toll on those Republicans who thwarted his leadership: "Poor Reuben D. Tucker [the Independents' leader] is almost to be pitied. His disasters came upon him in a cluster. He failed in his attempt to get into the Assembly, of which he was very confident—he has been turned out of the bank direction and will be dismissed as prosecutor for the banks. And, on attempting to get the [state] Attorney-General's office, did not obtain a single [legis-

25. Trenton *True American*, June 21, July 19, Aug.-Oct., 1813, *passim*.
26. *Ibid.*, Aug. 25, Sept. 22, Oct. 13, Nov., 1817; James J. Wilson to William Darlington, Aug. 26, 1817, Darlington Papers, Lib. Cong.; Samuel L. Southard to William S. Pennington, Aug. 11, 1818, Southard Papers, Princeton Univ. Lib.
27. James J. Wilson to William Darlington, Nov. 13, 1817, Darlington Papers, Lib. Cong.

lative] vote! So mote it ever be with those who . . . league with Federalists."[28] Wilson never let a political enemy go unpunished.

The 1817 attempt to undermine the Hunterdon Republican party was not unwarranted. Wilson, according to one hostile observer who expressed the feelings of many, ruled with a heavy hand, "and any who ventures to exercise his own judgement and vote different from the caucus nomination, will of course, be politically proscribed." This critic was even more candid in describing the scene at election time: "You are called on to come at the elections and act your part in the puppet show." The democratic facade of the county meeting, he maintained, did not alter the realization by a growing number of Republicans that the "election is already made while the principal actors are behind the curtain and pull the wire, so that each voter is mechanically fixed to vote, as the great master of the show may think fit."[29] There was no doubt about the identity of the great master.

The minority Republican faction made a final attempt to undermine the county meeting in 1819. Early in the year a group of Republicans discussed the possibility of abolishing the open county meeting and substituting a meeting of delegates elected on the basis of proportional representation. The ticket would be selected by representatives from the townships, the number of delegates per town to be determined "in proportion to the number of votes cast in the last election in each town." This effort came to naught, as had its predecessors.[30]

The county nominating meeting, if the *True American's* reports were accurate, had indeed grown unwieldy. From over three hundred delegates on an average by 1810, the number grew to about five hundred in 1815. Thereafter, the press of participants steadily increased, until, by 1818, almost a thou-

28. *Ibid.*
29. Trenton *True American*, Aug. 24, Sept. 28, Dec. 21, 1818.
30. *Ibid.*, Feb. 15, 1819; James J. Wilson to William Darlington, Oct. 20, 1818, Darlington Papers, Lib. Cong.

sand persons were reported to have attended.[31] There were approximately 5,500 eligible voters in Hunterdon County in 1818.[32] It appears, then, that about 18 per cent of the eligible voters in the county were active participants in Republican nominations at that point. No wonder the county meeting remained the cornerstone of the Republican organization and continued to hold sway as the nominating apparatus in Hunterdon until 1826, when the Democratic-Republican party in New Jersey finally passed from existence.

Hunterdon Republicans were at least as ingenious as their eastern neighbors in bringing voters to the polls. The county association organized in 1803 was an especially good engine for the task. Each adherent was enjoined to "disseminate correct information on public affairs among his fellow citizens."[33] Soon after its founding, the association was "very animated[ly] preparing to meet with every possible advantage, the next electioneering struggle."[34] At an early date party men pledged that "we will unanimously support, by all honest, honorable and constitutional means, the ticket that may be agreed upon by the present meeting."[35] A typical pre-election injunction emphasized that "it is the duty of the Republicans in every township . . . to organize themselves in such manner, that every Republican elector may appear at the poll."[36] It could be depended on, right down to the very end of the Republican era, that successful candidates in Hunterdon County were "very hard run."[37]

Getting out the vote was a particularly important task at the local level. Township associations were expected to meet

31. Trenton *True American*, Sept. 8, 1806, Sept. 5, 1808, Sept. 9, 1811, Sept. 11, 1815, Sept. 14, 1818. In 1819, about eight hundred men were reputed to have attended the county meeting. See J. J. Manners to Samuel L. Southard, Oct. 12, 1819, Southard Papers, Princeton Univ. Lib.

32. Worked out from the *Census for 1820* (Washington, D.C., 1821). Reprint of a return originally found in the American Antiquarian Society.

33. Trenton *True American*, Jan. 17, 1803.

34. Newark *Centinel*, Feb. 1, 1803.

35. Trenton *True American*, Sept. 5, 1803.

36. *Ibid.*, Aug. 15, 1808.

37. New Brunswick *Fredonian*, Sept. 4, 1823.

before each canvass to choose standing committees. If they did their jobs properly, these electioneering committees spurred on their comrades to "let not . . . *one vote* be lost—let every care be taken to urge to the poll every one who is well disposed to our Republican institutions. . . . Please to communicate these ideas to your Republican neighbors and fellow citizens."[38] That electioneering was essentially a local responsibility cannot be doubted. In 1813, Republican activists were reminded that "those who would support our ticket [should] meet at the usual places within their townships, at 2 o'clock, P.M. of the Saturday preceding the election, to make such arrangements as may be deemed most necessary and useful."[39]

Probably the best organized township in the county in a single given year was Hopewell in 1813. The town was "laid out in four districts, [and] a committee of vigilance consisting of eight persons [was] appointed to serve in each district, and the said Committee are . . . earnestly requested to use all fair and honorable means to induce their fellow citizens . . . to appear at the polls."[40] Trenton, however, took the honors for local electioneering year in and year out. The township association met annually to form campaign committees. These could be counted on regularly "to take measures for giving a full support to the Republican Ticket." When the canvas promised to be close, they really extended themselves. Each worker in town in 1815 was admonished not to "let one hour of the next forty-eight [the duration of the election] be lost. Let every minute, not necessary to sleep and refreshment, be employed to secure the election." Right down to the 1820's Republicans in Trenton employed "all due diligence" in supporting the county Republican ticket.[41] With local activities of this sort

38. Trenton *True American*, Oct. 26, 1807. See also *ibid.*, July 29, 1805, Sept. 8, 1806, Sept. 16, 1809; Newark *Centinel*, Aug. 9, 1808; James Linn to Ebenezer Elmer, Jan. 3, 1803, Gratz Collection, Hist. Soc. of Pa.

39. Trenton *True American*, Sept. 20, 1813.

40. *Ibid.*, Sept. 27, 1813.

41. *Ibid.*, Oct. 6, 1806, Oct. 26, 1807, Oct. 8, 1810, Oct. 3, 1814, Oct. 2, 9, 1815, Aug. 9, 1819, Oct. 5, 1822, Aug. 2, 1823; New Brunswick *Guardian*, Jan. 7, 1813; Trenton *Federalist*, Oct. 5, 1812.

a commonplace, it is no wonder, as William N. Chambers has so aptly noted, that "Jefferson's party became the archetype of a modern popular party."[42]

Neighboring Middlesex differed from Hunterdon in several respects: first, the Republicans lost in the former county as consistently as Hunterdon Republicans won; second, although the Fitz Randolph clan dominated the party organization after 1811, it did not do so as successfully and completely as Wilson did his bailiwick; finally, as we have seen already, the cornerstone of the county apparatus—the nominating machinery—was of the township delegate variety, and thus it differed fundamentally from Hunterdon's open county meeting. In several other respects, however, strong similarities are evident. Local organization, for example, was fully as complete in Middlesex as in the adjacent county; moreover, if the Fitz Randolphs did not fare so well as Wilson, they succeeded well enough to dominate the county organization until it weakened and fell apart beginning in 1817.

The Fitz Randolphs' claim to authority in Middlesex County was strikingly similar to that of James J. Wilson—in both counties editorial control of the local Republican paper was the keystone in the exercise of organizational power. The New Brunswick *Fredonian*, founded in 1811, was published thereafter by one or the other of Lewis Fitz Randolph's two sons, David and James. The isolated Republican triumph in 1811 boosted the family's political stock, and they took an increasingly active part in county affairs after that date. Robert Lee of Woodbridge, indeed, writing retrospectively in the *Centinel* under the pseudonym "Franklin," accused the Fitz Randolphs and their allies of manipulating the county organization. Like so many Republican printers, Lee averred, the Fitz Randolphs collected lucrative federal and state offices like the notaryship of the state bank at New Brunswick, the postmastership of New Brunswick, and the collectorship of the port of Perth Amboy,

42. William N. Chambers, *Political Parties in a New Nation*, foreword.

one of the most desirable political sinecures in the state.[43] William Tuttle, the editor of the *Centinel*, by publishing "Franklin" also injected himself into the controversy with the Fitz Randolphs. Accused of fomenting trouble in the party, Tuttle responded by denouncing his brother Republican printer for having become corrupted by the "effect of holding two snug offices." The Newark editor reminded his readers that "numbers of Republicans . . . [Lee included] have labored and tolied [toiled] before . . . James or David Fitz Randolph knew the county [Middlesex] . . . without ever receiving office, recompence, or reward."[44]

The leadership conflict between the Fitz Randolphs and Robert Lee, and the organizational difficulties growing out of it, was the most enduring internal weakness plaguing Middlesex Republicanism. Lee's political leverage emanated from Woodbridge Township, whose Republican party organization he dominated. No other New Jersey community matched Woodbridge for the zeal it exhibited during the Republican era; in a moment of exaggeration, and in more harmonious days, the *Fredonian* had labeled Woodbridge "without exception the most Republican district on earth."[45] Under Robert Lee's auspices, its Republican party was certainly the best township organization in the county and perhaps the state. However, the Woodbridge Republicans fed on controversy. Their political antics made the town at once the scandal and envy of every Republican center in New Jersey. For example, in the early summer of 1808, when many were guessing about the motives and intentions of George Clinton, Woodbridge presumptuously sent a committee (all expenses paid) to New

43. Newark *Centinel*, Sept. 19, 1820; Trenton *True American*, Sept. 23, 1820; James Fitz Randolph to Samuel L. Southard, Jan. 19, 1818, Southard Papers, Princeton Univ. Lib.

44. Newark *Centinel*, Sept. 26, 1820, June 26, 1821; New Brunswick *Fredonian*, Aug. 16, 1821; Trenton *True American*, Oct. 20, 1821. For a fine example of the Fitz Randolphs' ability to throw their weight around in patronage matters, see J. F. Randolph to Samuel L. Southard, Jan. 19, 1818, Sept. 5, 1816, Southard Papers, Princeton Univ. Lib.

45. New Brunswick *Fredonian*, Sept. 4, 1812.

York to ascertain whether Clinton would accept the vice-presidential spot on Madison's ticket.[46] It is doubtful if the committee even saw Clinton, for no answer was recorded.

Accordingly, the town was viewed as the black sheep of Middlesex Republicanism, but one that could not be dispensed with. "Woodbridge, of whose remissness you have sometimes complained, will this year do its duty," the *True American* announced in 1811. "That patriotic township will pour its hundreds to the poll, and give an almost unanimous vote for the Republican candidates."[47] Six months later, however, township Republicans attacked fellow party men in Middlesex for passively permitting the appointment of Federalists to the recently chartered state bank at New Brunswick. The pressure that Woodbridge applied helped to extend existing differences in the party and in a small way contributed to the Republican loss in 1812.[48]

The War of 1812 had dominated political discussion all over New Jersey. But Woodbridge Republicans went just a little further than any other town in demonstrating their patriotism. The town meeting appointed a "committee of ten of the most aged and respectable inhabitants," who were authorized to "make out a list of all those persons who, during the Revolution, were tories, and who are now federalists."[49] Woodbridge was one of three Middlesex towns to send their own delegates to the extraordinary Republican state convention at Burlington in July 1812.[50] The following April, a special township meeting was convened "to take into consideration the importance and necessity of forming an active and vigilant union, for the purpose of defending the Republicans against the attacks of external enemies, and internal foes."[51] The Republican

46. Newark *Centinel*, Nov. 1, 1808.
47. Trenton *True American*, Oct. 7, 1811.
48. Newark *Centinel*, Mar. 10, 1812.
49. *Ibid.*; New Brunswick *Fredonian*, Sept. 4, 1812.
50. Trenton *True American*, June 22, 1812.
51. *Ibid.*, Apr. 19, 1813.

party in Woodbridge, in short, convened at the slightest provocation.

Woodbridge party men were no less diligent in getting out the vote. In the canvass of 1808, the town was divided by the annual meeting into seven districts, with committees circulating in each area. Fifty men were employed to "superintend affairs relative to the approaching election," and to communicate with other towns in Middlesex County to "prepare [and] superintend the printing of, and distribut[ion] of . . . handbills and addresses to the electors of the county." The secretary of the committee was especially charged to "urge them [committee members] to the performance of the duties assigned them, particularly in bringing forward Republican Electors." On election day, committeemen in Woodbridge "distributed tickets and . . . attend[ed] the polls to keep illegal voters from voting."[52] A similar thoroughness was exhibited as late as 1819, when the town was divided into thirty election districts, with one person in each district responsible for turning out the vote in his section.[53] Following this election, Woodbridge Republicans tried to arrest the disintegration of the county organization by appointing a committee of fifteen to "visit all other townships of this county" in order to supervise a reformation of local organization based on the example Woodbridge provided.[54] Republicans from the town often were impatient with less skilled and less organized colleagues from other Middlesex towns.

Robert Lee was the individual who most often expressed this impatience. He did not reach the innermost chambers of party leadership in the county or state because he was not trusted by most party managers, yet he remained the town's leading Jeffersonian from the beginning until the end of the Republican period. It is difficult to imagine that the moving force behind the well organized, productive, and zealous Wood-

52. Newark *Centinel*, Sept. 20, 1808.
53. Trenton *True American*, Nov. 1, 1819.
54. *Ibid.*

bridge Republicans should never advance beyond his local position in the Democratic-Republican era, but this was the case. Like many another relatively unknown local leader among the state's Jeffersonians, Lee was to remain politically quarantined by his own party. Unlike most, however, Robert Lee did not long remain anonymous.

It was somehow fitting that the erratic town of Woodbridge should produce the "Don Quixote" of New Jersey Republican politics. The wealthy, eccentric, and dedicated Lee was forever tilting at political windmills. In his one and only early stint in the legislature, in 1811, he singlehandedly battled the Republican caucus on the bank question, until Mahlon Dickerson was moved to comment in disgust that Republicanism generally and the bank caucus particularly was "plagued with Robert Lee."[55] In 1815, ambitious for recognition and influence on the state level, Lee undertook an unsuccessful one-man crusade to repeal the state constitution and substitute for it one of his own making. He had an engraved form letter printed embodying the changes he wanted in the constitution and, at his own expense, mailed it to every Republican of any importance in the state.[56]

Lee wanted mightily to do more, but he was unable to gain election to the legislature after 1811, due to "deep intrigue, gross deception and base corruption," as he put it.[57] Woodbridge Republicans, in 1820, sought a place for Lee on the Republican congressional ticket, but failed again.[58] Two years later, his long-suffering Woodbridge supporters petitioned to gain an Assembly nomination for their hero. Lee was, they reminded Middlesex party men, "known to the county and the State for nearly twenty years as the firm, inflexible, undeviating supporter of the Republican cause and party." Once again he was left off the ballot.[59]

55. Diary of Mahlon Dickerson, Oct. 31, 1811, N.J. Hist. Soc.
56. Robert Lee to Mahlon Dickerson, Dec. 25, 1815, Mahlon Dickerson Papers, N.J. Hist. Soc.; Trenton *True American*, Nov. 1, 1819.
57. Trenton *True American*, Dec. 28, 1818.
58. Newark *Centinel*, Sept. 19, 1820.
59. Trenton *True American*, Aug. 17, Oct. 5, 1822.

The reason for bypassing Lee time and again was painfully clear even to Lee himself. He attacked anyone who disagreed with him, whether Republican or Federalist. His diatribes which appeared in the newspapers of New Jersey under the pseudonyms "Franklin" or "Sidney" always made colorful reading. Republican editors, with an eye to circulation if not to party unity, were glad to print them. In 1820, for example, Lee outraged the leaders of the Republican party by publishing an open letter to a leading Monmouth County Republican, asking him to lay his political cards on the table and announce who he was going to have nominated for Congress at the coming state convention. On other occasions, as we have seen, he openly broke with the Fitz Randolphs over the conduct of Middlesex County politics.[60] Such frankness was not well received by those who wanted to maintain the democratic facade of the party's structure.

To his friends and supporters in his home town of Woodbridge, Robert Lee was "the best political friend they ever had." Despite the attacks and ridicule to which he was subjected, the Republicans of the town more than once expressed their "undiminished confidence in the talents, integrity and patriotism of Robert Lee esq., as evinced by twenty years of steady devotion to, and support of, the Republican cause and party."[61] To his more moderate critics, Lee may have appeared a "little visionary or vain."[62] To his enemies, of whom there were many, he was "a little vain man, famous for manufacturing Constitutions and memorials, [who] has . . . all the bitterness and gall of disappointed ambition."[63] Loved or hated, he was never ignored. Robert Lee perhaps typified in the extreme those qualities that made Republicans strive to perfect the Middlesex organization and win the county, even in the face of repeated failures.

60. *Ibid.*, Sept. 23, 1820. See also *ibid.*, Dec. 28, 1818, June 29, 1819, Aug. 17, 28, Sept. 23, 1820, Oct. 20, 1821; Newark *Centinel*, Sept. 19, 26, 1820, June 26, 1821; New Brunswick *Fredonian*, Sept. 21, 1820, Aug. 16, 1821.
61. Trenton *True American*, Aug. 14, 28, 1820, Oct. 5, 12, 1822.
62. Newark *Centinel*, Sept. 19, 1820.
63. New Brunswick *Fredonian*, Sept. 21, 1820.

The cleavage in party ranks occasioned by the growing animosity between the Fitz Randolphs and Robert Lee contributed to the slow disintegration of Republican machinery after 1817. Between 1817 and 1820, too, the backbone of Federalism was broken. The need for a tight organization, anchored by an exceptionally stable county delegate convention, diminished accordingly in the eyes of its adherents. Thus, the convention as a party vehicle deteriorated after 1817, never to regain its former vigor. By 1820, torn by internal disputes, the organization generally was in a shambles, a situation on the county level all too familiar by that time to New Jersey Republicans.[64]

Republicans in Burlington County in South Jersey faced even dimmer long-term prospects than their Middlesex brethren with regard to surmounting enduring Federalist domination. A strong and original countywide Republican party machine, though it performed smoothly and well, did little in the long run to succor long-standing Jeffersonian hopes that Federalist strength in the county would "dwindle into insignificance"; even the most stubborn Republicans grew discouraged at the string of defeats that followed their efforts.[65] After many years of unremitting effort, the first cracks in the Republican armor in the county manifested themselves in the terse message that "no Republican Ticket will be run" in 1810. Again, in 1811, the Republican county meeting formed no ticket. The War of 1812 rekindled Republican enthusiasm and efforts, but to no avail. The Burlington association never cracked this Federalist stronghold, although it sporadically continued to try.[66]

Federalism in Burlington showed signs of weakening only after 1815, but by then the Democratic Association was itself too spent to enter the breach. Other county organizations were

64. Trenton *True American*, Sept. 23, 30, 1820, Oct. 20, 1821; New Brunswick *Fredonian*, Aug. 16, Sept. 1, Oct. 4, 20, 1821.

65. Trenton *True American*, Oct. 5, 1807, Sept. 5, 1808. See Table I, pp. 76-78.

66. Trenton *True American*, Sept. 10, 1810, Sept. 9, 1811, Sept. 7, 1812, Aug. 16, 1814, Aug. 28, 1815.

falling apart at the beginning of the "Era of Good Feelings," and the Burlington party met the same fate. It was too well structured to disappear entirely, but it lost its hegemony over the local Republican interest. In a final effort to retain control, the traditional association county meeting was opened in 1815 not only to members, but to all Republicans in the county. This was a sure sign, given earlier tight organization throughout most of South Jersey, that the local Republican structure was growing shaky. It was too late to attempt to broaden Republican responsibility in the county from within the organization, however, because the association was too reminiscent of earlier, more vigorous party strife; when the Federalists, as usual, swept the local elections in 1815, initiative passed from the hands of the association to an independent Republican movement bent on merging with the Federalists in order to form a ticket that would best look after Burlington's interests in the legislature. The more militant association nevertheless remained active in Burlington politics at least through 1820, although but a shadow of its former self. When the Federalists were finally compromised, the independent Republicans in the county were primarily responsible. The association, or what remained of it, probably supported the union forces that in 1817 joined with a part of the Federalist interest. In Burlington, at least, this latter development could be considered a victory for the old Jeffersonians—and it was the associators who had so ably laid the groundwork.[67]

Issues and Elections

Statewide politics from 1812 through 1816 were in many ways an anticlimax to the previous period. Republican victories in the counties, and the consequent return of the state

67. *Ibid.*, Aug. 28, 1815, Aug. 12, 1816, Aug. 24, 1818, Aug. 21, 1820. For the evolution of the union ticket—a combined slate of Republicans and Federalists—which eventually defeated the Federalists in 1820, see Anon., *To the Independent Electors of the County of Burlington* (n.p., Oct. 9, 1817), N.J. Pamphlets Collection, Rutgers Univ. Lib.; Assembly Minutes Papers, No. 1930, N.J. State Lib.; James J. Wilson to William Darlington, Oct. 23, 1820, Dar-

legislature to Republican hands in 1813, forecast the more general sweep that followed a year later. Tensions eased as the war continued, for the old issues grew rather tired with age; it was difficult, in short, to sustain the popular party enthusiasm that characterized an earlier era. Party adherence (at least among Republicans) sagged and did not long survive the end of war in any original or meaningful sense.

Foreign affairs continued to dominate party electioneering after the outbreak of war. The Republican party, striving to regain control of the pivotal counties that it had lost in 1812, and given pause by the embarrassing legislative defeat of that year, was wise enough to modify its appeal to the public. In 1813, therefore, Republicans projected themselves as the true peace men. The public was warned that "there is no way of obtaining an Honourable Peace but by a Vigorous War." This approach was best exemplified by the militant mastheads borne aloft by local Republican tickets: "Free Trade and no Impressment!" "Free Trade and Sailors' Rights!" "Don't Give Up the Ship!" "An Honourable and Equitable Peace!" The self-styled "Real Peace Tickets" still utilized the slogans of war, even in local contests. No statewide contest complicated the political situation, and these local appeals sufficed; the Republicans regained control of the legislature in 1813—they would never again lose it—by holding the solid Republican locales and winning back such counties as Hunterdon, Bergen, and Monmouth.[68]

Martial appeals were less in evidence a year later. Numerous references still appeared to our "war with a powerful nation," and venomous gestures were directed at "pretended peacemen," to be sure, but a new thrust was added to the fading war issues in 1814. Republicans were cautioned patriotically by the *Centinel*: "Many of our fellow-citizens are absent,

---

lington Papers, Lib. Cong.; *Town Meeting*, Oct. 9, 1820, N.J. Political Broadsides Collection, Rutgers Univ. Lib.; Trenton *True American*, Oct. 12, 19, 1818, Sept. 21, 1822, Aug. 30, 1823.

68. Trenton *True American*, Sept. 20, 27, Oct. 4, 11, 18, 1813.

doing military duty [on the Jersey coast]—and . . . double exertions will be necessary from those who remain at home [during elections]." A week later the same sheet clarified this point for its readers: "Nearly 5,000 of our fellow-citizens are from home doing military duty; and it is apprehended a vast majority of these are republicans."[69] Republicans, presumably, had finally cornered the patriotic market.

Hand in hand with the implied superiority of Republican contributions to the war effort went a kindred tongue-in-cheek generosity to their allegedly less loyal opponents. At the biennial state convention this new image was projected in a forceful address to the electorate: "Our political opponents call themselves the Friends of Peace;—we are willing to give many of them credit for the sincerity of their professions; but we also claim this credit for ourselves."[70] Gone were the fiery attacks and the offensive denouncements of Federalist aristocracy. The "solemnity of the crisis" was emphasized, but, because of the crisis, the Republican address averred, "[we] must be mild and conciliating. This is not the moment to excite the angry passions of party." The moderates of all parties were invited to compare the Republican pronouncement with that published "by the self styled Friends of Peace." The vitriolic Federalist presentation indicated that the Federalists had been caught by surprise. The Republican document, which was widely broadcast, was accurately described as one of "moderation, liberality, and an evident desire to shackle the fury of party spirit."[71] The Republicans sought to reoccupy completely the middle ground they had lost in 1812.

Despite the obvious politicking involved in the Republicans' taking this line, there was, in retrospect, a deeper implication to the appeals for moderation. The velvet glove in the

69. Newark *Centinel*, Aug. 23, Sept. 20, 27, 1814. See also the Trenton *True Amercian*, July 25, Oct. 10, 1814.

70. Newark *Centinel*, Aug. 16, Sept. 20, 27, 1814; Trenton *True American*, Sept. 19, 1814. The 1814 ticket included Thomas Ward, Lewis Condict, Henry Southard, Benjamin Bennet, Ezra Baker, and Ephraim Bateman.

71. Newark *Centinel*, Sept. 27, Oct. 4, 1814; Trenton *True American*, Sept. 19, 26, 1814.

shape of a grudging Republican admission that the Federalists after all also meant well for America was combined in 1814 with a touch of the mailed fist as well—witness the bellicose mastheads. The Republican party in New Jersey, apparently without comprehending the change, was less ideological than it had ever been in the past. This was the mark of a party in transition. A general reading of the 1814 Republican newspapers indicates that, with the passing of the banking crisis, ideological differences, such as they were, diminished. These differences may have been more apparent than real to begin with. It is certain in any event that the political scars engendered by Hamiltonian Federalism first and the choice of conflict between England and France (with heavy-laden ideological distinctions implicit in that choice) subsequently, healed rapidly when the issues relating to them faded from public consciousness.[72]

Apathy was one of the problems which, it is evident, the Republicans had not anticipated would arise from their half-hearted conciliation of the Federalists. If the old distinctions between parties were passing, there were few new ones to replace them. As a result, as one Republican press observed, there was "very great apathy in the Republican party" during the 1814 campaign. "Very little is said about it [the election], and still less done to prepare for it," the *Centinel* complained. At present, that paper concluded, "there is . . . great confidence in the Republican ranks."[73] The Republican effort to work both sides of the street in 1814 almost backfired as a result. The party barely eked out a close congressional victory, com-

72. Some feeling exists that what to twentieth-century readers seems to be extreme language was not so extreme to readers of the same material in the eighteenth and early nineteenth centuries. Such terms as "swinish multitude," "aristocratic gentlemen," and perhaps even "traitor," might have meant less to that generation than the terms mean to us. See, for example, Richard Hofstadter, *The American Political Tradition and the Men Who Made It*, 2nd ed. (N.Y., 1954), 29n. See particularly the discussion of these terms which, Forrest McDonald said, Charles Beard took literally, in McDonald's *We the People: The Economic Origins of the Constitution* (N.Y., 1958), 15-16.

73. Newark *Centinel*, Sept. 17, Oct. 11, and *passim*, 1814; Trenton *True American*, Oct. 3, and *passim*, 1814.

pleting the return to power begun in 1813.[74] Just as the Federalists never again would dominate a New Jersey legislature, so they never again would elect a congressman in the state. If ideological distinctions were passing, so was organized statewide Federalism.

The political torpor deepened in 1815. Foreign policy issues in New Jersey all but disappeared with the return of peace. Republicans were still reminded of the late hostilities by occasional slogans appearing at the tops of their local tickets; however, these were no longer militant. The most prominent new addition read: "We Have Met the Enemy and They Are Ours"—not necessarily true, but good political propaganda nevertheless. Republicans emphasized the merit of cooperating with the government now that the war was over; party men were reminded that the Republicans had been responsible for pursuing and "winning" peace, fighting honorably, and reducing taxes and the national debt.[75]

Even the *Centinel*, which had expressed misgivings about the lackadaisical attitude of the previous year, was sanguine in 1815: "We apprehend [Federalist] expectations are a kind of forlorn hope." The Republicans merely reminded Jerseymen that "we anticipate a stronger expression of republican principles at the approaching election than in past years. It will be increased by the general prosperity and confidence which our foreign and domestic affairs inspire." Periodic allusions to past issues did not overcome this sense of certainty. The Newark paper expressed what might be considered a valedictory for popular party differences: "Now the circumstances of the country are changed. The storm is overpast. The sun of prosperity appears; and public confidence re-animates the feelings of the nation. Should this state of prosperity continue, republican principles will advance—and as they ad-

74. Congressional election returns showed the Republicans triumphant with 17,859 votes to 16,697 for the Federalists—the last close election in a general canvass during the Republican era. See the Trenton *True American*, Oct. 24, 1814.

75. Trenton *True American*, Sept. 11, 25, Oct. 9, 1815.

vance—so will be the decline of federalism."[76] The *True American* cautiously waited a year; but, in 1816, Wilson also joined in tolling the end of popular party distinctions. In announcing that the Federalists would not contest either the presidential or congressional elections, Wilson editorialized: "Federalism . . . is in a hopeless condition in this State. We think the federalists have chosen the wisest course: they save themselves from the mortification of a probable defeat."[77] Federalism continued to exist locally, but political conflict after 1815 lost its sharpness and clarity.

The presidential and congressional campaigns of 1816 were anticlimactic; they appeared pallid compared to earlier party strife. Presidential politicking, such as it was, existed entirely on the Republican side, for no known Federalist opposition to James Monroe developed in New Jersey. The Federalists, the Republicans admitted, "have abandoned the ground." The *True American* cautioned, however, that "it is not safe to trust the presumption that they will be idle." Justification for this alarm was found in the immediate past. It was necessary to turn out for the legislative elections, so that the "power usurped from the people four years ago" could not be usurped again. "As they [the Federalists] have candidates [Rufus King for president] on nomination, the safest course for Republicans is to go to the polls and vote."[78] Among the admittedly scant allusions to the presidential contest in the press, it is surprising that no reference to James Monroe can be uncovered.

The state convention convened at Major Andrews' Inn at Trenton on September 26, 1816, to select congressional and presidential slates. Aaron Munn was designated chairman for the third time. Reports of the convention were brief. The address itself reflected the political equanimity that had settled on New Jersey since the end of the war. "Your Convention again addresses you," it began, "under auspices infinitely more

76. Newark *Centinel*, Sept. 12, 19, and *passim*, 1815.
77. Trenton *True American*, Sept. 23, 1816.
78. Trenton *True American*, Nov. 13, 1815, Oct. 7, 28, 1816.

favorable than when we last assembled." The end of the war also signaled the end of statewide party contests. Republican certainty was marred only by an evident concern about the state of local party machinery. Republicans were reminded of the "high importance of attending . . . county meetings," for America, as the last bastion of freedom against the return of European tyranny, was obligated to preserve its democratic institutions. The convention itself, Republicans were reminded, was proof of that democracy: "It is a pleasing presage of the future success and high standing of the Republican party in this state, to observe the numerous delegation appointed, and general attendance of members to the Convention."[79] By 1816, then, party battles were fought only in some counties. Stirrings of the old vigor, however, were still evident in the legislature.

The Legislative Caucus

Contrary to the experience of other components of the Republican party machine, the caucus not only maintained its vitality, it actually expanded its role in party affairs after 1812. After the Federalist victory in 1812, it was the caucus that took hold and led the movement to revamp party structure to meet changing conditions. Meeting in caucus early in 1813, the legislators drafted a form letter that was printed and sent to every Republican of any importance in the state. These key men were "requested to aid the Republican cause, by furnishing essays, from time to time, on political subjects, for publication." These literary gems would be issued through the Republican press or as broadsides. The intensive and well organized propaganda campaign that followed continued through the year the Republicans remained a minority party. The Republicans in the caucus thus began to regain the initiative lost with the advent of war.[80]

79. *Ibid.*, Sept. 23, 30, 1816.
80. Benjamin Ludlow to Samuel L. Southard, Feb. 16, 1813, Southard Papers,

The same 1813 caucus turned to the task of regularizing and making more flexible the party's apparatus. The party's poor showing, when it attempted to adapt itself quickly to the new format of the congressional elections of 1812 imposed by the Federalists, called attention to the lack of uniformity of local Republican machinery and the party's consequent rigidity and inability to mesh when confronted with a new political situation. In an attempt to "produce union and energy of action at elections," the legislative caucus bade Republicans throughout New Jersey to establish Whig Societies. Each township was exhorted to form a unit. The township organizations would together constitute a countywide party group governed by a single complement of elected officers. The caucus learned from its experiences in 1812 that "uniformity, and one general system, is, on many accounts, desirable."[81]

Qualifications for membership in the local party group were easily fulfilled: only a "good moral character" and an attachment to Republican principles and the United States Constitution were necessary. The township societies could meet as often as required by circumstances at the instigation of their own local officers; the county societies were required to meet at least once every three months. The function of the parent organization was to "superintend the township societies, and afford them such aid as they may require." Once each year the county Whig Societies were to send delegates to a state convention. This general meeting would "recommend to the attention of the whig societies, such plans for promoting the Republican interest, as may appear proper." A committee of correspondence for each county unit also would be appointed

Princeton Univ. Lib.; Ludlow to Mahlon Dickerson, Feb. 16, 1813, Mahlon Dickerson Papers, N.J. Hist. Soc. Ludlow chaired the 1813 caucus that adopted the printed form letters, of which the above citations are examples.

81. *Whig Societies*, Feb. 1813, N.J. Political Broadsides Collection, Rutgers Univ. Lib. All Republican members of the legislature, apparently, participated in forwarding the scheme. See also Henry Southard to Samuel L. Southard, Nov. 2, 1813, Southard Papers, Princeton Univ. Lib.; Trenton *True American*, Sept. 26, Dec. 26, 1814.

to coordinate the activities of the societies throughout the year.[82]

The plan proposed by the caucus was logical on paper but too ambitious in reality. County Republican organizations were too set in their ways by 1813, and leadership and power too firmly rooted. Only Monmouth County adopted the scheme in its entirety with any success. A few townships in South Jersey also formed societies, but these were of passing significance.[83] However, the project was noteworthy from another point of view. Failing to attain its announced goal, the Republican caucus nevertheless at least forced its compatriots to take another look at the party creation. The caucus, then, in practical terms, provided much needed leadership at a critical moment in Republican fortunes. In so doing, it generated a new unity of purpose when that ingredient was required. Also, the attempt to create Whig Societies marked the caucus as the fulcrum of party machinery.

If there was any remaining doubt about the last point, that doubt was quickly dispelled in 1814. The legislative struggle for a United States Senate seat in that year was a classic example of caucus politics at its best. The close-quarter fight indicated that body's pre-eminent role in determining the lines of political authority, the extent of that authority, and most important, who would wield it.

The caucus, prior to the joint meeting in October 1814, failed to agree on a senatorial candidate. James J. Wilson was given sixteen votes to thirteen for Mahlon Dickerson with one member abstaining. But nine of the minority in this instance refused to comply with the usual mandatory adherence to the wishes of the majority. The nine die-hards disliked Wilson with such intensity that in the joint meeting they continued to support Dickerson, who had returned permanently to the state from Philadelphia in 1808 and was now a justice on the New

82. *Whig Societies*, Feb. 1813, N.J. Political Broadsides Collection, Rutgers Univ. Lib.
83. Trenton *True American*, Sept. 26, Dec. 26, 1814.

Jersey Supreme Court. The others in the minority, following the usual caucus discipline, supported Wilson, giving him a total of twenty-one Republican votes in the legislature, but the nine Dickerson men refused to give in and openly bucked the party in the joint meeting.[84]

The Federalists' twenty-three votes were cast for John Lambert, the Republican incumbent who had voted against the War of 1812 and had been read out of the Republican party for his efforts. He was designated the Federalist candidate, probably in the hope that he would draw some Republican votes. A majority of twenty-seven was needed for election. Ballot after ballot was taken with the same results: twenty-three for Lambert, twenty-one for Wilson, and nine for Dickerson. The latter's backers joined the Federalists to defeat a motion by Wilson supporters to drop the low man from consideration, the usual procedure in such circumstances.[85]

If Dickerson could not cull a majority of the caucus' support, it was not because he did not try. The week the legislature convened he spent in Trenton seeing every Republican who might aid him in gaining the coveted appointment. He closeted himself with Governor William S. Pennington three times, Congressman Henry Southard once, and numerous Republican legislators (and caucus members), including Robert Rutherford of Sussex, Benjamin Ludlow of Morris, Aaron Munn of Essex, and many others. His efforts succeeded only in retaining the nine die-hard votes already committed to him. These, however, proved to be enough to stalemate the legislature, for the joint meeting was forced to postpone the election till its next session in February 1815.[86]

84. *Ibid.*, Nov. 7, 1814; Newark *Centinel*, Mar. 14, 1815; James J. Wilson to William Darlington, Nov. 8, 1814, Darlington Papers, Lib. Cong.; David Thompson, Jr., to Samuel L. Southard, Nov. 15, 1814, Southard Papers, Princeton Univ. Lib.

85. Newark *Centinel*, Mar. 14, 1815; Trenton *True American*, Nov. 7, 1814.

86. Diary of Mahlon Dickerson, Oct. 21-30, 1814, Rutgers Univ. Lib.; Newark *Centinel*, Mar. 14, 1815; James J. Wilson to William Darlington, Nov. 8, 1814, Darlington Papers, Lib. Cong.; David Thompson, Jr., to Samuel L. Southard, Nov. 15, 1814, Southard Papers, Princeton Univ. Lib.

After the postponement, Dickerson continued to seek votes, although somewhat less feverishly. Nevertheless, he returned to Trenton often during the three-month interim before the joint meeting finally decided the senatorial question. Meanwhile, Dickerson encountered indications that his candidacy was a lost cause. Lewis Condict, a supporter from Morris County and a former congressman, "fear[ed] from the proceedings at Trenton that it [Dickerson's appointment] will not take place. I very well know the force of West Jersey prejudices."[87]

According to his own testimony, James J. Wilson did not actively seek the Senate seat, but his friends were busy indeed on his behalf. Edward Yard, a Republican member from Wilson's home county, was the editor's caucus manager in the contest. Yard feared that another deadlock would cost Wilson the position. If the joint meeting failed to appoint anyone in time for the next Senate session, Governor Pennington, not one of Wilson's admirers, would be empowered to make an interim appointment.[88] Yard busied himself with securing Dickerson's withdrawal from the contest.

Speaking for twenty-one Wilson supporters in the caucus, Yard offered to make a deal. He candidly recapped events in the caucus to date in an extraordinary letter to Dickerson. When that body indicated an overwhelming preference for Wilson, Yard wrote, "it was then thought that the minority would as usual fall in and support Wilson." This did not happen, because Dickerson's friends, Pennington at the fore, "resorted to the shameful Intrigue of colleaguing with the Feds, to destroy the election at this time—which they accomplished. This created a Sensation of a kind that I shall not attempt to describe." Now, according to the floor manager, Wilson's

87. Lewis Condict to Mahlon Dickerson, Feb. 15, 1815, Mahlon Dickerson Papers, N.J. Hist. Soc.; Diary of Mahlon Dickerson, Oct. 21-30, Nov. 21, 1814, Rutgers Univ. Lib.; David Thompson, Jr., to Samuel L. Southard, Nov. 15, 1814, Southard Papers, Princeton Univ. Lib.

88. James J. Wilson to William Darlington, Nov. 8, 1814, Darlington Papers, Lib. Cong.; Edward Yard to Mahlon Dickerson, Nov. 7, 1814, Mahlon Dickerson Papers, N.J. Hist. Soc. Wilson also claimed that he had no organized support in the legislature, a claim that was not true.

adherents waited to see if Dickerson would accept such dubious endorsement. Yard added that his colleagues were disturbed at Pennington's remark that "there was not a man of Talents or of understanding who voted for Wilson," or the Governor's intemperate reference to Wilson men as "Clod Hoppers."[89]

Having stated his case, Yard turned to the business at hand, threatening: "If we are not Solons . . . not Orators, or Stammering Spouters, we . . . know when, and how, to control and counteract the underhand Intrigue and cabal of a few." Having digested this threat of caucus reprisal, Dickerson read on: "It was thought and said by several that something ought to be done during the Recess, to heal this Division. . . . And you were look'd to [to] do this—and to prevent any improper impressions to take place, injurious to yourself, who before this affair stood so high in the opinion of all." The not-so-subtle threat was followed by an equally evident hint of a deal: "Should you think proper to interfere . . . you can do a good deal and perhaps bring us all together again. Should you accomplish this I should be led to believe you would stand higher than ever in the opinion of all."[90]

Reading the handwriting on the wall, Dickerson withdrew his name from consideration, bowing to the superior power exerted by the caucus majority as others must have done in like situations. When the joint meeting convened in February, Wilson was elected to a six-year term in the Senate. All Republicans in the legislature concurred in the appointment.[91] By way of a sequel, Dickerson was designated governor the following October. In the understatement of the year 1815, the New Brunswick *Fredonian* noted that "Room is . . . given for intrigue."[92] Not long after, John Condit's term in the

89. Edward Yard to Mahlon Dickerson, Nov. 7, 1814, Mahlon Dickerson Papers, N.J. Hist. Soc. Wilson and Pennington apparently had had other collisions from time to time.
90. *Ibid.*; James J. Wilson to William Darlington, Nov. 8, 1814, Darlington Papers, Lib. Cong.
91. Newark *Centinel*, Feb. 28, 1815.
92. New Brunswick *Fredonian*, Oct. 19, 1815; Newark *Centinel*, Oct. 31, 1815;

Senate expired; Governor Dickerson succeeded him.[93] The caucus had quietly resolved a major power struggle; so far as the public was concerned, only surface difficulties showed. The party apparatus in this case, at least, was intact, functioning, and vibrant, even if the same could not be said for other components of the Republican machine.

Deterioration of the party organization keynoted the war and post-war periods, with the one exception noted above. The convention continued its retreat from the forefront of the party's apparatus. Most county organizations also either literally fell apart or weakened considerably. Even the party presses lost their old venom and sense of urgency. Only the caucus, the one cornerstone of the party machine not operating directly under the public's gaze, perpetuated its role, even adding vitally to that role as other party components wilted. Whether the weakened party structure contributed to the passing of the existing superficial ideological differences between parties, or vice versa, is debatable. That such distinctions between Republicans and Federalists passed so quickly out of sight indicated that these distinctions were more symbolic than real, after 1800, anyway. As the "Era of Good Feelings" got underway, nevertheless, political conflict continued—Republican infighting often replacing the former Federalist-Jeffersonian struggles.

Trenton *True American*, Nov. 13, 1815; Diary of Mahlon Dickerson, Oct. 26, 1815, Rutgers Univ. Lib.

93. Trenton *True American*, Jan. 27, 1817.

VIII

PATRONAGE AND A PARTY
MACHINE

———•———

LEADERS OF THE NEW JERSEY REPUBLICAN PARTY, CONSCIOUSLY
bending to the task of creating an effective political machine,
soon learned that a party was built by willing workers, who
were made willing by the emoluments of office. It became
one of the party's main purposes to secure and hold jobs for
those who worked for the Republican interest. And it was the
caucus that became the indispensable instrument for effectively distributing jobs. In no other area was party discipline
more evident. The caucus unhesitatingly removed Federalists
from long-held positions and painstakingly supervised the al-
location of rewards to Republicans. After 1801, to systematize
the dispensation of both state and federal spoils effectively,
authority was vested entirely in the caucus.

The Republican party's patronage policies for turning the
rascals out assumed different faces for different groups of supporters. Typical Republican election propaganda, broadcast-
ing as wide an appeal as possible, avowed that "Republicans
have been very liberal and indulgent" about replacing Federalist officeholders with Republicans, "far more so than the
Federalists were while in power." *Plain Truth*, a Jeffersonian

campaign pamphlet issued in 1808, thus denied any self-seeking with respect to party patronage, alleging also that "the most valuable offices in this state under the General Government are still held by the Federalists . . . [and] many of the Post Masters are Federalist."[1] However, if the audience was a group of rabid party men celebrating the Fourth of July, the Republican attitude toward appointments shifted abruptly: "No federal spies in a Republican camp—no arms put in an enemy's hands, or outposts trusted to his keeping—no premiums for political error or patronage to revilers or opposers of Government."[2]

Senator Ephraim Bateman observed, after long experience with Republican party men, "Let a vacancy occur, or even be hoped for, in any office or public employment to which even moderate emolument is awarded—and like the rushing of mighty waters there is a simultaneous press from all quarters towards the aperture."[3] This judgment appraised Republican job-hunting most accurately, with the one qualification that the "simultaneous press from all quarters" was directed at the legislative caucus, which adjudicated rival job claims with scientific precision.

Caucus Patronage and the Party Machine

The Republican lawmakers annually dispensed through their caucus 150 or more state jobs according to fixed standards of eligibility and specific allocations by county and region. When passing out jobs each year, they voted in the joint meetings of the legislature virtually as a unit more than 95 per cent

1. James J. Wilson, *Plain Truth, Addressed to the Independent Electors of the State of New Jersey* (Trenton, 1808), 1-5, N.J. Pamphlets Collection, N.J. Hist. Soc. This attitude reflected in the campaign tract enunciated the official patronage position for the Jefferson administration, but certainly it did not conform to reality. See Cunningham, *The Jeffersonian Republicans in Power: Party Operations, 1801-1809,* chapters two and three. See also Raymond Walters, Jr., *Albert Gallatin: Jeffersonian Financier and Diplomat* (N.Y., 1957), 155-69.

2. Trenton *True American,* July 8, 1805.

3. Ephraim Bateman to Samuel L. Southard, Mar. 22, 1824, Southard Papers, Princeton Univ. Lib.

of the time.[4] In 1806, which can be taken as an average year, the joint meeting of the legislature made 117 appointments to paying state positions, and 42 militia appointments that carried no stipend.[5] Most of these offices went where the Republican caucus thought they would do the most political good. In addition to such classes of appointments as local judgeships, justices of the peace, county clerkships, state bank positions, militia commissions, and legislature-controlled city posts, there were individual appointments such as secretary of state for New Jersey, state treasurer, clerk of the Assembly, and even the governorship.

Besides these state jobs there was a significant number of federal jobs available in New Jersey. At the beginning of 1802, there were 79 federal appointees in the state. By the end of 1816, the total had risen to 139.[6] Federal places, all remunerative, carried longer terms than the state posts, most of which were for one year. There were fewer federal positions available for frequent redistribution, but because tenure in federal jobs was longer, they were much more desirable. Republicans in New Jersey after 1801 had access to an increasing number of postmasterships. Other openings within the state included customs house supervisors, collectors, and clerks; internal revenue collectors and assessors; commissioners of loans and bankruptcy; and several lucrative and influential federal court appointments. There was also a superintendent and keeper of the lighthouse at Sandy Hook.[7]

4. *Minutes and Proceedings of the Joint Meeting*, 1801-16, *passim*.
5. *Ibid.*, Oct. 31, 1806, 1ff.
6. Lowrie and Franklin, eds., *American State Papers*, Class X, *Miscellaneous*. I, 261-319, II, 308-96. Cunningham, *The Jeffersonian Republicans in Power: Party Operations, 1801-1809*, 61, 63, quotes President Jefferson's statement in 1803 that there were "316 offices in all the U. S. subject to appointment and removal by me." As Cunningham points out, however, this figure omits the subordinate officers appointed to the customs service by the Secretary of the Treasury, and the postmasters, who were named by the Postmaster General.
7. Carl Russell Fish, *The Civil Service and the Patronage* (Cambridge, Mass., 1904), chapter two; J. M. Merriam, "Jefferson's Use of the Executive Patronage," [abstract], American Historical Association *Papers*, 2 (1888), 47-52; Gaillard Hunt, "Office-Seeking During Jefferson's Administration," *Amer. Hist. Rev.*,

While some positions were pruned from the federal service in New Jersey between 1802 and 1816, notably in the customs house, the number of postmasters in the state increased sharply. Forty-four of the 79 federal jobs in the state in 1802 came from the Post Office Department; by 1816, postmasterships comprised 114 of the 139 federal positions in New Jersey. Few of these jobs either in the postal service or in other departments of the federal government were very taxing. All permitted the recipient to remain in the state and, if he were so inclined, to carry on his party activities.[8]

How many party workers were appointed to these paying positions, either by the state or federal government?[9] What portion of the total number of officeholders in the state did they represent? What was the relative importance of federal and state patronage in the rewards allocated to party workers? Did the Republicans build and perpetuate a party machine by carefully distributing jobs to the deserving? A survey of active Democratic-Republican workers in the state from 1801 to 1816 discloses some interesting answers to these and other questions about the political use of appointive positions in New Jersey.

For the purposes of the survey, active party workers were conceived to be those Republicans performing some party function, whose names appear as such, in the Republican newspapers of New Jersey during the period from 1800 through 1816. A further qualification was introduced to avoid sampling those who may have been active for a very brief period: only those whose names appeared at least once a year for two or more years were included. An active party worker is defined as any Democratic Republican who served for at least two different

---

3 (1898), 288; Lowrie and Franklin, eds., *American State Papers*, Class X, *Miscellaneous*, I, 261-319, II, 308-96.

8. Lowrie and Franklin, eds., *American State Papers*, Class X, *Miscellaneous*, I, 261-319, II, 308-96; Fish, *Civil Service and the Patronage*, chapter two.

9. Local patronage is not taken into account, for information on distribution of local jobs is not available. In any event, local patronage appears to have been a negligible factor in New Jersey during the Democratic-Republican period.

years on township or county "electioneering" committees, standing committees, or committees of correspondence, who chaired township or county party meetings, or who served as delegate to county or state nominating conventions. The survey does not include Republican candidates for elective office *per se*, although as one would expect many of them fall into the category of "active party worker" in terms of the original definition. The reports of party activities on all levels appearing in the Republican newspapers of New Jersey from 1800 through 1816 reveal the names of 256 such active party workers.[10]

Three basic areas of patronage are examined here: remunerative state appointive offices, remunerative federal positions, and nonpaying state militia appointments; and each category is scrutinized to discover how many of the 256 identifiable party activists held state or federal jobs during two periods—1801 to 1809 and 1801 through 1816.[11] For the entire interval 1801-16, a meaningful total of 164, or 64.1 per cent, of the

10. The newspapers consulted for the names of the party activists were: Newark *Centinel of Freedom*, Trenton *True American*, Elizabethtown *New Jersey Journal*, all for the entire period. The Morristown *Genius of Liberty* (1800-05) and New Brunswick *Fredonian* (1811-16) also were examined. These constitute all the Republican newspapers in New Jersey for which adequate files are available. All appointments to state offices and militia posts are listed annually in the *Minutes and Proceedings of the Joint Meeting*, 1801-16. Federal appointments of Jerseymen to office were gathered from the following sources: *A Register of Officers and Agents, Civil, Military and Naval, in the Service of the United States, 1816* (Washington, D.C., 1816); Lowrie and Franklin, eds., *American State Papers*, Class X, *Miscellaneous*, I, 261-319, II, 308-96; *Executive Journal of the Senate of the United States* (Washington, D.C., 1829-69), I-III, *passim*.

11. The comparison between the periods 1801-08 and 1801-16 was selected to account for possible changes in federal appointive policies as a result of the transition from Jefferson to Madison. The nearly three months' differences between the end of the years 1808 and 1816 and the termination of the presidencies of Jefferson and Madison are not taken into account because the sources examined did not date many appointments, particularly those in the postal service. With regard to the 1817 hiatus, any errors would occur on the side of conservatism, inasmuch as no 1817 appointments are included. If these months could have been accurately accounted for, the figures cited might have been a few percentage points higher for federal patronage through the inclusion of additional appointments by the Madison administration in its waning days.

256 party activists were appointed to a paying or honorary post either by the federal or state government. By 1809, 95 or 37.1 per cent of the 256 activists, had already received their jobs.

An analysis of these statistics in terms of state, federal, and militia categories indicates that state appointments, particularly during Jefferson's tenure, comprised the lion's share of offices allotted to Republican activists. During the years 1801-16, of the 256 active workers 139 (54.3 per cent) held paying state offices. Prior to 1809, 85 (33.2 per cent) party men occupied positions carrying stipends distributed by the New Jersey legislature. The federal government through 1816 appointed 29 (11.3 per cent) activists.[12] Far fewer federal appointments were made during Jefferson's presidency prior to 1809; of the 256 only 5 (2.0 per cent) were elevated to the federal service. Twelve (4.7 per cent) more gained honorary but prestigious state militia commissions through 1816. Of these, 8 (3.1 per cent) were appointed by 1809. *Within these totals,* there were 16 (6.3 per cent) particularly fortunate party men who in the years 1801-16 held both state and federal offices. Up to 1809, only 3 (1.2 per cent) could claim this desirable double bounty for their services to the Republican cause.[13] (All the above percentage figures given in parentheses are, of course, based on the total of 256 party workers.)

These figures show that, excluding honorary militia posts, 152 individuals who were party activists held paying state or federal jobs—or both—between 1800 and 1817 and that 87 men held these positions between 1800 and 1809. Of the 152, 139 (91.4 per cent) were wholly or partly rewarded with re-

12. Thirty-one appointments actually were made. Two activists held two federal jobs each.
13. The latter figures for combined state and federal officeholding, 16 and 3 respectively, are already distributed through the totals for state and federal appointees. To strike a balance, these figures must be subtracted from the general sum inasmuch as the 16 were counted twice—once for federal office and once for state office. It should be generally observed also that, to an extent, if the figures for Jefferson's administration are smaller, there were somewhat fewer activists to reward, for the 256 figure encompasses the entire period.

munerative state posts. To 1809, the preponderance of activists in state offices is even higher: 85 (97.7 per cent) out of 87.[14] For the years 1801-16, 29 (19.1 per cent) of the 152 Republican officeholders occupied federal office. It is highly significant that this figure was considerably less for the years up to the end of Jefferson's presidency: only 5 (5.7 per cent) of 87 officeholders held federal office. (The percentages in each case add up to more than 100 because of the number of men who held both state and federal jobs.) Little of this increase can be attributed either to a growth in the number of federal jobs available during Madison's administration or to a rise in the number of "deserving" workers. The rate of increase in both instances is less than the rate of increase from Jefferson to Madison in the number of party workers receiving federal appointments.[15] If a "spoils system" is a system of rewarding active party workers with paying offices, it appears that, in New Jersey at least, federal appointments became a major factor in contributing to and maintaining such a "system" only during Madison's administrations.[16]

During the years from 1801 through 1816, an estimated 2,000 paying state posts were available for distribution in New Jersey. Nearly all of the positions at the disposal of the legislature were annual appointments. The average number of paying jobs available yearly was taken at 125. (There were

14. Sixteen held both state and federal positions in the years 1801-16. Three of these held both prior to 1809. The same caveat expressed in n. 16 applies here.

15. The rise of federal officeholding in New Jersey during Madison's presidency can be explained in part by Jefferson himself. According to Cunningham, Jefferson observed in 1804 that it took time to get rid of the Federalists in office. To the first Republican President fell "the drudgeory of putting them [Federalists] out of condition to do mischief. My successor I hope will have smoother seas." Cited in *The Jeffersonian Republicans in Power: Party Operations, 1801-1809*, 52.

16. In states where state patronage was not available to Republicans after 1800, for example in Connecticut or Massachusetts, it is clear that the same conclusion could not apply. This merely underlines the need for state studies of Democratic-Republican party machinery. See Cunningham, *The Jeffersonian Republicans in Power: Party Operations, 1801-1809*, 57. Paul Goodman's *The Democratic-Republicans of Massachusetts, Politics in a Young Republic* (Cambridge, Mass., 1964), contains an analysis of patronage practices in the Bay State.

117 paying posts in the state in 1806, not counting the few major state positions with tenure of more than one year. A small but steady increase in the number of places available after 1806 is assumed.) Because the legislators, guided by the caucus, were prone to renew old appointments, an average length of service for an individual in state office may be estimated conservatively at three years. Known Republican activists received 139 paying appointments, which if renewed on an average of twice, totaled approximately 417 paying state appointments in sixteen years. Thus at least 21 per cent of all state offices during the period surveyed probably went to Republican party workers.

The percentage of available federal posts given to active party workers in New Jersey may be fixed more exactly. At the end of 1816, there were 139 federal places in the state; 29 known activists held 31 of these posts. Thus, 22.3 per cent of the total number of federal appointees in New Jersey in late 1816 were known to be active Republican party workers.[17]

It is clear that the conscious efforts to build and strengthen the party machine by employing relatively sophisticated patronage practices was eminently successful.

The Mechanics of Distribution

The caucus was admirably suited to the task of supervising patronage. It soon worked out its own appointment procedures, including legislative courtesy and well-fixed criteria for designating officeholders. It allowed nothing to stand in the way of its effective control over available jobs in New Jersey. Thus, Republican legislators and party leaders, after their first state victory in October 1801, set about to establish their authority in this area, beginning the difficult task of ousting scores of Federalists from state positions.

17. Complete lists of state appointments may be found in *Minutes and Proceedings of the Joint Meeting*, 1801-16, *passim*. A full roster of federal officeholders in the state at the end of 1816 is contained in Lowrie and Franklin, eds., *American State Papers*, Class X, *Miscellaneous*, II, 308-96.

The caucus immediately made it clear that it would brook no interference from either Federalists or Republicans. Even a good Republican who bucked the ironclad rules of the caucus found himself cut off from rewards until he saw the light. Former Congressman James Linn, an important figure in Hunterdon County politics, was slated for an appointment as clerk of the supreme court. That office was vacated soon after the new Republican legislative majority took their seats in 1801. Contrary to what was expected of him, Linn refused to promise to remove Federalists from posts that would fall under his jurisdiction and appoint Republicans in their stead. The Republican lawmakers, Linn complained, reacted violently. "They were exceedingly enraged, and threatened to oppose the confirmation of my appointment unless I complied with their wishes." Linn called their bluff, one of the first Republicans to do so. He found the caucus members "in this instance . . . as good as their word" and found himself out of a job.[18] Nor was this the end of Linn's patronage difficulties. The caucus did not soon forget his challenge to its authority, and twice in 1805 he was passed over by the Republicans for an appointment to the supreme court. It was not until a decade after his initial refusal to adhere to caucus directives that he was finally granted the coveted judicial office.[19]

Republican complaints of the ruthlessness of the caucus procedure henceforth were made privately,[20] although other good Republicans were critical of the new patronage system, even when it dispensed benefits in their direction. Silas Dickerson, who had not the least cause to protest his treatment at the hands of the caucus, nevertheless found that "they [the caucus] seem determined to reward those who have been most violent and active whether they are possessed of virtue and

18. James Linn to Ebenezer Elmer, Jan. 29, 1802, Gratz Collection, Hist. Soc. of Pa.

19. Trenton *True American*, Sept. 22, 1817.

20. Silas Dickerson to Mahlon Dickerson, Nov. 27, 1803, Dickerson Letter Book, N.J. Hist. Soc.; Silas Condit to Samuel L. Southard, Jan. 24, 1817, George Holcombe to Samuel L. Southard, Oct. 17, 1825, Southard Papers, Princeton Univ. Lib.

talents or not—by which means improper appointments will and have taken place and disgusted the more moderate of both parties."[21] Republican Jeremiah Hand, the clerk of Cape May County, was turned out of office, the *Trenton Federalist* alleged, for promoting his "excessive love of economy. The repeated calls for contributions to defray the expenses of meetings, newspapers, pamphlets, deputations to Trenton, and other 'republican' measures, had fretted away his patriotism, to that degree, and so worried his economical principles, that he determined to give no more."[22]

Many other Republicans, on the other hand, took to the new system with relish, providing the caucus with the support necessary to insure its authority. The "Happy Farmer," for example, approved of caucus job dealing. He pointed out, in 1805, "that Republicans at their last joint meeting did make six or seven federal[ist] appointments." To the "Happy Farmer" this was proof enough "that we are actuated from very different motives from what federalists were when they had the power of making appointments."[23] Yet had the "Happy Farmer" taken the time to reckon, he would have found that the seven Federalists appointed totaled less than 5 per cent of all state openings under the jurisdiction of the joint meeting.[24]

In making appointments, the caucus customarily followed the practice of observing legislative courtesy. If it was possible to do so, patronage decisions were left to Republican law-

21. Silas Dickerson to Mahlon Dickerson, Nov. 27, 1803, Dickerson Letter Book, N.J. Hist. Soc.; Lewis Condict to Mahlon Dickerson, Jan. 26, 1813, Mahlon Dickerson Papers, Rutgers Univ. Lib. Many moderate Republicans agreed with Silas Dickerson over the years. Silas Condit described the caucus as "that invisible impossible body that directs our political movements and appointments." Silas Condit to Samuel L. Southard, Jan. 24, 1817, Southard Papers, Princeton Univ. Lib. Still another Republican even later noted, in looking back, "what a wretched, humbling state of things has existed in our state for years past. From the *Executive* to the *Constable*, there is scarcely an appointment made without bargaining or corruption." George Holcombe to Samuel L. Southard, Oct. 17, 1825, *ibid.*

22. *Trenton Federalist*, Jan. 14, 21, 1805.

23. Trenton *True American*, Jan. 7, 1805.

24. The assumption is that there were about 150 jobs available. There were 159 in 1806. See *Minutes and Proceedings of the Joint Meeting*, 1806.

makers and party leaders in a given county.[25] Reports circulated in 1806 conceded that "Republicans in the legislature have promised not to interfere in appointments in Federal counties . . . [but] to leave them to manage the affairs of their county in their own way."[26] Governor Joseph Bloomfield was annoyed in 1811 at the "interference" of two well-known Republicans "in the appointment of a foreign county."[27] A year earlier James J. Wilson, member from Hunterdon County, was chastised for "interfering with the appointments of [Burlington] county," thus violating a principal tenet of legislative courtesy.[28] Inasmuch as Burlington was a Federalist county, it appeared that, in theory, Federalist legislators governed appointments in their county. This rule of thumb, and its justification, were well expressed by the observation of the *Trenton Federalist*: "The appointments for Cumberland then proceeded in the usual way under the superintendance of Messrs. Crane and Burgin [Republican legislators from Cumberland] without let or hindrance. The Joint Meeting taking better for worse, whatever they chose to advance, and therefore if any wrong is done, the responsibility rests where it ought, upon the members of the county."[29]

While the legislative courtesy extended to Republican lawmakers and party leaders remained virtually unassailable, party considerations, in practice, often superseded the extension of similar legislative courtesy to Federalist counties, rules to the contrary notwithstanding; too many jobs, after all, were at stake, and too many good Republican party men, in the minority in several counties, would have been cut out of a share in the spoils. So, while a few Republicans in minority counties were deprived of appointments, it was not to the

25. Trenton *True American*, Nov. 24, 1806, Nov. 16, 1812, June 30, 1814, Nov. 2, 1818; Daniel Dod to Samuel L. Southard, Feb. 14, 1811, Southard Papers, Princeton Univ. Lib.

26. Trenton *True American*, Nov. 24, 1806.

27. Daniel Dod to Samuel L. Southard, Feb. 14, 1811, Southard Papers, Princeton Univ. Lib.

28. *Trenton Federalist*, Nov. 5, 1810.

29. *Ibid.*

advantage of the caucus or party harmony to leave all or even most positions in Federalist hands. Although, then, some recognition was accorded to Federalist superiority where it existed, it was only a token concession apparently made to justify the operation of *Republican* legislative courtesy. In practice, Republicans received the majority of jobs even in long-time Federalist counties.[30] In the joint meeting of 1808, this discrepancy was made all too clear. Councilor Frelinghuysen, Federalist from Somerset, told a Republican legislator from Morris that he should not "have the indelicacy to interfere with the business of a county he did not represent." Nevertheless, the Republican office-seeker in question from Somerset County was supported by the majority in his bid for a state appointment. Other Republican appointments in this solid Federalist county followed. "Mr. Frelinghuysen did at the last beg for one solitary appointment required by the legal representatives of the county, but even this was refused."[31] Such blatant wholesale violations of the principle of legislative courtesy were not always possible, however, and compromises often were rendered necessary. When a Republican from Federalist Cape May County came up for reappointment in 1805, a Federalist legislator from the county "got up and moved a postponement of the appointment, and, of course, poor Townsend [the Republican] as well as the Federalists on nomination [for the same office], from Cape May, was thrown in the back ground." A nonparty man was finally designated.[32] Despite these obvious and frequent Republican violations of Federalist legislative courtesy, some Republicans continued to complain about occasional Federalist nominations over their heads in strong opposition counties.[33]

It appeared that when a close two-party county went Fed-

30. *Minutes and Proceedings of the Joint Meeting, 1800-15, passim*; Trenton *True American*, Nov. 24, 1806, Nov. 16, 1812.

31. *Trenton Federalist*, Nov. 28, 1808.

32. *Ibid.*, Nov. 25, 1805.

33. Daniel Dod to Samuel L. Southard, Feb. 14, 1811, Southard Papers, Princeton Univ. Lib.; Trenton *True American*, Nov. 24, 1806, Nov. 2, 1818.

eralist, the courtesy sometimes extended by the caucus to Federalist legislators did not apply at all. In the interim, when a sometime Republican county was without party representation in the chamber, its interests often were guarded by a neighboring Republican delegation or a single kindred lawmaker; the continuity of appointments in that lapsed Republican area thus remained inviolate. Assemblyman Daniel Richman of Cumberland County protected the patronage interests of neighboring Gloucester in joint meeting after that county went Federalist in 1813. So grateful were his friends from Gloucester that the county's Democratic Association tendered unanimous thanks for his favors by means of a formal resolution.[34] Presumably, he had preserved political offices for some of them.

Legislative courtesy as such could not, of course, apply to major offices that transcended the county level. Appointments to the state supreme court, the United States Senate, and the governor's chair were subject to overriding regional considerations, however. The old cleavage between North and South Jersey continued to govern state politics in this respect. In the case of the gubernatorial office, South Jerseyman Joseph Bloomfield occupied it for the first twelve years of Republican hegemony (through 1812), and then it passed to North Jersey for a like period in the persons of William S. Pennington (Essex), Mahlon Dickerson (Morris), and Isaac H. Williamson (Essex). The two Republican United States senators from New Jersey were never from the same part of the state. When John Lambert's term expired in 1814, the new appointment, according to the caucus, had to derive from South Jersey, for the other incumbent, Senator John Condit, was from Essex County. In order to balance the state supreme court in 1802, "the fourth Judge should be in West [South] Jersey," cautioned Ebenezer Elmer.[35]

34. Trenton *True American*, Jan. 31, 1814. See also *Minutes and Proceedings of the Joint Meeting, passim; Trenton Federalist*, Nov. 5, 1810.

35. Ebenezer Elmer to ?, Jan. 29, 1802, Gratz Collection, Hist. Soc. of Pa.; Trenton *True American*, Nov. 2, 1818; Harold F. Wilson, *et al., Outline History of New Jersey* (New Brunswick, N.J., 1950), 364; Newark *Centinel*, Oct.

By observing legislative courtesy for county-level appointments and regional interests in filling major state posts, the caucus almost automatically resolved most state patronage conflicts under its jurisdiction. More important, jobs went where they would do the most political good. It was the existence of just such political ground rules in the caucus that made possible its growth and continued control of important areas of party activity for the entire Democratic-Republican period.

Supervision over the distribution of federal offices, although necessarily much more indirect and diluted with strong doses of authority from other sources, was also a function of the caucus. As much local control as possible over federal positions in New Jersey was necessary to party operations on two counts: first, most federal appointments were made on good behavior. To remove an appointee was not a simple matter for local leaders, for it entailed a good deal of red tape and time, and replacement was bound to create local party difficulties. Mistakes in dispensing federal jobs, then, were intolerable. Second, to achieve the utmost political return, the state organization found it necessary to exert maximum pressure on the president, his cabinet, and Congress. New Jersey's Republicans were well equipped to place their full weight behind supplications for office. Party authorities could only request that their choices receive federal appointments, and they succeeded only insofar as the federal government responded to the pressure party men applied. The need for a united system of seeking favors from the national government was obvious under these conditions.

Jefferson, on principle, was reluctant at first to turn out the Federalists, but, as pressure on him increased, he let down the barriers and made a number of party appointments in the states. Although Jefferson—in New Jersey at least—was less

1813, 1816, 1817; Lewis Condict to Mahlon Dickerson, Feb. 15, 1815, Edward Yard to Mahlon Dickerson, Nov. 7, 1814, Mahlon Dickerson Papers, N.J. Hist. Soc.; James J. Wilson to William Darlington, Nov. 8, 1814, Darlington Papers, Lib. Cong.; David Thompson, Jr., to Samuel L. Southard, Nov. 15, 1814, Southard Papers, Princeton Univ. Lib.

prone than his successor to reward party men, insofar as he initiated the practice of doing just that for the Republican party, so he carried the burden of the friction thus generated by both eager Republicans and disgruntled Federalists in New Jersey. The President's plight was clear. To the persistent New Jersey governor, Joseph Bloomfield, seeking an appointment for a deserving Republican in 1801, the President replied that it was "the case of one loaf and ten men wanting bread."[36] New Jersey, moreover, was typical of the other states in this respect, and the pressure applied by party leaders in New Jersey as elsewhere was very great.[37] In New Jersey, party demands for federal offices from Jefferson met with moderate success. Although Federalists still held national posts in the state until well into Jefferson's second term, the state's Republicans eventually received a lion's share of the spoils as a result of the highly organized patronage machine in New Jersey acting on the federal government. If the situation was even more salutary for Republicans under Madison, Jefferson still bore the giant's share of the task of removing the Federalists from United States offices in New Jersey, and so he also bore the brunt of their animosity. A Newark Federalist, for example, expressed sore disappointment that Jefferson did not live up to the promises of patronage moderation implicit in his inaugural address. The unhappy representative of the minority concluded bitterly, "it is now necessary that even

36. Thomas Jefferson to Joseph Bloomfield, Dec. 5, 1801, Jefferson Papers, CXVIII, 20360, Lib. Cong.

37. For examples of the kind of pressure applied by New Jersey Republicans to gain federal patronage, see Joseph Bloomfield to Ebenezer Elmer, July 6, 1802, Ely Collection, N.J. Hist. Soc.; Joseph Bloomfield to Ebenezer Elmer, Mar. 5, 1804, Miscellaneous Collection, N.-Y. Hist. Soc.; David Thompson, Jr., to Samuel L. Southard, Jan. 13, 1821, Southard Papers, Princeton Univ. Lib.; Joseph Bloomfield to Thomas Jefferson, Nov. 10, 1801, Jefferson Papers, CXVII, 20262, Lib. Cong. For numerous examples of pressure applied to the Jefferson administration from other states, see Cunningham, *The Jeffersonian Republicans in Power: Party Operations, 1801-1809*, chapters two and three; Fish, *Civil Service and the Patronage*, 50-51; Hunt, "Office-Seeking During Jefferson's Administration," *Amer. Hist. Rev.*, 3 (1898), 288; Walters, *Albert Gallatin*, 155-69; Nathan Schachner, *Thomas Jefferson; A Biography*, 2 vols. (N.Y., 1951), II, 673; Leonard D. White, *The Jeffersonians: A Study in Administrative History, 1801-1829* (N.Y., 1951), 394-98.

your [Jefferson's] Shoemaker and Taylor should *think* with *you*, that they may render you just and equitable services."[38] The new administration was on the spot from any point of view, as Republican party managers in New Jersey, like the Republican leadership in other states, set out to exert as much pressure as possible for federal jobs.

United States government openings in the states ultimately were filled by the president on the advice of his cabinet; in many instances the Senate had to confirm appointments. Although officially the state party leaders were voiceless in these nominations, the approbation of New Jersey's chief executive, speaking for his party, was desirable and necessary to the national administration for political reasons. Naturally, the acquiescence of the state's United States senators and congressmen was politic also in the interests of party harmony. These Republican forces in New Jersey, led by the caucus and using the lever of party favor to advantage, usually worked together to fill federal positions. In the infrequent instances when Republicans could not agree, the caucus was the final arbiter, and it retained its hold on the federal patronage process in spite of necessary concessions to other elements in the state party.[39]

The pattern described above was evident with regard to federal appointments made in New Jersey. When a federal position opened in a given county, the Republican leadership in that county, with the endorsement of the legislative caucus, suggested a deserving party man to fill it. Legislative courtesy among Republican lawmakers usually applied, just as it did

38. *Newark Gazette*, Aug. 4, 1801. For similar expressions see *ibid.*, July 20, 1802, and the *Trenton Federalist*, July 8, 1805.

39. Joseph Bloomfield to Ebenezer Elmer, July 6, 1802, Ely Collection, N.J. Hist. Soc.; David Thompson, Jr., to Samuel L. Southard, Jan. 13, 1821, Southard Papers, Princeton Univ. Lib.; John Condit to Ebenezer Elmer, Mar. 30, 1808, Gratz Collection, Hist. Soc. of Pa. The Republican members of the legislature were able to apply heavy pressure on their fellow Jerseymen in Congress, pressure to which Republican congressmen usually responded with alacrity. Indeed, there were instances when members of Congress displayed great deference to Republican legislators, unified by the caucus, in matters relating to federal patronage. See Joseph Bloomfield to Ebenezer Elmer, Jan. 20, 1806, William Helms to Jonathan Rhea, Dec. 25, 1807, Miscellaneous Collection, N.-Y. Hist. Soc.

in making state appointments. Local initiative was frequently preserved even with regard to federal appointments by this means. In many instances, the federal opening was regional in character, for example, port or tax collectors. When this was the case, the Republican leadership in the region that the job embraced offered the initial recommendation. This, too, usually was transmitted through the agency of the caucus. Once the appointment gained the support of the Republican legislators, it went unofficially either to the governor or to one or more members of the state's congressional delegation.

In practice, very often both the governor and members of Congress transmitted the appointment to the proper places in the national government. The governor frequently communicated with the president when the latter's personal approbation was necessary. The state's congressional delegation influenced the Senate and the cabinet. These dignitaries in New Jersey rarely *initiated* appointments, however. Exceptions to this procedure were federal appointments desired for personal reasons by the governor, senators, or congressmen from New Jersey. The caucus passed up initiative in some cases, so long as these officials were moderate in their demands. For the most part, the all-important initiative in federal appointments resided, then, with the powerful leadership in the counties or regions, acting through the caucus, and not with the governor or members of Congress.[40]

The caucus did not have to meet to exercise its influence; legislative courtesy made it possible to handle matters by correspondence. Before President Jefferson nominated a commissioner of bankruptcy in Salem County in 1802, the appointee was recommended first by three Republican leaders

40. Joseph Bloomfield to Ebenezer Elmer, July 6, 1802, Ely Collection, N.J. Hist. Soc.; John Condit to Albert Gallatin, July 21, 1803, Gallatin Papers, N.-Y. Hist. Soc.; Joseph Bloomfield to Ebenezer Elmer, Mar. 5, 1804, Miscellaneous Collection, *ibid.*; John Condit to Ebenezer Elmer, Mar. 30, 1808, Gratz Collection, Hist. Soc. of Pa.; David Thompson, Jr., to Samuel L. Southard, Jan. 13, 1821, Southard Papers, Princeton Univ. Lib.; William Helms to Jonathan Rhea, Dec. 25, 1807, Miscellaneous Collection, N.-Y. Hist. Soc.; Joseph Bloomfield to James Madison, June 6, 7, 1815, Madison Papers, Lib. Cong.

from that county, Jacob Hufty, Artis Seagraves, and Merriman Smith. It was then transmitted, with the approval of the Republicans in the legislature, to Ebenezer Elmer, congressman for the unofficial district embracing Salem County. Elmer, in turn, passed on the recommendation to the President. Jefferson then made the appointment.[41]

A year later, Secretary of the Treasury Albert Gallatin, apparently unfamiliar with the intricacies of patronage distribution in New Jersey, inquired of Senator John Condit if he could designate some good men to fill two collectorships that had opened up at the port of Perth Amboy. Condit replied that before he submitted any recommendations he must contact local party leaders who would name some deserving Republicans. Condit claimed that he did not know of any potential appointees but that local leaders might.[42]

The district attorney's office for the state was vacated in 1804. The Republican members of the legislature, led by Aaron Kitchell, supported Governor Bloomfield's nephew, Joseph McIlvaine, after holding a caucus. He was duly named by the President.[43] After Ebenezer Elmer was replaced on the congressional ticket of 1806, he returned home to Cumberland County, where he picked up the reins of local leadership once again. He was sent to the legislature in 1807. From this vantage point, he initiated federal appointments instead of transmitting them as he had done while in Congress. In 1808, Senator John Condit wrote to him, "I shall with pleasure favor your wishes respecting the Collectorship."[44]

The patronage hierarchy emanating from the local level served New Jersey Republicans well for at least two decades. As late as 1821, David Thompson, Jr., a local Republican

41. Joseph Bloomfield to Ebenezer Elmer, July 6, 1802, Ely Collection, N.J. Hist. Soc.

42. John Condit to Albert Gallatin, July 21, 1803, Gallatin Papers, N.-Y. Hist. Soc.

43. Joseph Bloomfield to Ebenezer Elmer, Mar. 5, 1804, Miscellaneous Collection, *ibid.*

44. John Condit to Ebenezer Elmer, Mar. 30, 1808, Gratz Collection, Hist. Soc. of Pa.

leader representing Morris County in the legislature, urged Samuel L. Southard to take a proffered seat in the United States Senate as soon as possible. His reason for pushing such a course on Southard was an enlightening flashback on the relative positions of party functionaries regarding patronage in New Jersey during the Democratic-Republican era: "If a law shall be passed this winter [by Congress] laying internal duties—I shall wish for your assistance in making these appointments in this part of the Country. I do not want any office myself—but there [are] some persons I should be willing to recommend. This is one reason why I wish you to accept the appointment of Senator and go on to Washington as soon as you can."[45] In federal office-seeking, congressional representatives from New Jersey carried out the wishes of caucus members.

Like his Republican brethren in Congress, the governor also reflected caucus wishes when seeking to fill federal positions. Although his authority under the state constitution was weak, with the united support of the state's leading Republicans behind him and acting more in the role of spokesman than decision-maker, the governor could apply substantial pressure on the president. In many patronage situations, then, the "governor recommend[ed] to the President" the desired appointees.[46] However, because of the weakness inherent in the office at this time and because of his dependence on the caucus for his annual appointment, the governor by himself exerted little leverage in matters of patronage. His position with regard to federal jobs, vis-à-vis the caucus, was, then, even weaker than that of the state's congressmen and senators.

45. David Thompson, Jr., to Samuel L. Southard, Jan. 13, 1821, Southard Papers, Princeton Univ. Lib.

46. Joseph Bloomfield to Thomas Jefferson, Nov. 10, 1801, Jefferson Papers, CXVII, 20262, Lib. Cong.; Joseph Bloomfield to Ebenezer Elmer, Mar. 5, 1804, Miscellaneous Collection, N.-Y. Hist. Soc. Occasionally requests for removals and appointments in New Jersey came directly to the President from party members in the counties. These were not acted upon, however, without first clearing them through existing channels. See Hunt, "Office-Seeking During Jefferson's Administration," *Amer. Hist. Rev.*, 3 (1898), 288.

If the caucus men seemed to dominate both federal and state patronage distribution, even their authority was by no means absolute. Substantial pressure was in turn placed on the legislators by their loyal constituents, as lesser party stalwarts worked mightily to secure the rewards of office. One experienced legislator, Benjamin Cooper, for example, was forced to walk a patronage tightrope while exercising his power of legislative courtesy in recommending both state and federal appointments to the caucus on behalf of his constituents in Gloucester County in 1824. His activities seemed fixed by tradition, so we may assume that his situation was typical of one that might have occurred ten years earlier. Requests for jobs, special favors, and subtle pressures were all applied by the local Republican party in the weeks before the legislative joint meeting convened. One active party worker forwarded Cooper a request on behalf of a brother in arms, disclosing that this potential justice of the peace "has been and is a warm supporter of the Republican Party—and I believe has done great in [his] neighbourhood for the cause."[47] The candidate himself wrote to Cooper's legislative colleague from Gloucester, "I solicit your kind attention to the choice of the Democratic Association [the Republican organization in the county] . . . Joseph B. Harker [the writer] . . . was taken up by the meeting for your consideration. I trust therefore that you will do what you can for me in consideration of money and time expended in support of the party."[48]

Cooper and his colleagues in the legislature could not readily appoint Harker, however. The incumbent justice of the peace, James Pancoast, was loath to give up his office. Pancoast's Republican supporters were numerous also, and they intimated that his reappointment "would tend to support and keep together the party in our county."[49] Cooper attempted to work out a solution by offering Pancoast a federal post as

47. James Hinchman to Benjamin B. Cooper, Dec. 2, 1824, Benjamin B. Cooper Papers, Rutgers Univ. Lib.
48. Joseph B. Harker to Thomas Chapman, Nov. 8, 1824, *ibid.*
49. P. J. Grey to Benjamin B. Cooper, Nov. 26, 1824, *ibid.*

a commissioner of bankruptcy in order to gain his resignation as justice in favor of the Democratic Association candidate. Both, then, presumably would be happy; Harker would receive his local judicial position, and Pancoast would be consoled with a lucrative federal appointment. Cooper's house of cards tumbled just as the caucus was about to convene. The would-be federal commissioner of bankruptcy allowed his greed to master his sense of party accommodation. Having already been assured of his nomination as a federal commissioner, Pancoast wrote to the harried Cooper that he was now willing to give up his justice's office provided only that Cooper "would think proper of appointing my son David J. Pancoast . . . in my place."[50] It was thus necessary for the legislature, at Cooper's instigation, to dismiss Pancoast from his local office, thereby antagonizing a wing of the party in Gloucester. Such were the pitfalls of party patronage that Cooper was forced to disappoint at least one party man while exercising his prerogative of legislative courtesy in recommending appointments.

Grass-roots pressures of this kind on members of the caucus were not uncommon. County meetings of the party were often held before the legislature caucused "to take into consideration the subject of appointments to office for the county."[51] At one gathering, copies of the proceedings were ordered "delivered to each of the Representatives of the county . . . who are hereby respectfully requested to use their best endeavor to procure the appointment of the several persons herein recommended."[52] A Republican leader from unrepresented Bergen County arrived at Trenton in 1808, as the caucus was about to convene, and, according to a Federalist onlooker, was "permitted to say who shall and who shall not be appointed to office. He brings

50. James Pancoast to Benjamin B. Cooper, Dec. 11, 1824, *ibid.*

51. See, for example, the Newark *Centinel*, Nov. 5, Dec. 31, 1811; Trenton *True American*, June 22, 1812; Joseph B. Harker to Thomas Chapman, Nov. 8, 1824, Benjamin B. Cooper Papers, Rutgers Univ. Lib.; *Trenton Federalist*, Dec. 1, 1806, Nov. 28, 1808.

52. Newark *Centinel*, Nov. 5, Dec. 31, 1811; Trenton *True American*, June 22, 1812.

a long list of persons for that purpose."[53] At the same time, a Republican manager from Monmouth, likewise unrepresented in the legislature, allegedly wrote "a letter with *instructions* not to suffer any federal character to be appointed to any office in the county of Monmouth."[54] Regardless of whether the local instructions to caucus representatives derived from party meetings held in the counties or from Republican managers in the towns, the proffered recommendations invariably put forward uniformly active party men.

The Federalists reacted violently to these appointment procedures, which, needless to say, necessitated the removal of many Federalists from office. Reasons given for these dismissals ranged from the frank party complaint to the artful dodge. Moses Kempton of Burlington was turned out because he was a "violent Federalist, and a rigid persecutor of Republicans," while William Watson, a Federalist from Gloucester, ostensibly lost his position to a deserving Republican for "nonattendance of his duties."[55]

Even if the contrived innocence of the many Federalist jeremiads is taken with a large grain of salt, they bear witness to the political nature of the removals and the continuing process of purging nonbelievers from office. Andrew Bell, a well-known Federalist, was dismissed from his lucrative berth as collector for the port of Perth Amboy on June 11, 1801. On June 12, Daniel Marsh, a Republican party manager from Essex County, turned up "from Washington" as his replacement "with the commission in his Pocket." Bell concluded bitterly that "the exterminating System is going on with

53. *Trenton Federalist*, Nov. 28, 1808.
54. *Ibid.*
55. Hunt, "Office-Seeking During Jefferson's Administration," *Amer. Hist. Rev.*, 3 (1898), 288; Newark *Centinel*, June 1, 1802. The removals from office continued through the entire Republican period, with a multitude of reasons forwarded for the changes. See Andrew Bell to Walter Rutherfurd, June 12, 1801, Miscellaneous Collection, N.J. Hist. Soc.; "Samuel Mickle's Diary," in Stewart, ed., *Notes on Old Gloucester County*, I, 180; Trenton *True American*, Dec. 23, 1811, June 15, Nov. 23, 1812; *Newark Gazette*, Oct. 7, 1800.

Spirit."[56] Equally striking is the following unadorned excerpt from Samuel Mickle's diary. This nonpartisan Quaker from Gloucester disclosed that he attended his Federalist friend Elisha Clark's "vendue" in 1805. "Party spirit has wrested ye [County] Clerk's office from him and bestowed it on Chas. Ogden," Mickle reported. Ogden was an active Republican worker of long standing. A solitary entry three days later informs that "Elisha Clark removed with his family to Philadelphia."[57] Initial Federalist reaction was succinctly summed up by one bitter minority member: the patronage system "is in fact . . . a system of corrupt bargaining."[58]

The calculated removal process continued in the second decade of Republican control. Federalists, one of that party's newspapers observed, "are proscribed in a lump, and the whole declared to be unfit for anything but hewers of wood and drawers of water."[59] The articulate Federalist attorney general for New Jersey, Aaron Woodruff, complained bitterly on his dismissal from office in 1811: "I thought that freedom of political opinion should not be imputed to any one as a *crime* nor bring upon him punishment. But with many others, I am taught my *mistake*, and find that a citizen in these times must resign his honest sentiments or submit to *ejection* from office."[60] An anonymous Federalist captured something of the Republican impetus to change when he noted that "were there one hundred offices, republicans, those pretended haters of office, would be found to fill them all."[61] After more than a decade out of power, another Federalist remonstrated in 1812 that "officeholders were heading Republican meetings" and therefore were using their positions for electioneering

56. Andrew Bell to Walter Rutherfurd, June 12, 1801, Miscellaneous Collection, N.J. Hist. Soc.

57. "Samuel Mickle's Diary," in Stewart, ed., *Notes on Old Gloucester County,* I, 180. For a similar example see the *Newark Gazette,* Dec. 22, 1801, Jan. 26, and *passim,* Jan. 1802; New Brunswick *Guardian,* Sept. 23, Oct. 7, 1802.

58. *Newark Gazette,* Mar. 16, 1802.

59. *Trenton Federalist,* Sept. 16, 1811.

60. Trenton *True American,* Dec. 23, 1811.

61. *Newark Gazette,* Oct. 7, 1800.

purposes.[62] By that date, it was doubtful if there were any Republican leaders who did not hold some public trust in the state; this buckshot complaint, then, found no dearth of targets.

Those positions that the Republicans did not fill they wiped out; on the other hand, many new positions were created, and economy on the state level was a virtue only talked about. The first Republican legislature in 1801 abolished sixteen judgeships in the state, offices which the majority claimed were exploited by the Federalists for political advantage.[63] Where they could, however, Republicans created new jobs to service party activists. One Federalist observed that the Jeffersonians had become adept at the "trade of coining justices of the peace," adding that "the office of a justice has become an office of great profit and power."[64] Another critic pointed out that these new appointees were unfit for office "as to character or abilities."[65] The creation of six state banks early in 1812, each with a legislature-appointed president and six paid directors, provided another opportunity for Federalists to denounce the majority for proliferating offices. "These banks," the editor of the *Trenton Federalist* proclaimed, "are intended for party engines, and will be made use of for that purpose, so far as they are capable of strengthening and perpetuating democracy in New Jersey."[66] Active Republican party workers saw many avenues of advancement open to them after 1800.

The Most Favored Few

It is also clear that some groups among the Republican activists were more favored than others. Family connections meant much both for the ascent to authority in the party and state and for the rewards derived therefrom. Party printers, because of the leverage they exerted in party matters, also found that

62. Trenton *True American*, June 15, 1812.
63. Newark *Centinel*, Mar. 16, 1802.
64. *Newark Gazette*, May 4, 1802.
65. *Trenton Federalist*, July 8, 1805, Mar. 10, 1806.
66. *Ibid.*, Feb. 3, 1812.

they constituted a well-favored group. Finally, as the party settled into its permanent shape, incumbent party leaders perpetuated their authority by taking care of themselves first and their faithful retainers thereafter. All in all, then, Republican patronage policies contributed to a remarkably closed and highly ordered hierarchy. That the engine thus created served the state well for a quarter-century is one of the remarkable ironies of the American democratic process.

Party leaders or their families were frequent occupants of appointive as well as elective offices. Because party managers and their relatives were best able to apply pressure at both the state and federal levels, they constituted the most favored group among the many Republicans seeking office. The insiders, then, were treated with special consideration. Elected officials, ex-elected officials, and their respective friends and relatives usually skimmed the cream off the top of the patronage lists. Because of influence, sinecures often were obtained for departing elected officeholders. Jobs and other favors blessed relatives of party leaders.

When William S. Pennington retired from the governorship in 1815, he was awarded a federal judgeship for the United States District Court comprising the district of New Jersey. The position was later described as "almost a sinecure. There were four terms during the year . . . [but] they rarely lasted, however, more than a day. No grand jury was ever sworn in his [Pennington's] court, nor were any indictments found. He held this office until 1826."[67] Ephraim Bateman, long-time congressman from South Jersey, put out his feelers on retiring for "any convenient [public] calling by which I can provide competently for the wants of my numerous family."[68] Ebenezer Elmer, who ended his congressional career in 1807, promptly received the lucrative collectorship of the port at

67. Whitehead, *Judicial and Civil History of New Jersey*, 413.
68. Ephraim Bateman to Samuel L. Southard, Aug. 7, 1822, Southard Papers, Princeton Univ. Lib.

Little Egg Harbour.[69] James J. Wilson, on retiring from the United States Senate in 1820, gained a desirable slot as postmaster at Trenton.[70]

Attempts by holders of political office to seek out appointive berths for relatives and friends were equally common. The Dickerson and Southard families, each with two members holding elective offices in New Jersey for long periods between 1801 and 1817, were well versed in the art of employing influence for themselves and their friends. The Dickerson family included Silas and Mahlon, both extremely influential in the party hierarchy and official governmental circles. Mahlon carried brotherly concern to an extreme. He sought army commissions for a third brother and a nephew and a military contract to repair weapons for still another brother. On another occasion, he asked his New Jersey colleague in the Senate for a "lift" in gaining the Essex County clerk's post—a five-year appointment—for one of his brothers. He was usually successful.[71]

The Southards likewise were a political family. Henry Southard spent most of the period 1801-1817 in Congress. His son Samuel served in the legislature and later in the United States Senate. When Samuel was just getting started as a lawyer in 1811, Henry, writing from Washington, prodded many friends in an effort to gain for his son an appointment as surrogate of Hunterdon County. Sometime later, both sought to obtain through favor a place of some sort for Samuel's brother Isaac. A friend of Samuel L. Southard, one J. H. Simpson, confided, in seeking help to obtain a desirable office: "As this office is almost a sinecure, and would interfere but little with

69. John Condit to Ebenezer Elmer, Mar. 30, 1808, Gratz Collection, Hist. Soc. of Pa.; *Executive Journal of the Senate of the United States,* II.

70. Daniel Coleman to William Darlington, Jan. 5, 1821, Darlington Papers, N.-Y. Hist. Soc.; David Thompson, Jr., to Samuel L. Southard, Apr. 19, 1821, Southard Papers, Princeton Univ. Lib.; James J. Wilson to William Darlington, May 8, 1821, Darlington Papers, Lib. Cong.

71. Aaron Dickerson to Mahlon Dickerson, Mar. 23, 1810, Lewis Condict to Mahlon Dickerson, Jan. 26, 1813, Mahlon Dickerson Papers, Rutgers Univ. Lib.; Mahlon Dickerson to Samuel L. Southard, Jan. 1, 1820, Southard Papers, Princeton Univ. Lib.

my other business, if I could obtain it without much exertions, I should be gratified. This office is honestly worth from 250 to about 300 dollars, but [Robert] Arnold says—he has made out of it for the past year about $800."[72]

Many other elected officials utilized the effective patronage machine of the New Jersey Republican party to encourage familial advancement. Joseph Bloomfield, governor for twelve years, helped his nephew and ward Joseph McIlvaine to gain many high-ranking militia positions. Bloomfield used his influence also to obtain four different paying state appointments and one federal office for McIlvaine between 1801 and 1817.[73] Congressman Ebenezer Elmer similarly exerted himself, in this instance unsuccessfully, to promote the appointment of his *Federalist* brother Jonathan to the New Jersey Supreme Court.[74] When a new postmastership opened up in South Jersey, president of the Legislative Council and future United States senator John Lambert successfully recommended his brother William to the position and sought support for him from members of the New Jersey delegation to Congress.[75] Republican legislators, a Federalist newspaper asserted, "have seized upon every office within their reach either for themselves, their relations or their particular friends."[76]

The Republican printers in New Jersey constituted another

72. Henry Southard to Samuel L. Southard, Feb. 10, 1811, Feb. 19, 1818, Isaac Southard to Samuel L. Southard, Jan. 20, 1818, J. H. Simpson to Samuel L. Southard, Feb. 9, 1821, Southard Papers, Princeton Univ. Lib. In the cases of both the Dickersons and the Southards, large collections of family manuscripts are extant, offering valuable insights into what appears to be a common practice in New Jersey politics in the first quarter of the nineteenth century. It has been recently established that, throughout the nation, officeholding and family ties went hand in hand. See the thoroughgoing analysis of national politics in this connection by Sidney H. Aronson, *Status and Kinship in the Higher Civil Service: Standards of Selection in the Administrations of John Adams, Thomas Jefferson, and Andrew Jackson* (Cambridge, Mass., 1964).

73. Newark *Centinel*, July 17, 1804; *Minutes and Proceedings of the Joint Meeting*, 1805-1806, 1810, 1815.

74. Ebenezer Elmer to ?, June 29, 1802, Gratz Collection, Hist. Soc. of Pa.

75. Henry Southard to John Lambert, May 3, 1802, Lloyd W. Smith Collection, Morristown National Hist. Park. Numerous similar examples could be cited.

76. *Trenton Federalist*, Oct. 21, 1805.

favored group; they were the recipients of multiple appointments which helped to keep them solvent. The four leading Republican editors were James J. Wilson of the Trenton *True American*, William Tuttle of the Newark *Centinel of Freedom*, James Fitz Randolph of the New Brunswick *Fredonian*, and Shepard Kollock of the Elizabethtown *New Jersey Journal*. All four divided the annual printing chores for the state, publishing the proceedings of both houses of the legislature and the session laws and filling other lucrative printing needs for Republican New Jersey. The extent of the favors available to Republican printers when their party was in power in state and nation can be judged by the example provided by the editor of the *Centinel*, who "persuaded" the Newark postmaster to transfer his advertisements of letters being held at the post office from the local Federalist paper to the *Centinel*.[77] Equally important, three of the four influential editors also were favored with numerous public offices. Only William Tuttle, who sought and received state and national printing contracts but drew the line at accepting public offices, did not take any public appointments from obligated legislators and congressmen. In fact, Tuttle on occasion became an outspoken critic of the officeholding propensities of his newspaper colleagues.[78]

If Tuttle declined to accept public trusts, his fellow editors were not so reticent. James J. Wilson, editor of the *True American* and father of twelve children, collected the largest number of offices. At various intervals between 1801 and 1817, he was clerk of the Assembly, clerk for Hunterdon County, surrogate for the county, Adjutant General of the New Jersey Militia (one of the few paying militia commissions), and president of the New Jersey State Bank at Trenton. Each job Wilson held for a minimum of two years and some for much longer.

77. *Newark Gazette*, Apr. 27, 1802; see also *ibid.*, Dec. 1, 1801, Nov. 2, 1802; New Brunswick *Guardian*, Oct. 7, 1802.

78. Trenton *True American*, Nov. 24, 1806; *Minutes and Proceedings of the Joint Meeting*, 1801-16, *passim*; Newark *Centinel*, Sept. 17, 1805, Sept. 19, 26, 1820, June 26, 1821; *Newark Gazette*, Dec. 1, 1801, Nov. 2, 1802; New Brunswick *Guardian*, Oct. 7, 1802.

The legislature capped its tradition of rewarding its favorite printer with public offices by electing him to the Senate in 1815. When he retired in 1820, he was favored with a lucrative postmastership at Trenton.[79] Wilson always felt, according to his Federalist counterpart in Trenton (who may well have been a little jealous), that his "labours in the democratic vineyard would entitle him to some fat office or post."[80] During all this time, it should be noted, Wilson continued to publish his paper.

James Fitz Randolph was not far behind Wilson as an editor-officeholder. Fitz Randolph, editor of the New Brunswick *Fredonian*, was blessed with two gainful federal offices. He was collector for the port of Perth Amboy and postmaster of New Brunswick for most of the period from the founding of the *Fredonian* in 1811 through 1816. Tuttle considered Fitz Randolph corrupted by the "effects of holding two snug offices." His relatives and friends were likewise rewarded.[81]

Shepard Kollock of the Elizabethtown *New Jersey Journal*, the earliest Republican paper in the state, was also aided with considerable outside support. At various times he was a judge or justice of the peace in Essex County or an official of the city of Elizabethtown, all three positions at the disposal of the legislative caucus. At least five different appointments came his way during the period.[82] If, as many editors claimed, their papers barely broke even or did not repay them sufficiently for their efforts, they found financial solace in the many offices that smoothed their way financially.

Historians have long generalized about the appearance

79. Trenton *True American*, Nov. 24, 1806; Newark *Centinel*, Sept. 17, 1805; Anon., *To the Republicans of the County of Hunterdon*, 2ff; *Minutes and Proceedings of the Joint Meeting*, 1802-1806, 1811, 1814; *A Register of Officers and Agents . . . 1821* (Washington, 1822).

80. *Trenton Federalist*, Mar. 10, 1806.

81. Newark *Centinel*, Sept. 19, 26, 1820, June 26, 1821; New Brunswick *Fredonian*, Aug. 16, 1821; James Fitz Randolph to Samuel L. Southard, Oct. 21, Nov. 9, 1820, and *passim*, Southard Papers, Princeton Univ. Lib.

82. *Minutes and Proceedings of the Joint Meeting*, 1804, 1805, 1809, 1812, 1814.

of patronage in the early national period without describing precisely either its specific relation to the state party machines or the extent to which it strengthened party efforts. In New Jersey, the Republican interest was not a party of yeoman farmers, but a party of officeholders. Nearly two-thirds of the identified Republican activists in the state were rewarded with some appointive public office between 1800 and 1817. There can be no doubt, then, that the Republicans utilized paying offices to create a standing professional cadre of party operatives, tangibly dependent on the success of the party at the polls and therefore willing to give their all for the party. Many of those rewarded were bound to the leadership by ties of family or friendship. More than 20 per cent of the state and federal appointees were veteran party workers who devoted their personal efforts as well as the weight of their offices to maintaining the party's position. To the activists the party was a source of money, prestige, and power. Thus the apparatus of the Democratic-Republican party in the township, the county, and the state acquired a degree of depth and permanence it could not otherwise have achieved.

THE PARTY OF THE PEOPLE?

———— ·•— ————

THE CAREER OF THE DEMOCRATIC-REPUBLICAN PARTY IN NEW Jersey extended from 1796 until 1826. Mobilized initially to overthrow the dominant Federalist regime, the party achieved its first major victory in 1800, and thereafter, except during the period of the War of 1812, it rarely faced a serious state-wide challenge. Ultimately, it met defeat not at the hands of its traditional opponents, but through internecine controversies brought on by the absence of an effective opposition. Durable and successful, the party owed much of its potency to expert professional leaders, and to organizational techniques they developed.

The party was organized in New Jersey partly in response to national issues and events. New Jersey Republicans were slow to coalesce, falling behind Jeffersonian parties that appeared early in the 1790's in New York, Virginia, and Pennsylvania, among other states. Party organization in these states, coming earlier as it did, influenced Republicans in New Jersey. Aaron Kitchell, for example, applied tactics he learned from Republicans in Congress, and the Penningtons ably introduced party vehicles like the democratic society and the party press perfected elsewhere, to take the lead in knotting the fragmented opposition into a coherent political organization. In 1796, as a result, the faction became a party.

From this secure base party apparatus was extended through the initiative of statewide managers to most of the state. In most counties, leaders were recruited who, like the party they dominated, blended a professional desire for office and rewards with sincere dedication spurred by reforming zeal. The men who were party leaders in 1796, or who thereafter entered the party's ranks, all dominated or coordinated county organizations. In their number were the Penningtons in Essex, Kitchell and later Mahlon Dickerson in Morris, Silas Dickerson in Sussex, James J. Wilson in Hunterdon, Joseph Bloomfield and Thomas Newbold in Burlington, and Ebenezer Elmer in Cumberland. These county managers, building upon their local authority, grew in stature as the party filled out, and, by 1801, constituted an integrated, conscientious statewide ruling bloc. By that date also, these men presided over well entrenched county machines. All of them, as both party managers and ambitious individuals, sought and attained public office and political power.

These emergent Democratic-Republican captains encouraged reverence for a cult of appealing personalities. The men on top personified the public image of the party and raised the esteem in which the party was held by the people. Pennington was a hero of the Revolution; Bloomfield, the man who turned against his class to combat Federalist aristocracy; Wilson, the much-maligned, crusading newspaper editor fearlessly deflecting Federalist abuse; Aaron Kitchell and Henry Southard, artisan and farmer respectively, both epitomizing the Republican success story. These and other personal images were cultivated in the Republican newspapers, and were basic to the Republicans' popular appeal.

Politicians like William S. Pennington, Kitchell, Elmer, and Bloomfield, were well known to each other. They coordinated their organizational efforts by frequent conferences and extensive correspondence. These men and others worked also through newspapers, broadsides, and pamphlets to popularize their cause. Leadership reached out from Essex and Morris counties along preconceived lines of endeavor, trying to implement a coherent organizational pattern prior to 1801. The party was their creation. The only grass-roots participation in the formation of the original party structure was in the nature of a response to smoothly functioning leadership. Clear organizational models emerged by region as a result.

The precise form of party structure within each county varied in time with local circumstances and attitudes, but there were three general types. In North Jersey, the open county meeting (with or without attendant county committees) and the delegate convention both appeared. In South Jersey, the democratic association, a specialized party form, and the delegate convention both were employed with success. On the state level, the state convention first (1800), and the legislative caucus later (1801-1803), emerged as the most important decision-making bodies. To these must be added the militant party newspapers in New Jersey. The *Centinel* and *Journal* first, the *Genius of Liberty* and *True American* somewhat later, and finally, late in the Republican period, the *Fredonian*, the *Sussex Register*, and the *Cumberland Whig* rounded out the spectrum of Republican gazettes. Newspapers were important adjuncts of party organization.

The explicit functions of all local and county organizations and the state convention (excepting the caucus) included the nomination of candidates for elective office, and the encouragement of voter participation through electioneering for party candidates. These party machines, again excluding the caucus, also provided the appearance of fulfillment of the party's democratic ideology: democratic free choice of the best people, contrasted with usually undefined Federalist "aristocratic" techniques. Finally, local, county, and statewide machinery helped to publicize current party issues.

Apart from these public commitments, party organizations existed to facilitate decision-making by party leaders. There was less true democracy in the groups than appearances indicated, for group democracy and a political party that was hierarchy-oriented were antithetical. Democratic practices invariably suffered and eventually yielded to strong party leadership. This fact was demonstrated repeatedly in succeeding situations throughout the party's history between 1796 and 1817. Nominations were manipulated; party addresses were drafted by the leadership, and sentiment was guided accordingly; electioneering was managed skillfully with the intention of getting out the right vote, not necessarily all the voters.

The only party apparatus not designed to fit any public mold was the legislative caucus; it was frankly exclusive. It never pretended to represent the will of the people, except in the most indirect sense. The caucus' major function was to oversee the distribution of virtually all patronage to deserving party members. This task was executed carefully for many years, with an eye to perpetuating organization. Secondarily, the caucus provided a forum in which decision-making powers were exercised. The caucus, unlike all other party apparatus, was open only to legislators and party leaders, preserving the privacy necessary for significant party decisions. The state convention, while it was intended to provide a democratic appearance for the party, in fact was used until 1806 as a forum for leadership decisions—a function which thereafter fell quite naturally to the secretive caucus. Finally, the caucus, as it grew more powerful, began to implement changes (or attempted changes) in party organization.

Party machinery rarely operated democratically in the sense that control actually resided with the people. It was a question, rather, of the party's ability to project a democratic image. The Republicans usually were eminently successful in conveying to the public the appearance of democracy. Party propaganda, resting primarily on party newspapers, was largely responsible for this mastery. Propaganda was used effectively to induce the voters to identify with the party and then to reinforce and sustain such identification. It fulfilled this function by perpetuating or exaggerating issues that aroused wide popular support and enthusiasm. Party doctrine helped also to build distorted images of party leaders. Newspapers and broadsides publicized both political and social party activities. In sum, propaganda enhanced individual identification with the party and furthered the democratic illusion at the same time.

Issues, then, became tools to magnify the democratic appeal of the party. Party newspapers and other propaganda outlets did not create issues. Rather, they exploited them. Language distorted true divergences in order to justify party distinctions. This was true of the vigorous assaults by Republicans on old Hamiltonian policies even after 1800, the continuing campaign against Federalist aristocracy and the defense of the agrarian way of life, anti-lawyer, anti-aristocrat feelings in the counties, the bank-stock issue of 1810, and the issues connected with the coming of the War of 1812. All were employed to justify the existence and continued use of party machinery.

Party leadership was vitally bound up with party propaganda, as was demonstrated by the close link between that leadership and the party's newspapers. Most publisher-editors were party captains in their respective counties and in the state. The Penningtons, James J. Wilson, Shepard Kollock, and the Fitz Randolphs all exemplified this connection. They were full-time professionals operating in a professional party situation.

Although the Republican party itself was not democratic, it did promote the spread of democratic practices in New Jersey. Machinery was created that reached into the township and even the neighborhood, thus involving directly many voters in the state. Political identifications and loyalties were stabilized effectively. In a relatively new political situation, this was an important factor in bracing democracy against the rude shocks of extended, over-divisive factionalism. Personal involvement and voter participation increased broadly and significantly throughout the state. Organized electioneering became an effective party tool, unifying to an extent political judgments by wholesale numbers of participants. Thus, while political divisions were clear, sharp, and permanent, political animosities were controlled. This fact tended to keep politics from reaching dangerous extremes, contemporary language to the contrary notwithstanding.

Permanent parties, then, provided a unity heretofore missing in fragmented local elections. They aided in stabilizing political practices even at the grass roots. Political questions were treated extensively in the party presses and undoubtedly promoted discussions of public affairs. Enduring machinery enhanced responsible attitudes in elected and appointed officials, because individuals who acted contrary to the public interest jeopardized their parties and not merely themselves. The clash of two political parties, on balance, strengthened and preserved democratic forms in the society of the state even while one, and probably both parties were themselves undemocratic. This observable contradiction is one of the ironies—and one of the strong points as well—of the American political tradition.

A number of factors explain the success of the Republican party after 1800. Four years of groundwork, mainly in Essex and Morris counties, aggressive leadership throughout the state, popular reaction to the Alien and Sedition Acts, the expansion in depth of Republican organization, greater propaganda efforts, and aid from outside New Jersey, notably from the professional Jeffersonian leadership in Philadelphia and later Washington, all strengthened the party and contributed to its longevity.

The party usually handled its mastery in the state well. In patronage and propaganda matters, it is true, Republicans used their power in a highly partisan manner. Federalists were turned out of state and federal offices and replaced by Republican party workers. Within a very short time after 1800, the rewards of political power belonged to the victors.

On the other hand, like the Jeffersonians nationally, New

Jersey Republicans made their peace with existing economic conditions and attitudes. No effort was made to retard commerce and other non-agrarian pursuits. No "revolution" was wrought. Only the tax on bank stock in 1810 could be said to have been a radical departure from the preservation of the status quo; it was the only example of "equalization" in favor of agrarians and mechanics—and it met the needs, at the same time, of a growing and increasingly diverse economy.

Acts of incorporation favoring economic diversity, particularly those chartering turnpikes and bridges, encountered no Republican resistance. The Jeffersonians and their successors were sensitive to legislation affecting the courts, legal fees, and lawyers generally, but despite minority support for it, there was no leveling or even major simplification in this area. Republicans by and large limited themselves to simple criticism of lawyers without doing much about them. The state constitution was not altered; suffrage laws underwent a much needed revision in 1807, but not as the result of partisan effort and without any obvious benefits accruing to any particular group. Republicans likewise were sensitive to laws affecting taxes in New Jersey, but this susceptibility did not eventuate in any radical departures in the tax structure of the state, with the single exception of the tax on bank stock. Preservation of agrarian life remained ideological. In reality, practical efforts to shift away from a wholly agrarian society were not prevented and often encouraged.

Diplomatic issues after 1806 received increasing attention. Generally, New Jersey Republicans were sympathetic to France (although not always willing to excuse that nation) and opposed to England. The embargo was supported dutifully, a mark of professional party commitment. The exigencies of the embargo and of the war era increased Republican respect for, and support of, home manufactures and economic self-sufficiency. This attitude tended to obliterate existing ideological differences between the parties.

Significant contributions were made to American party

development by New Jersey's Democratic Republicans. Much has been said about the place of the mixed caucus in the party. It was the major source for the calculated distribution of party patronage. Operating upon an unwritten premise of legislative courtesy in the counties, the caucus assured party workers of suitable rewards for services rendered. Undoubtedly, much of the organizational strength of the party accrued from this caucus practice. It was not illogical that, given this initial authority and source of prestige, the caucus would eventually provide the chief forum also for party decisions concerning leadership and doctrinal changes.

Another organizational innovation was the permanent state nominating convention. Beginning in 1800, it was the first continuous party nominating institution on that level in any state. Its functions and purpose were distinct from those of the caucus; the convention's function was nominative, its purpose propagandistic. In reality the Jeffersonians were highly centralized, but it still appeared to the public that they had returned to grass-roots democracy by opening up to the representatives of the people the designation of presidential and congressional tickets. That the convention appeared to respond to the popular will, while the substance was anything but democratic, was a clear tribute to the professional abilities of the party leaders.

The same democratic appearance within a most undemocratic reality existed in the democratic associations of South Jersey, and, to a lesser extent, in the county nominating meetings of North Jersey. The cosmetic touches characterizing most political parties nowhere were more evident than in the local party usages of New Jersey Jeffersonians.

Campaign techniques and organization for elections were other fertile contributions to the American party system. How original the Republicans' efforts were on this score must await additional studies and comparisons. But, in New Jersey, the use of newspapers and other printed matter, the creation of enduring party forms, the development of a personality-oriented leadership were all effective in providing the necessary popular exterior to a professional party. Locally, the county meeting, the democratic associations, and extensive local organization in close two-party counties, all helped to turn out the party vote on election day.

The decline of opposition weakened party organization. By 1817, nearly every county witnessed to a degree the deterioration of its local machinery, signaling the end of an era. However, organized statewide Federalism also was stymied effectively by the end of the war. The major Republican apparatus, the caucus, the convention, the newspapers, and particularly the party managers, remained intact to carry on the Republican tradition, in form if not in substance. But the decline of the local party organization marked the end of the original and formative period of Democratic Republicanism in New Jersey.

NOTE ON THE SOURCES

———•—————

THE MOST CONSISTENTLY USEFUL SOURCES FOR THIS STUDY WERE the weekly newspapers. The Trenton *True American*, virtually the official statewide Republican organ for many years, was particularly dependable. A complete run, covering the years 1801-1826, is available in the original at the New Jersey State Library at Trenton, and on microfilm at the Rutgers University Library, New Brunswick. The Newark *Centinel of Freedom*, in the collection of the New Jersey Historical Society in Newark and available for virtually the entire period from 1796 through 1826, was also a major source of information. Although a complete run of the Elizabethtown *New Jersey Journal* is available for nearly the entire Republican era at the New Jersey Historical Society, its utility is compromised by its relatively infrequent political coverage. An incomplete run of the New Brunswick *Fredonian* spanning the years 1811-1818, housed in the Rutgers University Library, also proves helpful. A similarly incomplete run of the Morristown *Genius of Liberty* for the years 1798-1805 may be used in the library of the National Historical Park at Morristown. These are the most valuable available Republican newspaper sources. Virtually intact runs of *Woods's Newark Gazette and New Jersey Advertiser* (1796-1807) at the New Jersey Historical Society, the *Trenton Federalist and New Jersey Gazette* (1798-1826) at the Historical Society and the New Jersey State Library, and the New Brunswick *Guardian* (1792-1815) at Rutgers University Library were the Federalist periodicals upon which I relied the most.

The manuscript sources for New Jersey politics in the Jeffersonian Republican era are widely scattered. One finds a letter here and there in a great variety of collections in the East. Few collections, however, offer meaty, extensive, and continuous coverage of New Jersey politics, and so the exceptions are extremely important. The Mahlon Dickerson Papers and Diaries, housed at both the New Jersey Historical Society and the Rutgers University Library, are useful; this is particularly true of the Dickerson Letter Book, a never-catalogued and long unused part of the collections of the New Jersey Historical Society. Spanning the years 1798-1807, it consists for the most part of a continuing exchange of letters between Mahlon Dickerson, then active in Pennsylvania politics but vitally interested in its New Jersey counterpart, and his brother Silas, sometime legislator and longtime activist in New Jersey Republican circles. The Benjamin Cooper Papers in the Rutgers University Library, although they deal with a later period (1824), offer valuable insights into patronage operations in New Jersey for the earlier era. The William Darlington Papers in the Library of Congress contain more than eighty letters from New Jersey party chieftain James J. Wilson to his longtime friend William Darlington, an important Pennsylvania politician as well as a distinguished botanist. The correspondence spans the years 1801-1824, and offers valuable new perspectives as well as significant confirmation of information first uncovered in the newspapers. The Simon Gratz Collection housed in the Historical Society of Pennsylvania is spiced with valuable letters to and from many important New Jersey Republicans spanning the entire Republican era, but with particular concentration on the period prior to 1805. Use of this huge collection is as frustrating as it is helpful, because only bits and pieces of the whole manifest themselves. The correspondence pertaining to New Jersey is usually isolated, offering little continuity. This observation does not in the least apply with regard to the Samuel L. Southard Papers at the Princeton University Library. Newly unearthed and catalogued, and massive in its depth, this collection offers a valuable goldmine to students of pre-Civil War American and New Jersey political history. Unfortunately for me, the collection is most sparse in the period in which I worked; a few letters date as far back as 1808, but the concentration of correspondence only becomes heavy in the 1820's, when Southard entered the national political picture.

Several published primary sources deserve mention. Two political pamphlets offer valuable information and viewpoints. Ebenezer Elmer's *Address to the Citizens of New Jersey* (Elizabethtown, 1807), found in the New Jersey Pamphlets Collection of the Rutgers University Library, contains a very able contemporary analysis of the public utility of a party system. The anonymously authored *To the Republicans of the County of Hunterdon* (Philadelphia, 1812) sheds light on both James J. Wilson's career and the lines of authority evident in the dispensation of patronage. Lucius Q. C. Elmer's *The Constitution and Government of the Province and State of New Jersey* (Newark, 1872), combines firsthand knowledge with relatively sound judgments to describe the public careers of many of the Republican leaders of the Jeffersonian period. "The Journal of Ephraim Bateman of Fairfield Township, Cumberland County," *Vineland Historical Magazine*, 13 (1928), 14 (1929), is a valuable and almost unique exposure of the attitudes of a young rank-and-file party enthusiast. Anyone interested in studying patronage practices for any state will find the multi-volume *Executive Journal of the Senate of the United States* (Washington, D. C., 1829-69) indispensable. Any appointments requiring Senate approval (and that included virtually all major ones) are listed, along with the state, sometimes the town, and the date of appointment (and often the date of termination as well). Used imaginatively in conjunction with other sources (e.g., newspapers) it can add significantly to our knowledge of party operations in any period. Copies seem to be in short supply; I found an intact set in the Government Documents section of the New York Public Library. The *Minutes and Proceedings of the Joint Meeting [Council] [Assembly] of the Legislature of the State of New Jersey*, published annually, does for state appointments what the *Executive Journal of the Senate* does for federal appointments. It also proved most useful in analyzing and evaluating party issues.

Modern secondary accounts of New Jersey in this period are slim. Walter Fee, *The Transition From Aristocracy to Democracy in New Jersey, 1789-1829* (Somerville, N.J., 1933) is useful as a very general history of politics for the state, but it contains almost no emphasis on party machinery and organization. A student of Dixon Ryan Fox, Professor Fee follows pretty much the interpretation and frame of reference of his mentor's classic *The Decline of Aristocracy in the Politics of New York 1801-1840* (N.Y., 1919). Fee's book is meticulously accurate, and although limited by a now dated approach it is still a relevant study even though it is more than thirty years old. Richard P. McCormick's *The History of Voting in New Jersey: A Study of the Development of Election Machinery, 1664-1911* (New Brunswick, 1953) is an excellent background source for the legal and electoral changes of the era as they touched on the state's politics. Many important recent studies have been written for other states, as indicated in the bibliographic footnote contained in the Introduction to this book.

INDEX